A Story of Love

MELISSA MALCOLM-PECK

WESTBOW
PRESS®
A DIVISION OF THOMAS NELSON
& ZONDERVAN

WestBow Press books may be ordered through booksellers or by contacting:

WestBow Press
A Division of Thomas Nelson & Zondervan
1663 Liberty Drive
Bloomington, IN 47403
www.westbowpress.com
1 (866) 928-1240

Scripture quotations are from the Revised Standard Version of the Bible, copyright © 1946, 1952, and 1971 the Division of Christian Education of the National Council of the Churches of Christ in the United States of America. Used by permission. All rights reserved.

ISBN: 978-1-9736-6165-8 (sc)
ISBN: 978-1-9736-6166-5 (hc)
ISBN: 978-1-9736-6164-1 (e)

Library of Congress Control Number: 2019906611

Printed in the United States of America.

WestBow Press rev. date: 05/27/2020

To see this book published and have it influence
people was one of your greatest dreams.
And now it has become our greatest dream.
We now see a new beauty in life, filled with more radiance and joy.
No, we wouldn't change a thing.
We have found a new life.
He works all things together for our good. All things.
And we choose to have grateful hearts for the
extra time we were able to share together.
You are our beautiful angel now.

We love you forever, Momma.
-Brenna, Meagan, and Jacqueline

You are destined to read this just as I was called to write it. It is not the book I thought I would write, nor is it the life I once thought I would live, but years have yielded enough wisdom to ignore idle thoughts. Purpose waits rooted beneath passing thought. I believe I wouldn't change a thing. There is joy now in all of it. Time has added that joy. For some of it lacked joy, it lacked compassion, and it lacked patience in the living of it. A few weeks ago, I looked at years of pictures of myself in a family scrapbook. I was strong and healthy. My hair was dark. I had no scars. I looked beautiful. But I was not smiling. I smile now in every photo. Finding life has offered me the gift of a smile.

-Melissa

For those who do not yet believe...
and for those who need to believe once more.

How Did You Die?

Did you tackle that trouble that came your way
With a resolute heart and cheerful?
Or hide your face from the light of day
With a craven soul and fearful?
Oh a trouble's a ton, or a trouble's an ounce,
Or a trouble is what you make it.
And isn't the fact that you're hurt that counts
But only how did you take it?

You are beaten to earth? Well, well, what's that?
Come up with a smiling face.
It's nothing against you to fall down flat,
But to lie there - that's disgrace.
The harder you're thrown, why the higher you bounce;
Be proud of your blackened eye!
It isn't the fact that you're licked that counts;
It's how did you fight and why?

And though you be done to death, what then?
If you battled the best you could;
If you played your part in the world of men,
Why, the Critic will call it good.
Death comes with a crawl, or comes with a pounce,
And whether he's slow or spry,
It isn't the fact that you're dead that counts,
But only, how did you die?

Edmund Vance Cooke

Book One
That Which Doesn't Kill You

Chapter One

It is five weeks since the first pain. It came without warning and exploded to such spearing intensity, I could not control my reaction to it. You imagine alarms wailing before your life collapses. You imagine knowing there is danger. But I hadn't kept the clues.

Night has fallen. I climb the stairs slowly. Part way up as I near the first turn, for the briefest moment there is a sense again of something amiss. But I am weary, and at the start, it seems easy to ignore. After a moment or two of a gentle burn in the center of my chest, I gaze into the bathroom mirror and look long into my eyes as I put down the toothbrush. How odd. This must be what heartburn feels like. But I've never had heartburn.

Fire leaps into the left side of my neck. It is not gentle now. There is only time to straighten from the sink. Then pain rolls with numbing pressure through my left arm. And I know. God help me, how could I not. There's a sickening sense of disbelief but no doubt. I know exactly what is happening to me. I am forty-three years old, and I am in trouble.

I manage the three long flights of stairs, going down as quickly and as calmly as I can. My husband stands in the kitchen, and I pass by him to sit in the family room. I can't yet say the words. The pain builds, bending me over involuntarily. I call his name. William appears instantly. The tone of my voice, I suppose. I try to smile. I try to straighten.

"I think I'm having a heart attack."

He stares at me in incredulously. There is no more time.

"We have to go," I say, struggling to stand.

A voice within warns that I will be incapable of walking within seconds. Then I think of our three little girls' asleep upstairs.

"Call Sara," I say urgently as I open the garage door.

She is our closest neighbor and friend. Sara can be here in minutes, yet my mind skips to what might happen before she arrives. The checklist billows from years of mothering until I shrink from it. I don't want to leave my daughters all alone, but I can't think about it anymore. There is enough pain without adding anything to it.

The silver Audi is in front of me, and I slip in. But I can't close the door; pain shoots past unbearably. Seeking some relief, I prop my legs across the dash. Relief does not come. I close my eyes, trying to erase what is happening. Trying to remove myself.

"God," I whisper, "Dear God, please, please help me."

I could howl in agony. I could scream, if I had ever once screamed in my life. But I hold it in, and it just keeps building.

William closes my door and starts the motor. The next minutes are the longest of my life.

The car catapults from the garage. We are still fifteen minutes from the emergency room at Boulder Hospital. Fifteen minutes. Dear God, I can't endure fifteen more minutes of this. Most of the trip will be down a steep mountain road with banked curves and sharp corners.

"How are you doing?" William asks.

"This is bad," I answer. "This is bad."

My left arm is completely numb, and I'm nauseous from the stabbing pain.

"I have to throw up," I mumble weakly.

William keeps trying to call the hospital from the car phone, but it isn't working. It always works. He lives on the thing, but for some reason, these calls won't go through. Unbelievable. This is all totally unbelievable.

I'm moaning now, crawling onto the car floor, trying to curl into a ball. The next instant, I'm back in the seat, straining against it. Back and forth, rocking and moaning. I can hear the sounds, but I can't stop myself from making them. And I can't stop this violent, searing pain. Back and forth. *This isn't me. I can handle pain.* I've learned to handle all pain.

Suddenly, I'm floating away, lifting from my body and the shattering pain. With a thought, I accelerate toward the release, but suddenly I remember the words I must say. Dear God, help me say them.

I reach out my arm, knowing William will see it. "I love you," I whisper. He finds my hand. We've been together twenty-five years, since

I was a girl of eighteen. There have been no other loves in my life. One love alone can generate tidal waves of emotion.

The frantic drive down the mountain rolls on in slow motion. Searing pain inside my chest pushes me past endurance. William squeezes my hand. Through the births of our children, he held that hand, encouraging me. Never once during childbirth did I find the experience more than I could tolerate. But this is far more excruciating. Fear smothers me, and controlling this fear and pain feels impossible. There is no hope of it ending except by dying.

It'll be over soon, I think. It cannot possibly go on much longer. I feel myself slipping away again, and this time, I say good-bye with a touch of my hand.

"Hey! Hey! Hey!" William shouts, as if he instantly understands. "Come on! You're not going anywhere, are you?" Panic strangles his voice.

I hear it from far away, yet the sound startles me. I've never heard panic in his voice before.

"I'm here," I answer weakly, regretting that I am.

"Keep breathing," he says loudly. "I want you to think about breathing." He clears his throat. "You're doing fine," he adds softly. He repeats the lie again.

I don't speak. I'm somewhere far beyond, detaching from him, from life, and from time. We're careening around corners, still going down a never-ending mountain. At moments I think I hear him calling. The shouted sound of my name jolts me back, but I leave over and over again, eager to escape agony.

Then suddenly, as quickly as it came, the pain recedes. It vanishes. And I sit shaken within some other reality. The monster is completely, inexplicably gone. Yet it diminishes me; as it flees, it steals a part of me. Part of my confidence, in my life and in myself, is ripped away in the wake of its passing. I sense my loss instantly.

Minutes pass until I try opening my eyes. The road looks damp, as if there has been an easy rain. I glance around, trying to orient myself with familiar sights of my hometown. I know it well, yet all seems new. Very new.

What day is it? Yes, it is Tuesday, July 1. It is one week and a few days past the summer solstice. Summer. That thought would normally bring a smile, for I begin yearning for summer just a few months after it leaves. The details of my dreaming grow richer by the end of winter, and by then, I think often of the colors, the gentle mountain warmth, and the birds that will return to grace my walks. Yet green grass shines under streetlights. I look up to trees alive with fresh leaves and outstretched branches. Everything is growing. The summer solstice approaches. Days will get darker now. They will keep getting darker now. Each one darker than the last. The night seems blissfully calm yet somehow surreal, as if I'm watching a movie. I can't sense myself anywhere in the picture. Everything appears in perfect focus ... Everything except me.

I glance at William, wanting to reach out to him, to connect with something strong and real. Looking at his profile, I realize how badly I have frightened him. He cannot comfort or reassure me now. I do not know how to reassure myself.

Please, William, don't look that way. I need to look away. I need to recall his face the way it used to look such a short time ago, just after dinner. Oh, William, where are you? The William I know is decisive and confident in every crisis. The William I know runs to the rescue before I can even begin to react, and I have thought myself quick. But I have jolted us both clear off our foundations. I have shaken you tonight.

The car keeps moving, and I suddenly remember one morning on this road. A little dog ran into the street from between two parked cars, and it was impossible to miss him. We both gasped at the sound as we skidded to a stop. I opened my door and started out, but William grabbed my arm and pulled me back in.

"Don't leave the car!"

I've never known anyone who loves animals more than William, and he did not want me to see and be hurt by what we both knew was there. So, I strained to watch his face as he bent under the tires to the dog, but I couldn't read his expression. And I could always read his expressions.

He stood, cradling the dog gently, as I moved into the driver's seat. All the way to the vet's, he kept telling that bleeding, whimpering, limp little dog that everything was okay. And I believed him, just listening to his confident voice. Miraculously, William was right about the dog. About a week later, body wiggling and tail pumping triple time, we returned him to his owner's arms. We'd caught each other's gaze as we got back into the car. And I was thinking at the time that the little guy might not have made it had he been hit by anyone less determined, or less able to focus on a good outcome. William is a very determined man.

I count on William's instincts and reactions in any crisis much like I used to count on my father as a child. I desperately need to hear his voice telling me as we approach that hospital that I will be okay, that I am going to be just fine. I need him fully committed to making it all be fine. But William is not talking confidently now. He isn't even talking. The startling contrast between the enthusiastic efforts he'd put into that dog and the heavy sounds of complete silence enveloping the car confuse me.

"It's better," I say quickly.

I turn to see him nod. He makes a turn to the right into Boulder Hospital parking lot. And I take a deep breath. I have a fear of hospitals. An irrational fear of doctors, especially male doctors.

Come on, I tell myself. You can do this. You've ridden out massive waves on a pitching, shuddering ship in a typhoon battering the South China seas with a smile and a meal in front of you. You can do this without your stomach heaving and sweat streaming down your sides. You stayed calm remember? You can do this. Surely, this time you can. But I cannot.

I feel like a condemned captive facing the final, fatal destination when I spot the emergency room entrance, brightly lit, just ahead. Quickly I look away. Thirty-foot waves are preferable to the level pavement leading to that door. Yet, I know I must be here. Positive thinking alone will not fix this problem. Fifteen minutes earlier, I'd asked William to bring me here. This place I avoid like the plague. This irrational me I avoid like the plague.

William pulls in front of the emergency room entrance, and the right front tire slams into the curb. William jumps from his seat and runs to open my door.

"I'm okay," I insist as he reaches for me. "I can walk."

Ignoring me, he grips my arm as he leads me in. I glance around. I hate this place. And I hate most that I am here.

I tell them I've just had chest pains. They usher me in quickly while William stays to sign paperwork. An IV needle plunges into the back of my hand.

"That's not too bad is it?" the nurse asks.

She is tall and built like a fullback. Looking up at her from the examining table, I feel dwarfed. I shake my head to answer her question, thinking an IV is a tangle in your hair compared to a falling tree flattening you. I already did the tree tonight. I doubt anything she does can make me wince.

I begin working on my breathing, working on keeping my fear under wraps while they're sticking round receptors to my chest with what feels like cold slime. This fear of doctors shames me and is something I would never reveal. It makes me feel two years old and just as inarticulate.

The emergency room doctor appears in my cubicle as they complete the EKG test. I try to describe what happened, but I'm not doing a good job. I wish he could have seen me five minutes ago. Then I would not need to explain.

The EKG report prints out. The doctor stares at me oddly.

"It's normal," he says dryly. "Completely normal. But the report isn't the whole story."

They will do blood work to see if there's been damage to the heart. He asks me more about my medical history and lifestyle. No, I don't smoke. I don't drink alcohol or do any drugs. No, I don't even drink coffee. No, there have been no heart attacks in my immediate family.

I have a clean diet. No garbage food. I have a lean, athletic build and have just started training for a triathlon. Though I haven't exercised with religious regularity since swimming competitively in high school and college, I've always been active. I use the treadmill, bike, and weights at least three or four times a week.

But two days ago, I completed a 5K race with Sara, and it drained me. It sickened me. I've never been a good runner, and Sara is. I'd forgotten my pulse meter and idiotically pushed too hard trying to stay up with her. I mention the race, my nausea and the exhaustion immediately following it to the doctor. He says it doesn't mean a thing. The troponin blood test comes back. In monotones the doctor explains the results show no heart damage.

"We could repeat the test in a few hours, but you have absolutely no risk for heart problems." Looking down the hall, something else earns his attention.

A few moments later, he glances back at me, "A panic attack is quite possibly causing these symptoms."

The brawny nurse frowns in my direction and straightens up as if I'm taking up valuable bed space. Yet, there aren't many patients here tonight.

My frustration instantly escalates. It appears they think I'm a hypochondriac. I can't stand anyone thinking of me that way. I look at William, expecting him to tell them I'm no neurotic. I want him to tell them that I'm certainly not the type to have panic attacks. I don't even know what type that is, but I don't wish to count myself among them. I want him to tell them I don't flinch or complain. Most of all, I want William to tell this man that I am the last person on earth who'd go to a doctor trying to get attention. I'm no whiner.

But William says nothing. His words flow copiously in every situation, but not now. We sit like silent stones, our blinking eyes offering the only signs of life. It will take me weeks to realize I've lost my voice. My fears have made me weak. Tears lurk ominously close, yet I refuse to humiliate myself further by crying in front of a man who suggests I'm being melodramatic. I will not cry.

And then, all the time I have spent in business comes to my aid. I learned not to cry years ago. I learned I could keep back the tears as long as I don't try to talk. If I talk, my voice will tremble and betray me. When I was a workingwoman, I used to pretend I was studying something in a file to get me through. It worked for me. Tonight, there are no papers to review, but I get very quiet. The tears will vaporize. They always do. I won't think about it, and they will pass without me sobbing.

Another doctor appears and introduces himself. His name is David Jamisen. He is attentive and polite as he asks me questions. In good humor, he mentions that he was sound asleep when they called him in. He smiled as he tells me what I've already heard.

The tests came back normal. I have no risk for heart problems. He tells me that this is probably not my heart. He talks to me about esophageal reflux, stomach acid backing up, and I'm thinking it takes a lot more than stomach acid to drop me to the floor and make me feel like I'm dying.

"Can stomach acid cause that kind of pain?" I ask. He pauses, and

I sense he is evaluating something. But he does not know me, and he does not know how I handle pain.

"Possibly," he says.

I sigh inside. This is my heart. I know it is my heart, and I know I can convince him of that if I could just get the words out. Why can't I just get the words out? I stop trying. Men take you seriously if you are calm and logical. They will at least give you a hearing if you appeal to logic and reason. But I can't speak, and I bear down on my silence, so the tears won't fall. Keeping them back takes all my effort. And I know this doctor has no idea of the battle I am waging.

"I won't kick you out," he tells me kindly. "But I think you're safe to go home." Then he pauses for another instant. His hesitation catches me and rivets me to him as he continues.

"Sometimes before a heart attack, there are people who have an ominous feeling. They feel something terrible is about to happen." I look away. "The choice is yours," he tells me, "if you think you should stay."

He is right on top of it. I've had this ominous feeling, as he calls it, for weeks. Two nights ago, I had a strange dream. There was a thick book and a voice telling me it was my Life Book. It was open, and I glanced at it. Then I woke without remembering what I'd read and wondered why my Life Book was open and being reviewed. Part of me understands.

There is more to this feeling. I'm at my peak, strong, and full of energy and purpose, but for the previous few weeks, I would stop in the middle of something thinking, I must finish this before I'm gone. Then I'd analyze the thought and brush it off as idiotic. But I am thinking of it all again. It's starting to make sense. Dr. Jamisen brought it up, giving me the perfect opening and opportunity, and still, I can't speak. I do not know him well enough to tell him these things. I glance at my husband. I have not told him these things either. If I do so now, he will laugh and roll his eyes. It's part of the package of those "airy fairy" subjects he hates, but the fact that I can't tell him hurts.

"You can stay," Dr. Jamisen repeats patiently, "if you think you should." He waits for my response.

He's soft-spoken and seems caring. His manner is nothing like the mask of the emergency room doctor, but still, I sense he's humoring me.

I know that I have woken him from much needed sleep. For what he believes is stomach acid. I don't wish to waste anyone's time.

I can't stay. The thought of staying in a hospital is a nightmare. There is no way I will choose on an elective basis if the doctor doesn't insist. There's no logical reason for him to insist. I am at zero risk for heart problems.

The pain seems long gone. The monster is far away and very unreal in this moment. "I'll go home," I hear myself tell Dr. Jamisen.

It is a dumb decision. It is dumb to silence your voice and what you know to be true. But I am thinking only of leaving a place that scares me. Of leaving people who can't possibly understand me. I will pay a price for my stupidity.

Chapter Two

William doesn't say a word on the way home. He doesn't have to. I feel his irritation with me, and I know he'd rate me just about as high as that emergency room doctor.

Why, after all the years, does each day bring a new need to prove myself to him? Past performances during stitches, broken bones, a drug free childbirth, and a car wreck mean nothing. I have become a wimp by making a big deal about stomach acid. Or a panic attack. His wife is now having panic attacks.

It is still Tuesday. Tuesday's child may be full of grace, but I have never felt less graceful. I climb the stairs at home, careful not to turn on many lights as I head into the girls' room, knowing Sara must be asleep in the back bedroom. We have three bedrooms for the kids, and yet they always chose to sleep together in Jacqueline's king-sized bed. I gingerly perch on the edge, careful to avoid a sprawling, little leg.

Jacqueline, our two-year-old, rests between her six-year-old sisters, Meagan and Brenna. They look like real life angels lying there. Breathtakingly beautiful little girls. Suddenly, the feeling of foreboding returns...clouding the scene and dominating me. Immediately I say a prayer that God will send His angels to watch after my daughters. Leaning over, I pull up disheveled sheets, laying them across shoulders and under chins. I turn away, and I linger at their door, looking back. But I'm unable to see my girls clearly, and I'm completely removed from myself. The whole film wavers out of focus and out of harmony this time. Nothing feels real except the dark heaviness of this feeling. I watch my hand slowly closing the door.

I'll take a shower. I'll take a hot shower and relax and then this terrible, idiotic feeling will wash away. I strip off my clothes, dropping them into a pile. Leaning into the shower stall, I turn the water pressure on high and the heat way up. It feels so good. Water always brings me home. I begin a routine that I've completed a thousand times. I will not complete it tonight.

The pain hits full force. My chest. My arm. I double over grabbing my left arm as I stumble out.

"It's happening again!" I yell at William. Panic strains my voice. I know this excruciating agony, and I cannot stand it. I cannot stand it again. I grab my robe and barely make it to the bed. I sob from the pain and my own awful stupidity. I shouldn't have left the hospital. I knew I shouldn't have left.

William leans over me. "Get me back," I moan. "You've got to get me back."

But I can't move this time. I am incapable of walking even half a step.

"Call an ambulance," I plead, but I'm thinking the same thing he is. It will take them twenty minutes to drive to our house, if they can even find our house in the dark. And it will be another twenty minutes getting back down to the hospital. It's too long. I need help now. Dear God, I desperately need help now.

William reaches down to pick me up. His arm tightens around my left side and he lifts. I cry out. Without thinking, I push away frantically, slipping through his arms and off the bed onto the carpet. He stands over me, and I sense him trying to figure out how to get me up without hurting me. He's 6'3" and lifts weights regularly; but I weigh 135 pounds, and I am not a barbell. It isn't going to work.

I turn on my side, vomiting on our white bedroom carpet. The mess I'm making is meaningless to me, though I've struggled years to keep this rug spotless. My body begins shaking violently, uncontrollably, suddenly icy cold but breaking out in a drenching sweat.

"William," I sob, "I have to get to the bathroom." But there is no way. There is nothing left in my stomach and nothing left of my dignity. I roll over onto my back. Please God. I can't stand this anymore.

William says he'll get the nitroglycerin tablets they gave us at the hospital. Footsteps race down the stairs. He is moving fast, I think. And I am alone again. Alone with a pain too awful to believe.

"Hurry!" I scream. "Please Hurry!" So, I've become a screamer now.

I don't even care. The seconds are endless. The suffering is endless. Why is he taking so long?

But I know he isn't taking long. Frantic steps charge up the stairs. Losing consciousness, I feel him slipping the pill under my tongue, and for a few seconds I cling to the hope that the pain will stop. But there's no stopping it. I hear the moaning continue.

I'm drifting farther away. My noises quiet. My writhing slows way down.

William tells me he's going to wake Sara. She can help him ease me off the floor without hurting me. But moving off the floor doesn't seem so important to me anymore. I'm leaving my body again. And with this new release comes a measure of relief.

From far away, I hear Sara's voice. My sweet, pregnant friend has left her husband and her two-year-old daughter to come to our house and keep our children safe. I'm not able to open my eyes, yet I feel her concern.

"Look at you," she whispers, her voice breaking with emotion. She bends to my side.

They have me off the floor in a second. William gathers me into his arms like a broken, limp, sweaty doll.

"Can you put your arm around my neck?" he asks me gently. I know it would help immensely, but I can't. I can hear him, but I am lost. I can't move a muscle, and I can't answer. He carries me from the bedroom and toward the stairs.

"Don't drop her," Sara says beseechingly. "Just don't drop her."

Drop me. Please. Just drop me right over this railing if it will end the pain. William carries me quickly down the stairs, through the house and to the car with Sara at his heels. Somehow, I am aware of images as we move past all these rooms, and yet my eyes are still closed.

Sara opens the car door. William slides me across the backbench seat. Sara bends close to my ear. "I love you," she whispers, and I hear her voice break again.

I try to move my lips. "I love you, too," I tell her and yet, I am not sure she can hear me. I am not sure I can hear myself.

William starts the car, but Sara hovers at my side. "I'm worried about you," she tells me. Her voice lifts tenderly, filled with concern, but I can't answer or reassure her. I've passed worry a long, long time ago. She closes the door.

This trip down means nothing to me. I have no concept of time or the corners or the speed William is driving. Another shattering blast of pain radiates my entire left side, the side I am lying on. If only I could roll over, could roll onto my back, to remove this spear twisting me inside. But I can't move. I lose consciousness sometime on the drive down. It is 2:30 in the morning. July 2nd. I have just had my second "panic attack."

Chapter Three

The car door opens. Hands pull me out. A faint prick of an IV goes into my hand. Someone touches me. I am naked under the long white bathrobe, but I don't care who sees me, I no longer care who touches me. EKG receptors once again stick on my chest.

I realize the pain is gone. Mercifully, miraculously the pain is gone once again, but I still can't move or even manage to open my eyes. This time, it's harder to come back. I've been much farther away. I can hear the emergency room doctor saying, "This is hard to ignore."

But within minutes, he will ignore what he sees. The EKG indicates another normal reading. I am nowhere near normal. Does this take a genius to assess?

Suddenly the doctor's voice grows harsh when he speaks to me. I'm not used to people talking to me like this. He startles me with his roughened tone.

"Melissa, tell me what happened."

I flinched involuntarily. "William can tell you," I whisper.

"No," he insists, continuing belligerently. "You need to sit up, open your eyes, and we need to have a conversation about this. You need to tell me in your own words."

I listen to him in confused disbelief. This cannot be happening. Does he actually think I'd be lying here if there were any way I could sit up? I have never been in more need of help. I search for a shade of compassion in his voice, for any indication he cares even slightly that I am lying inert before him. Why is he so combative?

It can't be personal, I tell myself. Maybe it's a technique. The last time I'd come in, he didn't bother to hide that he thought I was a hypochondriac, perhaps now he thinks I am acting out what he'd seen on TV shows, and his anger was designed to ferret out fakers. But I don't watch any shows.

"Melissa!" he snaps, as if calling a dumb and disobedient dog. "I told you to sit up!"

And my temper flares unexpectedly. I haven't lost control of my temper with a stranger in years, but it's raging instantly inside me. One thought drives me. I am going to find a way to walk out of here, right now, even if it kills me. And it is going to take a far better man than this one to stop me.

My anger has bypassed all fear of doctors. Taking a deep breath, I open my eyes and rip off the oxygen tube feeding into my nose. I struggle to sit up. The effort brings pain and instant tears to my eyes that I can't will away.

"I see this is hard for you," he tells me in the same infuriating tone.

I slowly turn to look at him. Just yank my chain one more time, buddy. You'll find a pit bull at the end of it.

One ... two ... three ... four ... five. I try to muster more patience. He has misread me, and I am thinking then that he has a medical degree but little intuition. What he's lacking can't be measured by IQ tests, it can't be taught, and it is what separates those who excel from those who memorize. Intuition is badly needed in an emergency room. And it is sorely lacking tonight.

A stream of words I would never use, flow to my head. Not even now. I glance at William, ready for battle, but get no response from my partner. *I would speak up for you. You're always ready for a fight.* Yet the night has badly bled you, I see that clearly. Very well, sit there stone quiet. I can take care of myself.

I look back to the doctor, steadily. This is his ship. He's the captain. A mutiny seethes before him, yet he stands oblivious to it all. His eyes remain dull and indifferent to it all.

I am breathing heavily and trembling from the rage rolling through me.

"You need to change your tone," I tell him, every word clipped in perfect match. I don't blink as the seconds pass. You don't blink when the gauntlet shows, and you never talk first. You wait ... just as long as it takes.

But there is a change. A subtle shift within his eyes. I've been in too many negotiations not to notice the softening. He begins talking again. Nicely this time. For the first time. Trying to convince me it is important that I tell the story in my words. It is a moot point by now. He is no longer rude. I am up. My eyes are wide open. We are indeed having a conversation, and I could care less if I passed or failed this test he runs on me.

He asks me politely to put on the oxygen. I nod because I am willing to give ground too. That's the way you play. He leans closer to help put it back around my ear while I consciously try to think better thoughts about him. Thoughts are all I can control. I don't want to leave anymore. I just want someone to help me. Dear God, can I just get a little help?

Despite my efforts, good thoughts feel hard to muster. I know I must somehow be contributing to what I have against doctors. I take responsibility for it. I just can't seem to change it. Except for childbirth, I've been able to limit contact with them. I don't get sick. I make sure I never get sick. Positive thinking and alternative medicine have helped me. But my fear, coupled with a few weird experiences I've had with doctors, make normal reactions exceptionally difficult. A bad cycle, and I can't break it tonight.

Sitting there, I remember when I was twenty-two and talked myself into going to the university health center for a routine check-up and a pap smear. It'd taken me months to bully myself into going. I hated the idea of a strange man touching me, but I'd told myself I was idiotic for feeling that way.

He's a doctor, I'd kept telling myself. He sees this stuff all the time. Then, after the pelvic exam, while still lying on the table, the young gynecologist with an English accent asked me out for a date. A slight slip in protocol.

I'd started trembling as I dressed, and I trashed the card he gave me—the one he'd written his home phone number on. That was the last time for ten years that I got anywhere near a male doctor. The memory of it still makes me cringe.

Then at the age of thirty-two, I began having episodes of chest pain. They would only last a few seconds, but they'd stop me cold. A glass would drop from my hand. Will insisted that I had to go in and find out what was causing it. I did go and met with a cardiologist. He lifted the half smock that was covering me from the waist up, stared at my bare breasts for a slow six seconds and then lowered the smock and told me that I was far too young to have heart problems. Since there was no family history of heart disease, there was no reason to do any tests.

"Women your age rarely have heart problems," he said. That was all.

I wish he could have managed that revelation while I still had my clothes on. I remembered dressing, feeling like a total fool and thinking I'd rather die than ever be seen by another male doctor. I didn't explain to William what happened until years later: He would not have let the incident end without a major confrontation. All this plays out again in my mind.

Let it go. Stop thinking about this garbage. It helps nothing. Just let it go!

As the doctor leaves the cubicle, the nurse comes closer. The same nurse from my first visit, wearing a profoundly perturbed look on her face. She stops beside me, tight lipped. Finally, she speaks.

"We gave you nitroglycerin tablets and you were told exactly how to use them. Don't you remember? I told you to take one, wait five minutes and then if you still had pain, you were told to take the second pill."

She pauses and I nod, wondering where this is leading. The nurse continues.

"Then you were supposed to wait another full five minutes and if it still didn't help the pain, you should have taken the third one. After that, you could have called us. But you shouldn't have come in until you used all three of them."

I don't bother to respond to the lecture. It all seems so moronic. I've been chastised enough by these people. What can I tell her? I came directly in because I was dying. I'm sorry no one can figure that out. Yes, ma'am, I do usually follow instructions exceedingly well, but it just didn't seem appropriate this time. The first nitro pill knocked me out, and if William had forced the other two under by tongue, I'm sure I'd be dead by now. But next time, I'll try somehow to do better.

Staring up at her and that irritated look on her face makes me feel like I've entered the twilight zone. Dear Lord, how do I get out?

I hear the ER doctor on the phone, probably talking to Doctor Jamisen again. Waking him up again. *But it's their job!* It's their job. The doctor explains something about the way I came in and about my pallor, which he attributes to the nitro tablets.

Of course, he wasn't there in my bedroom when I collapsed. And I know he doesn't believe there is anything really wrong with my heart. I am the weird woman with normal EKGs and normal troponin levels.

The doctor maintains his politeness when he returns, and I have a firm grip on my wayward temper. He reiterates that there probably isn't anything seriously wrong, but they decide to put me in the hospital for what is left of the night. They'll do some tests tomorrow. I know they are tired of me. The feeling is mutual. It is 4:00 a.m. The night is nearly done. I'm wheeled upstairs. I suggest to William that he goes home and gets some sleep. We'll talk in the morning.

Soon after they've settled me into the hospital bed, I get hooked up to a smaller version of an EKG. The nurse assures me they'll be monitoring me. Is this supposed to make me feel any better? I have zero confidence in these machines. I have even less confidence in the people operating them.

I don't sleep, but then I'm a mom. I've put in plenty of sleepless nights. One more feels like no real loss. Activity increases as the suns rises. Visitors come for my diabetic roommate, and there are breakfast and blood pressure checks for me.

I'm holding on to a semi-slow frustrating burn. There have been no other pains, but I know they will come again soon. I sense it. I sense both the monster and the time bomb inside that will bring it back to life, and I realize I must do something quickly, but I can't figure out what else to do.

Another physician calls on me. He seems friendly. But it is the same story. There is nothing wrong, and I should go home and put this behind me. They've repeated the troponin test two more times to be on the safe side. All three of these blood tests are normal and indicate no damage to my heart. The doctor orders an ultrasound before my discharge. He suggests a treadmill stress test as soon as possible, within twenty-four hours.

"But there's nothing to worry about," he says, smiling confidently. "You have zero risk for heart disease. Likely esophageal reflux."

Stomach acid again. What's missing here? I keep asking myself as he talks. I've never had stomach acid, but I'm betting I could handle it with a Tums and a change in attitude. And I know it isn't stomach acid that has dropped me to the floor twice. These are bright men. I must have somehow failed to communicate some vital piece of information they need. If I could only go back and do better, I would, but I don't know exactly what I did wrong.

Watching this doctor, I wonder if they all believe I'm a complete idiot. Do they think I am exaggerating the pain or simply inventing it? How in the name of God can another M.D. come to me with a straight face and tell me to just go home and forget it?

Would you forget it? I wonder. Would you treat it as insignificant if the same thing happened twice to you in one night? You'd jump right up from the floor, wipe off the puke, and the drenching sweat? You'd ignore the crushingly numb left arm and the scorching pain, and you'd just go about your day, telling yourself it was stomach acid? And your next thought would be to just put it all behind you and get on with your life. Somehow, I don't think you'd do that. Yet, you are telling me to, so I must conclude that it is not the symptoms you dismiss. It is me having them. And that leaves me believing you must think I'm either a liar or a hypochondriac, and I am neither. But you don't know that, do you? And somehow, I think if I were a man you would take my story seriously. You would take me seriously. That is the bare bottom line of this infuriating struggle. It galls me.

Please do not pat my head next. For I will lose it. I'm on edge. Too close to the edge. I smile wanly at the physician. Within the hour I'm complacently doing the ultrasound on my heart.

"It all looks great," the technician volunteers cheerfully. "A doctor will check it, but it looks completely normal, except for a prolapsed mitral valve. That's nothing major," she explains.

I thank her. I'm discharged from the hospital. Will has already dropped off my Jeep and my keys and had someone take him to work. I slide into my car to drive home.

"Do something," the voice inside urges. "You must do something quickly."

What? What am I supposed to do? I've been to the ER twice. Enduring a doctor who lacks compassion and common sense, an irritated nurse who schools me, and two specialists who tell me my heart is fine. What else am I supposed to do? Something. There is always something. Think.

Then a little something comes to me. I look to the one bright spot in my medical history, Richard Porreco, MD. A well-known and respected obstetrician and a high-risk specialist, he is the only doctor who has ever known anything about me.

I was seven months pregnant when I found my way to his practice. Will had set up a meeting for us. And I was dreadfully nervous. I couldn't believe I was sitting in front of another male doctor. For something like this of all things? How do women talk themselves into this and tell themselves it's okay? I can't do it and pretend they aren't really men and that they don't well, really look. Those two doctors, long ago, ripped that delusion permanently from me. No, I thought, I can't go through with it. But how am I going to have these babies?

Dr. Porreco sat in front of me. I was eyeing him with suspicion. It didn't matter that women were flown in from six states seeking this man's expertise. I heard myself sounding nervous, and still I couldn't stop myself. I told him I just wanted to talk. I didn't want him to "check anything."

Dr. Porreco leaned back in his chair. His voice was gentle and there was no pressure. There was no judgment. As he talked, my shaking slowly subsided. I listened to his words as I studied him. I recognized his intensity, and I respected it. He took time with me, time I knew he was short of, and I kept listening to his voice, and he listened fully to mine, as if I were the most important patient he'd ever had. And as I sat there beside him, watching him, he had my trust. Dr. Porreco earned my trust. It was that simple. I had no doubts. He told me he'd take me as his patient. I told him I'd take him as my doctor.

I had dreamed of a home birth, a dream that went out the window with the discovery we were going to have twins and the realization we lived too far away to get help if something started to go sour. I would have been willing to risk my life in order to avoid the hospital and doctors, but I couldn't risk my twins. I stood up, and with a smile and a handshake, our meeting was over.

"Twenty-seven weeks is getting a little late with twins," Dr. Porreco had said with a laugh as I turned to leave. And I laughed too. I knew it was late. I just couldn't force myself in a day earlier. He had this amused, I-have-seen-and-handled-everything look on his face. And I believed it, because he had just handled me. Effortlessly.

In time, I learned that I had not made a mistake trusting Rich Porreco. Sometime that first month, I started calling him by his first name, and it was not due to a lack of respect for his profession. It helped my fear with the doctor thing and he took it all in stride. "Hi Melissa, it's Rich Porreco," he would say whenever he returned my calls. Not once did he refer to himself as Dr. Porreco. He knew he was a doctor, but he never needed to put that distance or discomfort between us. I figured all along he had my number, but I didn't mind.

As high-tech as he was, we had an understanding. It was going to be as natural a birth as possible. As natural as it can be in an operating room, with numerous specialists standing by. I covered my fears in a deep, back drawer, knowing if something went wrong, there was Rich. But nothing went wrong. There are times you can will things to work out well. That you can clearly change outcome by intent. I'd practiced it in business a hundred times with success. Will and I were willing a good birth. Rich was willing it. And God had granted it all. Together we'd made it through the twins' birth, and, later, two miscarriages, Jacqueline's birth, and the hemorrhage immediately following it.

I was watching his eyes when the bleeding started. Watching as he glanced at the Pitocin drip, then once again at the bag that was used to induce her birth. It was still hooked to my IV. And I knew Pitocin is used to slow bleeding.

"We're down one unit," he said to his nurse. His voice was calm, his expression completely composed yet I saw just a flicker of concern in his eyes. Firm resolve was there too. Iron resolve that I know well. The kind of resolve that instantly erases everything else. Rich Porreco could get real serious, real fast. I saw that in his face that afternoon.

Will was at my side, holding the baby, casually chatting, completely oblivious to the fact that I was bleeding. And Rich was talking and answering just as casually as he kept working quickly. I never told him that my mother almost bled to death following a delivery. It hadn't ever come to my mind. But it came to my mind then. That simple fact that women used to die with some regularity during childbirth.

Within another minute, he had the flood stopped. When our eyes met, I wanted to tell him that I knew I'd probably be gone if he hadn't been there. That a home birth in my case might have just turned into a home death.

Rich Porreco was articulate with explanations, and quick with decisions, but there was something more I sensed. That's what I am remembering today. Once when I went in with what turned out to be false labor, before he sent me home, Rich had asked me, "What do you feel is going on?" What did I feel?

I stared for a moment at this man who worked so successfully with women. And I had to grin. I loved that question. Because I understood then why I had put my faith in him. He had all the medical credentials one could hope to have, yet he had instincts too. Instincts and intuition. He was weighing every fact before him, listening with his head and his heart. Exactly what I needed. That balance made all the difference.

And now I need him again. My sense of doom grows like a rising, mountainous thundercloud. I know Rich Porreco will believe me if I tell him I'm in serious trouble. He'll understand I wouldn't go to the emergency room twice on a whim, and he'll know if I tell him that I was writhing on the floor in agony, that something is seriously, seriously wrong. He knows how I can handle pain. He saw me smiling through natural childbirth.

Jacqueline's birth had caught him in his shirtsleeves. He'd stopped in during labor to see me and made a comment to the nurse that I was still smiling and to up the Pitocen. He didn't bother to examine me because his years of experience told him I could not be smiling through natural childbirth, but he was wrong. The nurse ran to get him just a short time later, and he stuck his head in the door.

"Do I have time to change?" he asked me.

"I think so." And he did. Barely. How did I know? I didn't do this everyday.

He called me stoic once. Being stoic is just part of having a Marine for a dad. A Marine who fought in three major wars, who saw a lot of men dying and hurting. A father you love very much, whom you don't ever, ever want to think of you as weak or complaining. My dad was a stoic, and it's not an easy thing he passed to me, but I shouldered it instantly because of the look on his face when I was a little girl. A look that said Malcolm's do not show pain. Not even when there is a lot of it. They stay strong, they clean it up, and they say they're doing okay. And only if someone asks. Repeatedly. I got it Dad. *Semper Fi.*

Rich I need you now, and somehow, I have to get through to you because you seemed to understand me instantly. The doctors that I'm dealing with now do not. I need to talk to you or have you refer me to someone who'll believe something is really wrong. Because something is terribly, terribly wrong.

⊰❊⊱

My phone is ringing, and I pick it up. William tells me he has reached Dr. Porreco's nurse, Mary Lou, and she's just given him the name of a cardiologist. I feel relief. But it will be extremely short-lived. Nothing is flowing easily. Nothing even flows.

Mary Lou has recommended a woman cardiologist in Denver, and I would go that instant, but I can't get in to see her: She isn't in my insurance group, and her receptionist tells me that I'll need a referral from my primary care physician before I can make any appointment, even if I'm willing to pay out of pocket. But I don't have a primary care physician who knows me. He's just a name on an insurance card I've only taken out of my wallet once.

I'm back home now, sitting at my desk, and I finally get through to my primary care physician, Dr. Lucas. It quickly becomes apparent that he won't even consider referring me.

"As far as I'm concerned, the specialists in Boulder are excellent. There is absolutely no indication you need to get another opinion."

"I'm sure they're excellent," I tell him. "But in my case, they're making a mistake."

Dr. Lucas cuts me off abruptly, "I am extremely busy, and I think it's best if you change to another primary care physician." I agree.

We hang up. I stare at the phone for a few minutes trying to calm down. I've watched Will play a lot of baseball. I've watched and cheered for countless hits and phenomenal catches far out in left field. Now it's the World Series, bottom of the 9th. My team's one run down...bases are loaded, 3-2 count. And I finally understand what striking out with bases loaded feels like deep in the pit of your stomach.

Okay. Okay, you still need to do something. Just keep thinking. Just find a physician in the same insurance group who will refer you to the cardiologist Rich's nurse recommended. Do it. It takes another three hours of frustrating phone calls to locate a primary care physician who will refer me to this cardiologist. I stand up from my desk wearily. I have an appointment the following afternoon with a nurse in the new doctor's office who says she could refer me. The doctor is far too busy to see me for at least a week. *I don't care; just give me the referral. Please, so I can believe I've done something to stop this avalanche that's bearing down on me.*

Chapter Four

Thursday morning on July 3rd, almost two full days since the first attack. My friend Christine is watching the children while I shower, dress, and drive the twenty-five minutes to Broomfield for my appointment with the nurse. I fill out new patient forms and wait to meet with her.

It proves to be a quick meeting. She is obviously rushed and has squeezed me in between appointments. I give her a brief story of my chest pains and my recent visits to the emergency room. She listens to my heart and tells me it is normal except for a slight murmur. She takes my blood pressure. It is low, 90 over 55, but then it's always low. Next, she tells me she wants to take blood for a thyroid check. I give my consent. I don't care at this point. If she wants blood, she can have it. I just want the referral.

"This is not your heart," she informs me methodically, as she fills the last vile. "Have you heard of panic attacks?"

I manage to maintain a straight face. Yes, *I have heard of them; and if this keeps up, I may finally have one.* I press for the referral. She said she'll give it to me, but nothing will happen until after the upcoming holiday weekend.

"Please," I ask, pleading, "Please see what you can do. I feel that I need to get in right away." These words flow from the heart effortlessly.

The nurse glances out toward an employee lunchroom table that is laden with mounds of goodies and decorated red, white, and blue. An office party. I am keeping her from an office party.

I leave the building and open the door to my Jeep. I have failed again and know it. There was a time in my life when I did not fail like this. What am I supposed to do now?

I start the car and call Christine to tell her I'll be home soon. In the background of her cheerful voice, I hear my kids playing. They seem far away, and their raucous laughter feels even farther.

Five minutes down the highway is the town of Louisville where my father was born and raised. I notice Avista Hospital sitting prominently on the hill to my right, then I look back to the road before me.

Then it hits. The same violent pain hits at sixty-five miles an hour. I know it intimately. I know the pressure in my left arm will reduce me to a helpless shadow of myself in moments. The agony in my chest will collapse me. Somehow, I have to get off the highway. I wince as the breath is knocked out of me. Oh, please help. I don't want to hurt anyone. I slow down, putting on the turn signal to veer off the road, but I see the Louisville Exit directly in front of me. I take it instead of pulling the car over and stopping.

I think of William. The office building for our new company is only five minutes down this road. If I can just make it a few more miles, I can make it to...A thought comes to me that this road leads to Avista Hospital. I keep driving as the pain escalates. I call William on my car phone; the receptionist puts me through immediately.

"It's really hurting again," I try telling him.

But the pain peaks and words won't come out right. My left arm is gone again. For the third time. Completely numb, useless, hanging limp and curled in my lap, and I'm driving with my right hand trying to make the turns. I will not hurt someone.

Unexpectedly, I take a turn to the right, away from William and our office building. I am driving somewhere as if I am led. Glancing around, I tell William I am near the hospital. We say goodbye quickly. I can't believe I am going there. But the pain feels so terrible I desperately want help again. Please. Please, can someone help me this time? I try dialing the phone again but remembering my home number now seems impossible. I keep repeating the number aloud, trying to punch it in, trying to concentrate and focus most of my attention on keeping the car within my lane. I have to redial three times before I get the number right.

"Christine? Christine," my voice breaking. "I can't come home. My heart is hurting." I hang up the call.

The emergency room looms in front of me. I turn off the car. The pain is easing off. Right then...in an instant...it just disappears. Okay.

Just relax. It wasn't as bad this time, and it didn't last nearly as long. I am able to get out of the car and make it in on my own. A male nurse walks toward me.

"I've just had chest pains."

Without hesitation, he leads me to a cot in the emergency room and flawlessly puts another IV into the back of my hand. Another EKG machine gets hooked up. But the pain is completely gone. There is another readout from the machine. Another normal. How is this possibly normal?

The emergency room doctor on duty appears, Dr. Davis. I start talking to him and telling him what has been going on. I answer his questions. I realize it is coming out reasonably coherent. Somehow, I must get through to someone right now. He seems to care that I am having a real problem. He seems to be listening to me as if he believes I might be having a real problem. We talk easily with each other.

"I want to call Dr. Jamisen," he says.

"Please don't. It won't do any good. He was very nice to me, but I'm sure he'll think I'm having more mental problems, not physical ones."

Dr. Davis leaves, and he is on the phone a long time before he returns. Will arrives, and I reach for his hand as we look at each other. I see his concern. I'm sure he sees my frustration.

Dr. Davis walks to my side again. "Dr. Jamisen believes there is some real reason for this pain." He tells me gently, "And I don't think you'd keep going to emergency rooms if there wasn't something wrong. We'll find it."

I exhale. Okay, I can deal with this. I can deal with this. Just give me a chance. I can prove I'm not a flake, if you guys just give me a chance.

Dr. Jamisen first wants to rule out blood clots in my chest. I agree to have a chest X-ray and a VQ scan, which will show clots. I agree to see Dr. Jamisen later that afternoon for a treadmill stress test. He's told Dr. Davis that he doesn't want me to leave the hospital until I've done the stress test and that he'll drive to Avista to administer the test as soon as he's finished seeing patients.

"Okay," I promise Dr. Davis. "I won't leave."

I suggest to William that he might as well go back to the office to get some work done while my tests are completed. Not long after William leaves, a young technician wheels me in for the X-ray. I'm just glad the pain has gone again. It doesn't even cross my mind that the violent pain has come in pairs. I have a few more minutes of ignorant peace.

⋛⋚

I take off the Celtic cross I always wear around my neck, and the X-ray finishes quickly.

"Do you notice anything?" I ask anxiously.

"It looks normal," the technician whispers, "but I'm not really qualified to tell you anything. A doctor will have to look at it."

Sitting in a wheelchair, alone for a moment. I close my eyes. "Dear God," I pray softly. "Please help me. Please just help them figure out what's wrong with me."

I hear the woman return; I open my eyes. She wheels me back down the same hall. At the end of the hall, an odd and overwhelming sense swarms me. An instant later the pain hits. It is here again. Devouring my chest. Oh Lord.

I leave the chair and climb back into the cot in the emergency room. I don't say a word to the technician. It is completely quiet in the ER. I am quiet as the monstrous pain takes over again.

Looking to my right, I see the male nurse who has been so pleasant. Time subtly shifts. I hear Dr. Davis on the phone. The nurse pivots as if in slow motion and stares at me. With my hand, I start a spinning gesture of an airplane propeller speeding up - the pain taking off again. He instantly understands. I watch him interrupt Dr. Davis's call and then I look away. I look up at the ceiling. Breathe, Melissa. Try to breathe.

Instant agony again. I struggle to control myself, to stop myself from crying out from the blasting force of this shattering pain, I am not in the car with my husband, or in my bedroom, and if I can find any way to keep myself together, I still need to try.

My left arm is gone once more. Numb yet somehow it feels squashed flat to the bone between a heavy vice. But it is the stabbing knife in my chest again that wracks me. Sitting on the table, I am rocking slightly. Still fighting to breathe through this.

Suddenly, Dr. Davis is beside me. Standing very close and talking softly to me. I turn to him. The concern within his eyes melts me. He is with me. I am not alone this time. Without needing words, he is telling me he'll do everything he possibly can to help.

I know he can sense I am trying to hold it together. I know he realizes I am hurting, bad. This is the fourth time now. The fourth time in a day and a half. Then I start crumbling, and I just want him to hold me, to please make this stop happening. My eyes rim with tears, and they break free, trickling all the way down my cheeks. I wipe them away quickly with my fingertips. It's okay, I tell myself, letting the rest fall. It's okay. He'd probably be crying by now too.

Dr. Davis calls for an EKG again. It arrives quickly.

"Try to hold still," another technician tells me.

I realize she has no idea how hard it is to hold completely still through this kind of excruciating pain. But I hold still while the test is completed. And the EKG's completed for the very first time while I am actually having pain.

Dr. Davis reads the report and says simply that there is a change registering on the machine. I don't understand what the change means, but it's capturing his attention. It is just the exact same excruciating pain to me. Yet everyone is moving quickly now.

My breathing degrades once more to moaning on each exhale. Dr. Davis puts his arm around me and gently leans me back onto the table. I shut my eyes. I need to close my eyes to block some of this out. I ask him to call my husband.

"Call William," I repeat over and over again. I need to see him. I want him with me. I float away.

Dr. Davis is calling me. He is only inches from my face telling me something. Looking down on my chest, I see my hands there curled up grotesquely like frozen claws. I watch his lips. Yes, he is trying to tell me something.

But I can't understand him. *I would do what you ask, but I can't understand a single word you are telling me.* I am not afraid: I feel strangely calm. I am leaving again.

Chapter Five

A nitro pill slips under my tongue. Someone unzips my jeans. I lift slightly trying to help as they slide down. They are not snug; they come off easily. I have this mental image of the struggle they must have trying to remove the skin-tight ones. Then I figured they don't struggle, they just cut it off.

Will is suddenly on my left. Finally. I reach out my arm, and his presence brings me back slightly as his fingers connect with mine. His presence brings me back slightly; making me feel it's safer to be here.

"I love you," he tells me.

Somehow, I understand Dr. Davis has called the Flight for Life helicopter. It is a quick drive to Boulder, but I guess it isn't quite quick enough. He tells William they don't want me caught in traffic. He says something about the caliber of people that will be on that helicopter.

Flight for Life arrives. Lori, the nurse, takes charge of me. Talking to me, shifting me over to her lines and monitors. It is done quickly. Smoothly, precisely. I am being loaded onto the left side of the helicopter. Lori leans down, talking to me, and I open my eyes. She has her flight helmet on. Our eyes make contact. She makes sure they make clear contact. You are good at what you do, I think. You are very good, Lori. Thank you for your kindness. I can feel her caring even through the thick helmet that separates us. I keep watching her eyes. Her eyes are willing me to stay. Willing me to keep watching her and to keep on trying.

"How are you doing?"

"I'm okay,"

"How's the pain?" She will ask it several times during that short flight to Boulder.

"It's easing off some," I say softly.

"No, give me a number one to ten."

"A six," then I hesitate. "Maybe a seven," I add, trying to be more honest.

I have known tens the past two days. I have known twenty plus. But I don't bother Lori with this information.

I'm still not afraid. Everyone is doing the best they can. I am doing the best I can. I have lived my life the best I can. But this is way out of my hands, my "need to control things" hands. A sense of peace enfolds me. A relief in relinquishing my pack to let others take control. There are things being set in motion I do not understand. Other people are taking charge of my life and whatever remains of it.

Later, Dr. Jamisen will tell me he was in his office still seeing patients when the fax of my EKG came across his line. He will say that it is the worst EKG he has ever seen. This time, the machine finally registered my massive heart attack. He makes the decision to call in Flight for Life and leaves immediately to meet me at Boulder Hospital.

⋑⋐

The helicopter lands. I glance out the left side as they unload me. I am home. Boulder. People crowd close along the sidewalk. The hospital again. I don't want them staring at me for something like this. They wheel me to the door. I close my eyes, pulling inward. I have seen enough. The rest blurs.

Something startles me. I lift my head, as a man on my right works near my groin. He looks at me and says he is sorry, but he has to shave me completely. He seems genuinely apologetic. I drop my head back down. "It's okay," I say softly. "There are worse traumas."

And then there is an image of Dr. Jamisen at the end of the table. Saying something to me about "finally presenting myself."

For an instant, I don't want to see him. I don't even want to look at him. For a split second I feel he has somehow failed me and failed to believe me when I needed him most.

"I don't know what you mean by presenting myself."

There is a tone to my voice, and I've put it there intentionally. But I do know exactly what he means: I know it is just a medical term, but I am thinking I have tried to "present myself" numerous times to you guys.

Why do I answer him rudely? I wonder instantly. He's done nothing wrong. He made the best call he could with the facts he had. He's done nothing but be polite to me during the little contact we've had.

The pain is too much to stay. I feel myself drifting out of my body again. Before I can go completely, I feel a few sticks of a needle and something clamps hard onto the outside of my left thigh, pinching me. It hurts a little. Some of it hurt a little. I don't want to stay and feel anymore.

My rings are eased off my fingers. A woman's voice asks me about my wedding ring. I'd taken it off two months earlier, but the indentation in the flesh of my finger must have still shown. A nearly perfect 2 carat marquis cut diamond sits at home in a dark and securely locked box. I'd taken it off after an argument I'd had with William. It is something I've never done before, but after it was done, I could not force myself to put it back on. It might have been easier to do, if he'd ever noticed that I wasn't wearing it.

Sara and another close friend, Jan Mako, noticed it was missing the first day. I didn't need to say anything. A woman understands why another woman takes off her ring. And I am thinking this nurse will understand too. She will know even though she knows nothing about me. But she might know about love. And the hurt that comes with it sometimes.

She slides off my favorite "good luck" ring that I wear on my wedding ring finger. I've worn this gold ring with the raised woman's head since I was fourteen years old and discovered it in my Mom's jewelry box. It never leaves me. Mom finally presented it to me as a gift for my sixteenth birthday. Of all the things I own, this little ring means the most to me. I don't know why I've slipped my good luck ring on that finger, the one that is said to connect most directly to the heart. I want to wear something there. I am not trying to attract men. Dear God, I can do without the attention of men.

Now she eases off my father's gold signet ring I wear on my right hand. He was a combat office in the Marines, who fought in World War II, Korea, and Vietnam and wore his "good luck ring" on his little finger. Never once was he injured throughout his thirty-three years with the Marines. My father has been gone one year, ten months. I loved him dearly. The ring swings loose on my finger, but it stays and comforts, offering reminders of a powerful presence who was tender at home. Tender and always loving to me, never once raising his voice in anger. Always letting me find my own path.

"Just use your own good judgment," he told me repeatedly when I was growing up. I hadn't wanted to ever disappoint him, yet I'd felt unequal to the picture he held of me. A rare bond linked us. It was love. Unconditional love. And I have sorely missed its healing power since he's left me. Oh Dad, I still miss you terribly. But I remember your love. I will always remember.

A month before you got sick, I woke with a premonition that you would soon be gone. I struggled to prepare myself. But how do you prepare? I'm still grappling with the gaping hole his absence has left in my life. Filling in edges that keep falling back in when I least expected it.

I'm lying on that table wondering if I'll be with my Dad again soon. I open my eyes, but I do not sense him with me. At times I know with certainty that he is near, watching over me. He never failed me once when I needed him. Dad, are you here? Daddy, I can sure use some help here.

I don't want to die, but I realize it isn't my decision. I say another prayer for my children: I don't want to leave them. So much remains to share with them. So many things I want to teach them, and I am suddenly worried, knowing they are completely dependent on me.

If I die, my little Jacqueline won't even remember anything about me. She won't remember my face, she won't remember the sound of my songs, she won't remember the years we've spent pressed together. That knowledge hurts. I never did anything for praise or remembrance; I did them because they felt right to do. But no thoughts can convince me that dying now weaves the brightest future for my three little girls.

I'm lying there hoping I'll get the chance to see them once more. Nothing else feels important anymore. All the rest, all the stuff that seemed so important to get done, doesn't matter anymore. Nothing else is important. It is the kids and knowing my mom will be broken by my death. Dad's passing left a deep loneliness none of us could salve. And her quick assurances and easy smiles do not hide the truth from me. Now she will have to bear this new heartache.

It is too soon. It is too much. I am her baby, one of her pillars. She will miss my nightly calls. Oh, Mom, I'm so sorry. I should have told you last night about the pain I'd been having, but I didn't want to worry you. And now the chance is gone, and we can't even get to say good-bye. Forgive me, Mom.

Psalms 61: 2-5

Hear my cry, O God,
    listen to my prayer!
From the brink of Sheol I call;
    my heart grows faint.
Raise me up, set me on a rock,
    for you are my refuge,
    a tower of strength against the foe.
Then I will ever dwell in your tent,
    take refuge in the shelter of your wings.

Selah

Chapter Six

I sense William enter the room. I turn my head, trying to locate him as he walks somewhere along my left, yet I can't find him through the shifting haze.

William tells me later that when he arrived at the hospital, a nurse blocked his passage into the cardiac cath lab, explaining that it was a sterile environment similar to an operating room. Families weren't allowed in. William asked the nurse if she would just ask Dr. Jamisen. She did, and he quickly granted permission.

"Just don't touch anything in blue," Dr. Jamisen says, indicating the sterile areas.

I can't see Will, yet I'm certain he stands close. I focus toward him, instantly feeling his belief that I'll be fine. I can almost sense his intentions focusing a new reality, and I allow myself to be drawn into it. I allow myself the notion that if such potential can be coaxed into creation, William owns the power to do it. Half a lifetime, I've witnessed his intention. Let it be, I whisper silently to myself. *If it is God's will too, let it be.*

I know Dr. Jamisen is talking. Trying to explain things. But I can't retain any of his words long enough to make sense of them, yet I hear his voice. I hear the depth within his voice, and for some reason I will never understand, I trust him suddenly and completely. I believe in him and his fervent desire to help me. I feel safe in his hands. It feels safe like being in Rich Porreco's hands. And I hope this will be a good outcome for him, because as I'm lying here I can't stop thinking that it will bother him more than a little if I die on his table today.

He's working hard to save me. It's the first time he's seen something like this, and he will later say he hopes he never sees it again.

Dr. Jamisen works with absolute focus, Will recalls later. Studying him, he could see adrenaline running, and he could see too that he was using it well. Dr. Jamisen's talent stands apparent to even an untrained eye. But I do not know any of these things now.

The left main artery of my heart, the one coming directly off my aorta has dissected. Spontaneous dissection it is called, meaning there is no immediate proceeding trauma or known cause for the disintegration of the interior layer of that vessel. The first three episodes of excruciating pain are a result of a flap that has torn open within the inner most layer of the artery. Each time the tear opened, it totally blocked the flow of blood to the front of my heart. Three times that torn flap impossibly, yet miraculously, returned into a normal position on its own, allowing blood flow to resume within the artery. Allowing every test to appear completely commonplace.

But the fourth time, the flap continues tearing down inside the inner layer of the artery, like a peeling onion, unwinding far along within the vessel wall. And the left anterior descending artery, the one doctors call "the widow maker," which branches off from the left main artery to supply blood farther along the heart, is also dissecting halfway down its length. The serious injury within these two major coronary arteries deprived the heart muscle of blood long enough to create a massive heart attack. No blood can flow past the damaged, dissected arteries to nourish this crucial area of my left ventricle. The primary pumping chamber of my heart is dying.

Dr. Jamisen asks William to leave. He tries to fish an angioplasty wire through my collapsed artery to get the blood moving and to feed my heart. He is acutely aware that every moment is bringing me closer to cardiac arrest. Every moment is critical. Every passing moment leaves more of my heart muscle damaged.

He tries to get the wire through to reopen the artery, and I am a world away while he's doing it. He has to get the wire through to reopen the artery and to give me a chance at living for a few more moments.

Dr. Jamisen gets the wire through, then guides a balloon along it, which he inflates to reopen the vessel and reestablish blood flow. Finally, my heart is nourished.

And there's his voice again. There's Will again. I have this sudden thought that perhaps Dr. Jamisen believes I can make a decision. That he wants me to make some critical decision.

"I'm sorry," conscious once more of my words, "I can't focus. You'll have to tell William."

Awhile later, I turn my head to the left and I realize I'm watching William and Dr. Jamisen. Backs are toward me and they are talking under the TV monitor that shows my beating heart. I can hear them, and I watch William pivot suddenly and look directly at me. Then he motions to Dr. Jamisen that they should talk privately. They disappear from view. I close my eyes. All alone with my thoughts.

I'm not afraid, William. I want to tell him that I am not afraid. Dr. Jamisen isn't saying anything that you need to protect me from. I know it's bad, but I can look under the tires this time. Yet I understand his desire to shield me from any more of this discussion. It's grim.

Emergency open-heart surgery is my only option. I understand the words, but I have no concept of the surgery or the recovery period from such an operation. I'm glad I don't know. The decision has been made for me. It is Will's right to make this call. It would have been my right if he were lying here in my place.

He reappears and bends down, kissing me lightly on the lips. I'm thinking it's harder for him than for me. And I'm thinking I'd rather be here on this table than having to watch him on one. I've taken off my wedding ring, but I still love you. I would still give my life to save yours. And you would do the same for me-I know that. I've always known that, but that fact has never made it any easier.

Will is gone, and I sense they are trying to shift me to the left. To shift me onto another table. I want to help them. I say something about being sorry I am so heavy. They laugh about that. It is a silly thing to say, and I know it. But I'm thinking about William trying to get me off the bedroom floor. And then I remind myself they scoot men across this table who weigh a hundred pounds more than I do. They can handle me easily. This is my last conscious thought for the next ten hours.

I will learn the following events later. Dr. Davis waits in the wings of the cardiac cath lab, studying my heart on a monitor. William and Dr.

Jamisen talk again. Another heart surgery already scheduled is bumped for mine. A man prepped and on the operating table is taken off.

William is brought into the side room for a discussion with the doctors. Dr. Davis and Dr. Jamisen. He tells the surgeon that he just wants to know the person doing the emergency open-heart surgery can handle the pressure if things do not go well. He wants someone who can still hang in there and get the job done. He tells them both that the doctor who had operated on his father right before he died had been scared and it showed. William doesn't want someone with paper nerves cutting open his wife. He looks long at the cardiac surgeon and finds the quiet, intense eyes of a gentle gunfighter. Dr. Davis tells William he understands his concerns and that he'd feel exactly the same way if it were his wife.

As Will leaves, he thinks if things can possibly go right, they will go right for Dr. Jamisen and Dr. Davis. He has no doubt that they will do all they can to help me.

The operation starts at 6:30 p.m. and is expected to take about four hours. William settles into the ICU waiting room. Over the hours, my mother, sister, brother, and sister-in-law join him there.

William lies to my mother. Telling her without hesitation that my condition isn't life-threatening. She believes him without hesitation. He thinks it's best that way. He doesn't want anyone's fear corroding the reality he's holding on to, and he sees no reason to worry her. He cares for her greatly, and she is eighty years old and has been through enough of late. My father would have approved. Mom waits confidently as the hours pass.

William sends them all home around eleven. He continues to wait as hours pass the approximated four hours. The dissection is more extensive than anticipated.

The surgery takes seven and a half hours. Dr. Davis has finished a triple bypass. Two additional coronary arteries: The diagonal and the left proximal circumflex have also dissected. I started bleeding, a very unusual complication from standard medication given to me in the cath lab to reduce the risk of clots. My heart has been seriously stunned by the massive heart attacks, but they will not know the extent of permanent heart muscle damage until later. I have survived the operation, but there is more to come. Thank you, God, for keeping me ignorant. I do not believe I would have had the stomach for it.

Chapter Seven

I wake deep under heavy water. Dazed, I lie there a moment. Up, I tell myself. You must pull up. With that thought, I pull and kick with all my strength, struggling for the surface and the air and the light to lead me from the thickening darkness. But I can't move.

With a jolt, I realize where I am and what has happened. And then, still underwater, I try to breathe. But no matter how hard I try, I can't draw in any air. I am suffocating. I start choking and gagging. The choking doesn't stop. The suffocation doesn't stop. It goes on and on. But I don't die.

Something is sticking down my throat. I can't talk. I sense Will on my left, but I'm absolutely frantic. Desperate. I must find a way to let him know. He has to help me. Oh please, please help me Will!

"I CAN'T BREATHE!" I mouth to him in rising panic. He understands me. Thank God. He will fix this somehow. Quickly, it must be done quickly. I can't last much longer. I hear him telling the nurse that I can't breathe. I cling to his every word. I hang waiting for help. But the nurse doesn't help me.

"She's fine," the nurse says impatiently. "They all say that."

And I understand instantly by the apparent lack of compassion in her voice that she has never had this pipe wedged into her throat. She should try it, I think. It should be required training. I gag repeatedly, nearly vomiting, until she runs something down the pipe that stops the gagging. I wish she could run something down the pipe to stop my feelings.

I lie there unable to move and long to hear kindness in her words. I long for her to tell me ... The surgery went well, Melissa. This part will soon be over, and you'll feel better ... I need to believe that I can feel better. I keep listening, but rhythmic rasping of machines is all I hear.

I yearn for the gentle touch of a soothing human hand. But the nurse completes her tasks robotically as if I am just a body, like I am a piece of dead meat mechanically prepared for an oven ... clean ... swab ... cover. I sense her consuming disinterest from the depth where I am lost. William tells me later he would like to strangle her.

The following two days show me islands of absolute powerlessness and absolute panic. I exist marooned there now. I have not known such things before, but I learn of them. I grow more hysterical each time I wake; each second of consciousness rivals eternity, and it is torture, the perfect form of torture. I wonder if they do this to people in prison camps to get them to talk; I would do anything, sell myself out, sell out my country or anyone I loved, just to stop this. Just to die. Right then. But I can control nothing. They have tied me down tightly. How long, I wonder, how long will they keep me alive like this? I hear myself moan. A low desolate cry; yet it does not do justice for despair.

Sometimes I leave for an infinite black hole where I quickly lose myself. I remember nothing of where I have been when I return to the islands. I remember only that the void is painless; quiet, without thought, without suffering or fear. Returning means returning to excruciating agony, for each time I wake, each time I struggle up to consciousness, I wish I haven't. The pipe instantly subjugates me. The God-awful sound screeches, searing into every cell. I mouth at them to take it out. I must speak. I try. Not a sound comes out. *They've taken my voice.* Oh God, I can't even talk. *What has happened to my voice?*

Write, I tell myself. I must write somehow, or I will go utterly mad. Calm down. You must try to calm yourself. I try writing with my finger. William sees me and quickly calls attention to my efforts.

Tube out! Tube out! I write over and over again. And over and over the nurse refuses. My legs and hands are still tied. I am strapped down and pinned tightly to the bed.

"You must keep your legs straight," the nurse says callously, whenever I discover if I can move.

After one of my failed attempts for freedom, Will tells me gently leans over saying, "The tube can't be taken out because you are producing too much blood into your chest tubes. They might have to take you back to surgery."

Oh, Dear Lord. What can I do? What can I do to end this? I do not know how to control my bleeding. I do not know how to stop this torture. I give up. I quit. Isn't that enough? Please, God, help me find a way to let William know I can't last like this and keep my mind. I'm going insane, I silently scream over and over for hours. I am going insane!

My mouth and throat are set on fire. They are the desert. I write that I need ice. Of course, I am refused. I fall in and out of awareness and dream of ice. I dream of ice and cold, cold apple juice. *Let me die.* Please, please just let me go; don't keep me trapped here with this suffocating machine inside me endlessly breathing for me when I want to stop, I want to go. Now. I can't stand this. Please. Please just take out this tube!

I write again. *T...u...b...e...* spelling the letters out painfully, blindly, on my thigh.

"Tub?" The nurse asks blankly.

My God woman, what have I been writing for endless hours? She must be an idiot, I decide. I write the word over again, carefully making sure I add the "*e*" at the end.

"Oh, tube," she says somehow sadistically, and she hesitates a long, endless time while I hang twisting within the cavernous pause... "Well, it's not coming out."

Oh God! Help me! Please!

And then I hear a man's voice I have never heard before. Yet somehow, I feel I have heard him, that I know him. Dr. Davis asks the nurse if I am aware of what's going on.

"Yes, very aware." And I know her comment is a complaint. I wonder if he knows her well enough to understand. *You would have to be trapped here as her patient to truly understand.*

Yes, I call to Dr. Davis in my mind. *I am aware. I'm aware of my utter helplessness, of this hated tube garroting me and of a new pain building in my chest.* From my distorted lands, I try to communicate with Dr. Davis about the pain in my chest. I write that it spreads like the heavy pressure during a heart attack. I hear as William deciphers my scrawl perfectly.

"I don't see how that can be," the doctor says. "I've never had a patient tell me something like this."

I feel him trying to understand. I can't actually see Dr. Davis. I can't see anything, though my eyes keep opening and closing. Yet I sense things fully and have strange visual pictures. And I hear with perfect clarity. My hearing is unimaginably heightened, and I clutch at it like treasure. It's all that remains of a world I used to know and walk in.

Dr. Davis' voice is slow and calm, with a hint of a slight Southern accent. I am riveted to its soothing gentle sounds. I don't want him to leave me. Please stay. He is the man I need to talk to. He cares. Instinctively, I feel that he cares.

He knows nothing about me and is still caring an anchor rock solid in his voice. I kept writing about the pain on the piece of paper. Even this drugged, it feels like it's growing.

Soon after his voice leaves, Will gently explains that I am going back for another open-heart surgery. They need to see if a suture on the bypass graphs has torn or if there is another reason for the bleeding and the fluid building up inside my chest. His explanations mean nothing to me. I don't understand what was done the first time.

I don't know that Dr. Davis will reopen my sliced skin and muscles and undo the six stainless steel wires that were holding my split sternum together; and that he will open my rib cage with a chest spreader again and examine my exposed heart to determine what is going wrong. I don't know enough to be horrified by the thought. But I wake once to see dark red blood in a plastic bag hanging directly overhead. Blood dripping into my lines. Exhausted, I close my eyes. Just stop thinking about it. I'll die without the blood, I tell myself. But I don't even care anymore.

Chapter Eight

I am lost within the void during the second open-heart surgery. I wake again not knowing if it is over or still ahead of me. Then I hear William talking into my left ear, telling me the surgery is finished, that I am in recovery again. Dr. Davis removed a large clot and two and a half liters of blood and fluid from my chest cavity, but the bypass graphs were sound and there was no active bleeding discovered. The second surgery is completed.

The breathing tube ordeal and my struggle with it continues. Tears pool in my eyes as the nurse instructs me, "You just have to find a way to deal with it. Find a way to remove yourself from this time and place."

I hear her words and imagine she once memorized them from a training manual. But I don't believe the manual suggested delivering the message with such profound, unveiled irritation.

"They tell me it's like breathing through a straw," the nurse explains to Will.

No, I think, as the tears kept trickling. Breathing through a straw would never make me cry. Will knows that. *Slow strangulation and the hopeless dark depth of being tied tightly and buried alive for days makes me cry.*

I try to imagine the nurse by the callous, bored sound of her voice. I get no picture except her checking her nails, between yawns. Her comments come too easily, I think. I have known about visualization techniques as a way to control one's attitude for years. I am conscious of my thoughts and the immense power of them. But I can't visualize drugged. I can't concentrate.

I want to tell her this. I want to tell her that I am doing my best. I ache to communicate. Maybe she would like me better if I could talk.

Maybe she would know that I still feel things, but I can't say a word. I am utterly vulnerable and at a machine's mercy. And it holds no mercy.

On Saturday afternoon, the nurse collapses something and slithers the thick tube out from my chest and throat. Two days seem a long, miserable lifetime. I retrieve my voice.

"Thank God," I say hoarsely, and then I quickly ask for the ice and apple juice.

Magically, something I ask for appears. I can make something happen. I find William's eyes, and focus intently on them, telling him it was the worst thing that has ever been done to me. The worst thing I have ever, ever endured. And I'd thought nothing could possibly top those four heart attacks.

"Let me go," I tell him quickly, fearing I might not be able to speak for long. "Let me die before you ever keep one of those breathing tubes in me for so long again." A funny look freezes on his face. And I know why. It has been on my mind too. Constantly.

A respirator kept his elderly, dying father breathing in intensive care for three weeks before we finally asked them to stop. Three weeks! And all I could think about as I was lying there suffocating was, I hoped Bill wasn't feeling this, or anything close to this, in the name of trying to help him.

We are ignorant at times, utterly barbaric even, and still we think ourselves compassionate. Allowing people to leave their bodies naturally, when it's time to go, is compassion. Deciding when to stop extraordinary measures is achingly difficult, but stretching out a patient's suffering, and both prolonging and dramatically increasing their suffering with these machines is monstrous. Just because we can, does not always mean we should.

⚬⚬⚬

My next three days in intensive care blur together. I don't know that I am being treated aggressively with medication to combat pulmonary edema: fluids are accumulating in my lungs. A constant moaning somewhere too near reminds me I haven't died. Listening to it, I wish once more that I had. I try to look around the dim room, wondering if they have locked me into an asylum. I'm not sure. Low, pitiful moans arrive in relentless waves, varying in volume, but never pitch. It's not me. No, I don't believe it's me. Someone else cries out in darkness, all night, the pain lingers, faceless, yet far from unfelt, for I understand agony in ways I once did not, and the desperate loneliness within this fellow human's suffering hurts as deeply as my own. I wish with all my heart I could go to this stranger, to help somehow, yet I can't move. You are not alone. I call this over and over in my mind. *I am with you*, I tell him.

Let me sleep, I think, grimacing, please make me sleep, so I don't hear or feel anything anymore. The next time I wake, I listen intently, straining for the neighbor's noises that had become part of me. It is quiet. Relief sweeps over me briefly until comprehension comes. And then, still, I relish the quiet. I do understand what this silence means and yet freedom from heart-wrenching sounds makes it selfishly bearable to be awake.

I hear Dr. Davis unexpectedly. I hear him come closer, and I catch sporadic visual images I can't retain. I give up trying. It's easiest just resting my eyes and absorbing his voice. I'm comfortable listening to his gentle voice.

He takes out the "C" clamp from the femoral artery in my right groin. It was placed there during surgery to put more pressure on the artery to control bleeding. Nothing hurts as he works; it just feels like something literally being unclamped from inside me. And then his words fade away and a sandbag secures the spot. Someone tells me not to move for eight hours. It's okay, I'm not moving much anyway.

Dr. Davis' voice visits again later as he works on my left side, removing the intra-aortic balloon pump he's placed into the artery in my groin to help my heart work more efficiently. The pump suddenly springs from me like a cork from champagne. William and Mom's laughter mingles with Dr. Davis'. I listen to everyone; but I'm not part of the group, or part of their laughter. I am just a body everybody works on.

For several minutes, I feel Dr. Davis' hand pressing against my femoral artery, and when he is sure it is safe, his hand lifts and another sandbag settles heavily into place. Another eight hours.

"Lie perfectly still," he tells me. "If something suddenly hurts or feels wet, let us know." No problem.

When another eight hours end, my legs are untied. I still can't move much but just knowing that I can helps. No respirator and no restraints. Progress, and a minute measure of sanity returns.

I am more conscious, mostly of the time, although everything around me still flickers without focus. My new nurse Terry catches my attention. I discover comfort in his constant presence and his words, and the compassion carried within them. Comfort comes wrapped in the soft assuring tone of his voice and in the kindness of his touch. Terry makes me want to be awake more. I am beginning to see again. Beginning to be able to speak and to express myself. Without my knowledge, my lungs improve.

My back hurts terribly. I have never been flat on my back for so long without moving or shifting position. The surgeries and chest spreader have badly torqued my spine, and my back throbs continually. I don't want to mention it.

A car accident ten years ago left my neck and upper back seized up stiff as plywood. I've been sleeping on a cervical pillow for years, and it's the only thing that keeps my hands and arms from going numb while I sleep. I do not have my pillow. I want my pillow. It seems so trivial, so childlike, yet it hurts.

"How are you doing?" Terry asks, leaning over me with a concerned expression. "Is something wrong?"

"My back is hurting," I admit. Why do I complain about my back, I wonder. I hurt all over. Come on, tough it out.

Terry moves from my side. I can't lift my head, and my vision is still unstable, but I sense him bringing lotion. Near the bed a top pop opens, and the scent of Vaseline Intensive Care sweeps over me. Terry gingerly eases me onto my left side, but I tighten as my split sternum screams. I realize that he's seen my face by the way his hands on me freeze for an instant, and I am sorry for it. Sorry I am so weak I can't control myself any better than this pathetic behavior.

Terry is just trying to help, I remind myself. And now he must feel badly that he hurt me. But his hands move again. He rubs my back, and it helps, except the pain down the center of my chest doubles. Terry rolls me over again.

"Thank you," I say very softly. Boy, that sounded lame, I tell myself. Be a little more enthusiastic for Terry. He's trying for you.

Terry keeps pulling up the long tubes that are inserted into my chest, checking the amount of liquid within them. The tubes drain into something on the floor that pumps constantly. Just watching him work,

I understand he wants the output of liquid to slow down. No one needs to explain this measurement forms a key indicator of my progress. Terry wants the liquid to decrease. He wants me to get better. I want it to decrease in order to see my kids again. But part of me believes I won't get better. Part of me knows I am never going to make it home, because I am already gone.

I know with certainty my will is gone, and I remember what it felt like, stoked and blazing steadily inside me. I cannot track the faintest trace of it anymore. The working of time and excruciating agony has swept it cleanly away, just as it has cleanly swept me. I am a changeling.

The shock waves of uncontrollable pain and finding the remains of me diminishing to an invalid in a matter of days slams hard, jolting my body and my mind. But lying there constantly reliving the agony of the heart attacks and the memories of being cocooned around a respirator demolish my once stable emotions. I understand that I am now helpless. Helpless to understand what has happened to me and most importantly, powerless to stop it from happening again. As far back as I can remember I have believed in my ability to have a positive impact on the events in my life. That belief formed the membrane in all that I was. To the me I once was. With all structure ripped away, I do not know who I am anymore. I know only that I lack the critical raw materials needed to rebuild.

Why should I keep struggling to stay? Dying has to be easier than all of this. And what of anything good in me remains? Doing my best was never good enough before. And I was competent and successful. Now, my best will never be more than mediocre. I don't see how I can handle that. And I know Will won't.

Oh God. This weak woman flattened in bed is a complete stranger. She is supposed to be me. I know that. They call her by my name, but when will they learn she isn't me?

Where can I begin to find myself? I don't have a body to return to. The body in this bed isn't safe to be in anymore. Something could happen again anytime. And I far prefer leaving quickly than suffering the pain of another heart attack or being choked and endlessly, slowly suffocated by a respirator. The unplugged respirator pumps my biggest fear: I know if I stay here too long, it will be secured inside me again. I will fall asleep and wake with it living inside me once more. And I will go insane instantly if that happens. I could go insane just imagining it.

William sits near me. I flutter my eyes, and see he is here, always here, working on paperwork for the business. I sense him beside me, even when my eyes close. He brings music and tapes and my best loved books. He offers to read to me, but I feel too sick and too weak to want to do anything. Even listening is too laborious.

He says one of the nurses told him I'm so pretty, and they don't often get people so young and pretty in intensive care. It is kind of him to tell me that. I would have thought he must be making it up, but he would never have done that out of kindness. I can't imagine anyone describing me as pretty now. And though people usually think I am years younger than I am, I feel far from young anymore.

I try to perk up each day when Mom approaches the bed. I owe her that. I owe her far more than that. My earliest memory of childhood was the feel of a hand patting my back steadily, patting away fears steadily, as I tried finding sleep. I know it was Mom's hand. She was always there. She was the laughter and the fun, talented at every sport she taught me, and knowledgeable with homework she reviewed with me. Her encouraging eyes inspired me to do my best. For Mom and Dad both, I wanted to excel from an early age. I worked hard and learned how to keep people smiling by doing well. Anything else hurt too much.

Mom bends over me, and I brighten for her. I know she is strong. She's always been strong. But if I saw one of my kids looking how I know I must look, I would faint. Period. She must feel the same, but she musters a smile for me while making pleasant conversation. The chest tubes inside me bubble loudly. Mom talks over them.

Oh, Mom, I'm so sorry. I love you. I'm sorry I was too dumb to figure out how to stop this from happening. First, we lost Dad, and then my sister, Sharon, was diagnosed with terminal cancer. What has happened to us? I want to be strong for you, to be there when you need me, but now I've caved and given you more to worry about.

So much for your golden years. Yet you stand tall beside me, joking and chatting with me just like we are sitting around the kitchen table. Without this you'd be bowling or playing golf or duplicate bridge and winning at all of them. Dad would have been proud of you, but then he was always proud of you. And you will keep going because slowing down brings too much time to think. Too much idle time brings too much pain. I idle now and understand your hurry.

❧

The last day of intensive care, Sara gains admittance. Let her in, I tell Terry when he asks permission. Sara seems like family to me. In truth, she's my sister.

She leans down to peer at me. I haven't seen the radiance in her grey-green eyes for five days. We usually see each other daily. Sara laughs with me. She asks about that odd pumping noise and the tubes coming out from the bed, and I tell her she doesn't really want to know.

"Okay," she says cheerfully. "You're probably right."

"Trust me." I reply, simply.

Sara will admit later that looking at me like this is one of the hardest things she's ever done. But it doesn't show on her face today. All that shows is that she's missed me and that she's thrilled to see me. We're joking like the battle is over and we've won. In that perfect peaceful moment, it feels as if it is. In that peaceful moment, I don't realize that it has only just begun.

"Don't you ever scare me like that again. That was awful seeing you that way in the bedroom."

"It was a great moment. Hallmark like." I grin at her. "I'm just glad you work out, or I'd still be on the floor."

"That part was easy, you're such a little thing."

"Oh yeah," I say laughing, "five foot nine is real petite." And then I mimic her voice. "Don't drop her...just don't drop her."

"Oh, Shut up."

"And I remember you kept trying to get the last word in. You wouldn't close the car door."

"Well, I was afraid it really was the last word."

I smile at her. "No, we're still yakking."

Sara leans down to kiss my cheek. "The kids are all doing great."

"Thanks for taking care of them. I know they're thrilled to have more playtime with you. Just tell them I'll linger here for their benefit as long as I possibly can."

She frowns at me. "I'll be back to visit tomorrow."

"I know...You'll do anything to get out of the house."

⫷⫸

Terry stands near later that day when I feel a tingling sensation spreading steadily across my face. Suddenly I am scared.

"Terry," I call nervously. "Something's happening."

"Morphine," he explains. "I just gave you some, and you're very sensitive to it."

I had no idea he had given me anything. I lie on my throbbing back and realize for the first time that I must be getting a lot of drugs. Morphine. That's pretty substantial stuff. I haven't asked for it. I haven't once asked for anything, but it must just be given, and I drift with it. But again, this isn't me. I never take anything. The person I used to be never took anything. She ate organic foods to avoid pesticides and steroids. I chose a drug-free root canal. In that moment I understand I must be getting these injections constantly. So now I'm on heavy drugs. But there's no fight in me. Not an ounce of fight, and I just don't care. Shoot me up again.

⫷⫸

It is late afternoon, July 7th. The date makes me nervous. Silly things like that make me anxious, but seven has always been meaningful to me. Sevens and I go way, way back. It was my dad's special number too. And he died when he was seventy-seven. I wish I hadn't noticed the date. Today is the seventh day of the seventh month, and Terry is getting me ready to leave ICU. I'll be transferred to the surgical ward.

"How long do you think I'll be there?" I ask.

"About a week," he tells me. Terry is busy in the room, handling my tubes and lines.

"Terry?"

"Yes?" He comes to my bedside.

"What was that moaning noise I heard for so long?"

He pauses a few seconds. "A young man broke his neck diving into a pool." He hesitates again, longer this time. "His buddies thought he was just horsing around, so they kept drinking instead of getting him out right away."

Our eyes lock together. There's more to this story, and I know it. I know Terry's holding back.

"You're not supposed to tell me what happened to him."

Terry nods.

"He died," I say.

Terry nods again.

"I'm glad," I whisper. "I'm glad he didn't have to suffer like that anymore."

Terry begins working again at the end of the bed as I lay there imagining the mom and dad who sent their promise to the future away to break his neck in a shallow pool. A few days ago, a stranger's voice had shattered their hopes and made mockery of years of watchful eyes and loving care. They must weep now, in some lonely house filled with overgrown space, two people grieving for their lost son and for their lost dreams. As I watch Terry I am thinking that when a body is hopelessly damaged with no chance for a quality existence, dying is a kindness. Oh Lord, may his parents someday understand the merciful blessings within a quick death. I only wish it had been quicker still.

Closing my eyes, I try to close off memories of the young man's pain. I move a few aching inches in bed, yet despite my best efforts, that night returns with an unwanted persistence and carries once more those sounds that haunt my darkness. The dying man returns with a heartbeat. I sigh deeply. I don't believe his parents understand anything except they've just lost their son. Few parents could. Not unless they heard what I heard. And I couldn't wish that for them either. But in that moment, I still see no cruelty in his passing. Just the waste. Cruelty would be weeks and months and years of such moaning inside and out. Life can be hard and harder yet to understand sometimes. And sighing again, I wonder what waits ahead for me.

Then I notice Terry studying me carefully. His hands, which hold the end of my chest tubes, rest unusually still. I shift gears instantly, dropping the maudlin thoughts. I don't want Terry regretting being honest with me. Honesty should always be applauded, never penalized. I know that better than most and getting past this mood quickly is the least I can do.

He explains that he is ready to take the catheter out. I've been so removed from reality; I didn't even realize there was one in. By Terry's new hesitation, I sense he is trying to prepare me for some discomfort. But thinking about it too long isn't going to make it any easier for either of us.

"Oh, just go for it," I tell him, managing a thumb's up. He pulls quickly, like ripping a very large band-aid off. There is a slight burn for an instant.

But then I know pain in that area, for I have struggled with bladder infections and crystals. Living with a constant burn that lasted days before it faded, only to have it flame up again days later.

"Imagine sitting on a Bunsen burner," I told a friend who'd never experienced a bad bladder infection. One of life's real treats.

Terry is watching me for a reaction.

"Oh, come on. That was nothing," I tell him, with my best tough guy look.

"Well, it's always worse for men," he adds defensively, resuming his work.

"Yeah," I say, starting to smile. "Cause women only have a couple inches of urethra and you men all have ten to twelve."

He stops what he is doing again. I see him processing.

"Wait a minute," he says finally and then we both start cracking up.

It's a measure of what I feel for Terry that I can joke with him about such things. But Terry has bathed me and cared for me in intimate ways I could never have imagined a man doing. And Terry's hands were the gentlest, his voice the most kind.

William and Mom arrive for another visit just as Terry tells me we'll walk toward the elevator. This will be a first. The first time I've even been off my back since I arrived in the helicopter almost a week ago.

Terry helps me sit and shifts my legs until they drop over the side of the bed. The effort blanches me. He stands close as I camp at the edge of the bed. The wheelchair is a step away. But Terry said I'd be walking. I'm sure he did. I am supposed to take hold of the handles on the back of that thing and actually walk. He can't mean it. *I can't imagine even sitting here much longer without passing out.* Walking is not going to work.

I look away from Terry's scrutiny. How will I ever get back to where

I was? I stare down and my gaze halts at my hands. They are shaky and boney; they are the hands of an old woman clinging to a bed for support. And somewhere in that instant, I know that I won't ever get back to where I once was, and that is the simple, honest truth. The truth hurts. The truth could make me cry if I linger longer with it. Come on, don't think about it. Just take a breath and don't start thinking like that. Take another breath.

Terry expects me to stand. His eyes don't leave me. If he wants me to do this, I can give it a shot. And if I can't handle it, he can peel me off the linoleum. Wordlessly, Will puts down his papers and steps to my other side.

Terry's hand tightens on my left elbow as I start to rise. That simple motion takes all of my effort and what is left of my balance. In my mind I hear my dad saying, "Weak as a kitten." Yes, Dad, I'm as weak and shaky as a newborn kitten now.

I can't even come close to completely upright. A crooked crescent is as straight as I am going. I don't dare look at Mom or William as I inch painfully down the hall. I don't want them to see me like this. And I sure don't want to catch their expressions right now. I'm not sure if I would find pity or disgust, but I don't want either. If I could crawl into a hole, I would.

Terry tells me that he once had someone who made it all the way to the elevator.

"Please don't tell me that," I say to him.

I know he doesn't understand. He seems like a calm and reasonable man, but I was once a perfectionist, and I was competitive. Even this diminished, I obviously still stick with both curses, for I find myself suddenly wanting to do better than the best he's ever seen. This is sick stuff and I know it, but I can't shed it.

"Really Terry, if you tell me that, I won't feel good unless I make it to the elevator."

"I don't care," he says oblivious to what he's stoked in me, "When your pulse hits 120, you're sitting in the chair."

I am close to that now. A few steps before the elevator, my pulse tops 120. My performance disappoints me. I was hoping somehow, I might make it.

As I sit, it dawns on me that the elevator game must be one Terry plays with all of his patients. To push them a little harder. But no one has ever needed to push me. I could push myself up and right over any mountain. I don't need help with the pushing, for I am crumpled and already tumbling fast down the side of a cliff. What I need is help figuring out how to stop.

Terry bends close. I realize that he is looking at me; and I gather my thoughts before I turn my eyes up to meet his, knowing that if I give him my best dimpled smile, he'll stop worrying.

"I'm fine," I insist. I exhale slowly and fully try to rid myself of the faintness and nausea nudging me. Terry is still staring; I am still smiling. Finally, he nods. Great. I can con Terry. I should be real proud.

"You're quite a trooper," Terry says as he pushes my wheelchair the rest of the way. The elevator opens at the second floor. Cardiac care is on the right. The cancer wing lies on the left. We turn right and travel to room 207. Terry touches my hand softly. I don't want him to leave. I don't want anyone else to look after me. And then he asks me to come back to see him, making me promise him.

"Promise me you'll bring your kids so I can meet them." I'd like to do that someday. But I'm not really sure I have a someday left to live.

Chapter Nine

William and Mom stay long enough to see me settled into bed. Flowers start arriving. Cards keep arriving. I am exhausted, but I need to get up repeatedly to use the bathroom. Now that the catheter is gone, I can't walk there without asking for help. I hate asking, but I can't get myself out of bed. There's no way to take a step without the looming potential of falling, so I push the call button and when help arrives, I shuffle with my IV pole, my lines, and my chest tubes dragging behind me. I've become Scrooge's dead partner Marley ... chained, completely drained and still hanging around. What a mess.

Unexpectedly, I catch the first glimpse of my face in the bathroom mirror and wish I haven't. *It can't be me.* I don't know myself. My skin is the color of old paste, except for the six-inch purple bruise that covers the right side of my neck. Huge black circles dominate my eyes, faintly reminiscent of an owl. Well, I guess that part is okay. I've always loved owls.

A ponytail sticks straight up from the top of my head, making me look like a cockatoo. I remember Lori gathering my hair and putting a rubber band around the thick dark mass of it when she was trying to get it out of the way in the Flight for Life helicopter. It's still in the same position, only matted now. I look away and carefully avoid my reflection for another two days. *I'm alive,* I tell myself, trying to think of something positive. *I just don't look it yet.*

⚛

I miss Terry. I have to get used to the new floor and the difference in attention and response times. Terry was always with me, or seconds away. Now if I push the buzzer to ask for help getting up, I wait awhile.

They're trying, I tell myself. They have more patients here. Terry only had you.

I feel needy. It's not normal for me to feel needy. But what is normal anymore? They put you under, and then you wake up when everything is different. Everything about you is different.

I glance up to the television set and stare at the blank screen. At home it remains hidden behind thick wood panel doors and off limits to the kids. We're planning to toss it. But right then, it's just what I want. I don't have any ability to concentrate. I've lost all my drive. TV seems the perfect companion. I reach for the remote to turn it on. It comes to life, spontaneously controlling the room and my uneasy thoughts. Another drug as sure as any tranquilizer. I lie there pacified, watching for endless, mindless hours. Knowing that I have sunk low but am unable to turn the channel I'm stuck on.

Friends and family arrive in ceaseless shifts, warming me with their attention. Receiving their brightly colored flowers remind me of the ones I've just finished planting at home. I hope someone waters them in the midst of all this trauma. Flowers wilt quickly in Colorado without water. Imagining them dying before they have much chance to live hurts me more than it should.

"You look tired," a nurse says. "I'm putting a sign up that says you can't have visitors for a while and need to rest."

I don't argue. Talking to so many people, trying to act like you aren't hurting when you are, trying to act like you remember how you used to be is fatiguing. I want to see them, and yet she is right: I need to rest more.

But I think of my dear friend Jan and wonder if it would be okay to ask if she could come by to untangle my hair. I can't lift my arms to brush it. Jan has thick curly hair: she'll know how to deal with it. And if she doesn't, I'll have to cut it all off.

I hesitate. It's the asking for help thing again. It's the needing help and admitting it. Oh, come on, she's your best friend; you can call. I shake my head and gingerly stretch for the phone, but simply reaching for it takes my breath away, so I lean back, clutching the phone and recovering a few moments before trying to dial her number.

Jan has hovered by the phone for the better part of a week, making countless calls to William and to intensive care. But William is stonewalling, assuring her and everyone that I am fine. Yet fine is not what Jan feels deep in her heart. And when she can't get any answers from the hospital, except the label "critical condition", she asks a friend who is a nurse at Boulder Hospital to check on me. The nurse talks to her coworkers in intensive care and tells Jan on the Fourth of July they didn't expect me to survive.

Jan said, "No way, we aren't going there. Don't you even say those words." She kept holding the intention that I'd make it, her prayers circling continually with that thought.

Jan and William have become an unlikely pair, both clamping onto the thinly stretched strings of my marionette, both willing me to remain on stage. But I'm not sure I can keep on acting, though my lines are well memorized.

Later, much later, when Jan tells me about asking the nurse to find out how I was doing, I question why she requested information from the nurse if she didn't really want to know. She tells me simply she needed to know what she was dealing with, she needed to know exactly what she was up against, but she sure didn't need to buy into it. And she's right: it is three full days past Independence Day. And I'm still here.

The phone at my ear rings twice. Jan answers, and I tell her who I am because I fear she won't recognize the weakness that is now my voice. We've been close for six years and have shared ourselves deeply with each other, yet at that moment I have to tell her my name. It is all that remains.

"I'll be right there."

Then I close my eyes. She's coming. And I sleep.

It is heaven to see her, yet when she arrives, I'm too tired to talk. Too tired to do anything but sit and think about breathing. She nods and tenderly squeezes my right shoulder. I would pat her hand that rests there, but I can't move my arm that high. Jan works through my hair nest with gentle patience and an entire bottle of de-tangler, smoothing the hopeless mass effortlessly into an orderly French braid. Her voice lifting like a song as she works. Thank you, Jan. If only life could be like that.

⚜

Sara comes by nightly to visit as promised. My spirits lift at the sight of her. Tall and beautiful with a heart as golden as her hair, she brings a care package with a brush, razor, hair products and other items that used to seem like necessities.

She stands at the bottom of my bed while we both grin at each other. I'm in the hospital gown and the sheets are pulled down to the bottom of the bed. Then she notices my legs for the first time. They aren't too pretty anymore either.

Both calves were cut during heart surgery to use the veins during the triple bypass. The incisions running along the inside of each shinbone look very obvious. The cut on my left leg is about six inches long. The cut up my right one measures at least nine inches.

Sara inspects the wounds, her eyes moving back and forth from one leg to the other. Something is bothering her.

"They're uneven," she says, continuing to scrutinize them with a look of distaste. Then she shakes her head, jokingly. "Only a man would do something like that."

We both laugh, but I feel protective of Dr. Davis.

"He was harvesting veins, not making an artistic statement." I look down at my legs.

"If you'll notice, they're quite straight, and I think he did a great job."

She looks totally unconvinced. I try again.

"Sara, I wouldn't want my left leg cut up another three inches just to even them out." I pause. "Would you?"

She is actually thinking this one over, and the look on her face makes me start laughing again, and I'm clinging to my chest, trying to stabilize it to lessen the hurt.

A few seconds pass until Sara can ignore my legs and sit beside me on the bed to tell me what is going on. She tells me how much she misses me and what I mean to her and that she can't begin to imagine life without me. Our fingers lace together. We can't let go of each other as the tears start. She tightens on my hand, and I look down, savoring the sight.

There is nothing I wouldn't do to help Sara. No distance too long to cross if she needed me. And there is nothing I could ask of her that she wouldn't willingly give. I have come far to attract friends like Sara and Jan. It was not so very long ago that things were different. Very different.

Dr. Jamisen drops in unexpectedly while Sara is sitting on my bed, and I make introductions awkwardly, tripping over his name. But this is the first time I've seen him since he was standing at the end of the cot right after I arrived in the helicopter, and I'm suddenly nervous. I don't want to think about that day, or any of it, or about how I felt when he'd failed to believe me. Seeing him forces me to remember. But Dr. Jamisen is chatty and friendly and within minutes he makes me forget I am in the hospital.

"I wonder why I didn't go into dermatology," he says smiling. "The hours would be easier, there'd be no emergency calls in the middle of the night, and if some patient called with an itch, I could just tell them to scratch it."

He makes us laugh. I need to laugh. And every time I do, I have to hold a pillow to my chest incision to ease some of the pain laughing causes. But it's a good pain, and I willingly pay the cost.

Dr. Jamisen talks of other things. "I've known young women who've had heart problems and have recovered fully. I will give them your number and have them call you once you're home. There's no reason to believe this will ever happen again."

And as he talks, a small flicker of hope kindles within me. For that instant, I am hoping that he's right and that I will live the long, full life I'd once envisioned. It seems a distant dream, yet as I listen, he draws me in.

Dr. Jamisen leans against the wall while he talks, and I recognize his fatigue. I have leaned against many a wall in my time; in just the same way he is doing now. But there is no hint of fatigue in his voice as he talks. He stands in surgical scrubs, it is late, and he must have had a very long day. And still, despite the hour, he has stopped by to check on me and to pass on hope.

They feed you three times a day here, yet it's the nourishment that

Dr. Jamisen offers that provides the best chance to sustain me. I wish I could swallow it whole, yet I am afraid to believe him. Afraid of the disaster that comes when I count on anything too much. When I need anything or anybody too much.

⚜

Tuesday morning, I can't force down more than a bite of breakfast. Weakness suddenly overtakes me. I lean my head back and sink lower in the chair they have propped me in. Something is wrong. I called a nurse. She takes my blood pressure. It reads 70 over 30.

"You're fine," she informs me.

Oh, please, let's not do this routine again.

"I am not fine," I say and there is that testiness in my voice infused by fear.

Fear is making me think mostly of myself.

"How do you think you'd feel at 70 over 30?" I ask her, and then I drift.

The feeling scares me. I reach for my pulse, but I can't find it at my left wrist. I can always find it quickly. Oh God. I have no pulse. The fear quickly escalates. Making me sick to my stomach.

Aren't you dead when you don't have a pulse? And when do they stop saying you're fine, when you start molding?

"I am not fine," I insist again.

The nurse patiently tries to calm me. I know I am panicky, but it won't go away. I know the way I am letting myself go isn't helping. Now, I think, now I'm the type of person to have a panic attack. Last week I wasn't.

I just want someone to help me feel better. I just want to get out of this hospital and get back somehow to my life before it all fell apart.

"The heart monitors are fine," she tells me enthusiastically.

"Please, please don't tell me that."

I drink more water. I want to see Beth Kelly. I ask for her. She is Dr. Davis' nurse, his eyes and ears, as she's called it. I instantly felt drawn to her organized, professional, and bright personality. Beth moves quickly with confidence, and I figure she can handle herself in tough situations. Like someone I used to know. I need Beth to tell me that I am doing okay. I've lost faith in my body. I've lost all faith in myself and in my ability to deal with fear.

A nurse delivers a potassium pill. The last blood check shows I am low, and I swallow it quickly. I try to hold on, and I wait for Beth Kelly.

Over the next hour, I begin feeling better, and by the time Beth arrives to check on me, I know I've lost that wide-eyed, "deer frozen in headlights" look. Exuding energy and empathy, Beth helps me relax, helps me believe all these bizarre sensations are normal. Just part of the healing process.

Oh please, Beth, let me borrow your strength and vitality. Let me feed off them a while. You see, I've lost mine. And there is something in your brown eyes that I used to see in my own. But I see nothing shining in mine now but fear. Fear stares back boldly in the mirror, taunting me whenever I have the guts enough to look.

⋇

Alone in my room, I try to figure out what caused the weakness. Was it just the low potassium? Perhaps the pain pills I took the night before also contributed to the problem. I react so strongly to medications; my first thought focuses the primary blame for my lost ground in their direction. I don't want it to be my heart. I want it to be something I can do something about. And I can do something about discretionary pain medication.

I decide to go without any additional pain pills, though they cut the worst of the pain down to a constant, blaring ache. I don't like dizziness, and if there is even a remote possibility the weakness has anything to do with those pills, I don't want to take them. I don't want any more of them. I can deal better with pain.

They've already weaned me off morphine, and I immediately start turning down all offers of pain pills and sleeping pills. And I am hurting. Well, I'm not a complete dolt, I expect to hurt, but I could do hurting. This is excruciating. I shift constantly in bed, trying to invent any position that makes tolerating this easier.

Late that evening, a nurse appears in my room and suggests Tylenol for the pain. I look up at her. Woah, how'd you guess? She stays there, wisely not saying another word, just holding out the pills in her hand.

I have to smile at her, and then I nod and take her offering. Any other choice seems sheer stupidity. The Tylenol helps ease the bite, and I am thankful for her initiative, for I never would have asked. But I can deal with this level of pain. I can deal with more if need be to keep the dizziness and weakness at bay.

I have a harder time coping with the nightmares. It is difficult to fall asleep, and when I do, the nightmares start. I am afraid of them, desperately afraid of sleep for fear I'll never wake again; and I'll live orphaned in that alien world forever.

They are real, live, horrific nightmares, and I have never imagined anything like them. This is altered reality. They are vivid. Horribly vivid. Vibrant colors grab my attention and slow motion, amplified action terrified me. During waking hours, I relive each moment with frightful clarity. Bizarre, hideous, obscene creatures flock to me, mobbing me, pawing me, trying to overpower me... No, they are not like dreams at all. I cannot make myself believe they are dreams. They are real on some strange nocturnal, demonic dimension I have gotten trapped in. And they feel real, far more real than what I am experiencing in daylight hours.

Exhausted, I drift off to sleep and the details of another nightmare begin engraving my mind in perfect clarity. Grotesquely shaped beings mob me and terror builds, freezing me until I find a way to shake myself out of it. I race out frantically, but I can't run fast enough. My heart pounds uncontrollably, and I break out of the horrible place. I wipe sweat from the bridge of my nose as I glance at the clock in the hospital room. It must be morning. But it is not. I can't believe what the clock is telling me. I stare in utter disbelief. Only twenty minutes has passed since I last looked at it. Since I fell asleep and reentered the strange world. I leave the lights blazing bright for the rest of the night. I can't risk sleep. I can't risk going back.

It's just the after effects of these drugs, I keep telling myself. It must have something to do with the morphine I am coming off. I'll try sleeping again when all the drugs are completely out of my system. I can't risk going back into that monstrous world that I visit each night.

⚜

Dr. Jamisen stops by to check on me again. He sits in the chair beside the bed, quiet for a moment as he flips the pages of my chart. I am quiet too, watching him scan quickly.

He turns the paper as he casually suggests that I take the sleeping pills if I can't sleep. I need to heal, he tells me. I have said nothing to him about not sleeping, but then I realize I didn't need to say anything. It must be documented in the charts. Most everything they are interested in dwells within the paperwork. What is not lies written plainly in my face.

Even if my all-night vigils are not recorded, I know I must look tired. I am. Dr. Jamisen turns to me, examines me with a glance. A moment later without any visible effort, in a calm and factual voice, he says, "There's absolutely no reason to believe another artery will dissect. You'll be back to where you were," he insists. And I feel his determination again. I feel his determination willing me to believe. Giving me again what I lack most.

He reads me effortlessly. And I never used to be so transparent. I have never imagined myself so transparent. But he is right on it again, yet I am wondering why there is no reason to believe another artery won't go. We have no idea what made the first one go. Three others did the same thing. Why wouldn't another artery dissect? I think over and over. Why are you telling me this? You can't possibly know that it's true. But somehow you make me want to believe you. You make me want to believe.

I listen, but I don't trust myself to talk to Dr. Jamisen. I do not trust my voice. Tears flow dangerously near. I am deeply discouraged, and I sense he sees it in me. It is a solid indication of where I am that I do not even try to hide my discouragement.

But he keeps talking, telling me that my body has had a terrific assault and that it will just take a little time. Dr. Jamisen stands and smiles, and he asks if I have kids. We both discover we have twins the same age. We keep talking a few more minutes, and I realize my mood is lightening, and then just before he leaves, he says I can use makeup on my scars. He glances down, dabbing invisible dots lightly on his chest, as if demonstrating how easy it would be to put it on. I have to smile as he looks up at me, for I am suddenly feeling the need to reassure him. I know men cringe at being thought of as sweet, but all I can think for a few minutes after he leaves is how sweet it was of him to try to encourage me.

He can't know that I've never worn makeup on my face, and I am not likely to buy it for my chest, yet he must have thought it might be the scars that were bothering me. And he is right, but it is the ones that don't show that are the most disfiguring. They are the ones demanding attention, yet they need no makeup, for they have been well covered for far too long.

I glance out the window, to the foothills, and my eyes traveled aimlessly along ridges and valleys spreading out before me. I lie alone again with my thoughts, knowing another night is fast approaching. Nights are the worst. There are visitors during the day. But nights you are always alone with nothing to distract you from yourself. I turn the television on.

❧

Beth Kelly and another nurse come to take out the chest tubes. It will be good to have them gone. I hate the idea of them pumping inside me. William's head bows over a computer manual when they arrive for the procedure, and we both decline the suggestion that he leaves. He's not squeamish and there is certainly no part of my body he hasn't seen countless times. I know he'd rather watch this. Watching closely helps him understand. William wants no mystery around him.

It helps me not to watch: I can appear coolly composed if I don't look, and I understand all I need to know without any closer scrutiny. I've seen enough of those three tubes hanging out from my body while I drug them along with me on endless trips to the bathroom. I look away. Some of us need mystery.

Will scoots his chair closer and leans in. The plastic tubes are about three-quarters of an inch in diameter. They enter my body in a horizontal row below my breasts. Beth doesn't tell me they'll hurt coming out. I can figure that out. She gives me detailed instructions on what I am supposed to do, how I am supposed to breathe before the tubes are pulled, and I listen closely, though I suspect her lesson is at least partly intended to give me something to think about besides long plastic tubes being pulled out from my chest. I've already made up my mind that I am going to make this easy on Beth. I can do this I know, I will do this, without a groan or even a grimace.

I shift my mind elsewhere right before the first one is pulled. *Okay,* I coach myself. *That's one. Only two to go. No sweat.* The pain wasn't too bad. The middle was the worst. The longest.

"Almost there," Mary says encouragingly as she pulls. And then it is out.

A moment later, a flood of fluid gushes from the wounds. Soaking me to the waist and my lap below. This could make me queasy if I look at the open wounds. I wonder if the flow is bloody. Don't look down, I caution myself. My eyes stay steady on Beth, on her quick, calming eyes and on William's intense, unblinking blue ones.

Beth pulls on the stitches to close the holes and laughs as she tells me how some people are such babies.

"One man leapt off the bed when I pulled his first tube out," she says shaking her head.

"Leapt off the bed," I say in admiring tones. "That was quite energetic of him."

I know I don't have the strength to leap anywhere. Offer me a million dollars, and I could not leap off this bed. Even offer me my health back, and I could not leap off this bed.

A nurse helps me take my first shower the next day. It is tiring beyond belief. Both physically and mentally demoralizing, before I even step in, for as I strip off the light hospital gown, I get the first full glimpse of my nude body. And if this doesn't make me throw up, nothing ever will again.

A "terrific assault" is an understatement, if I've ever heard one. It looks like I've survived a full-blown autopsy. The chest incision is all I can look at for the first full minute. I just stare, trying to understand this belongs to me. Trying to understand the way it runs about eight inches in a straight line down the center of my chest. Trying to understand this huge scar is part of me. A little below the massive rip lays three horizontally stitched seams from the chest tubes. Seeing them from this angle, I realize that Dr. Davis has tried to place them with some thought to symmetry. Sara would approve.

Then I lean out to look at my legs and notice the first signs of infection. A distinctive dark pink painted the wounds and all the surrounding flesh about an inch away from the incision. An infection is not what I need. Looking overlong at all these scars is not what I need.

I step in and let the water trickle down me. The nurse tells me it is supposed to be lukewarm, not hot, which it unfortunately is. Cool air continually drifts around the sides of the little plastic curtain, chilling me. I start trembling. This will have to be fast. I can't raise my arms enough to wash my hair anyway.

Shivering, I stand there, trying not to look at myself anymore, but the color captivates me, and I can't look away. I can't stop scrutinizing the rest of my body. I am purple. I hadn't comprehended the extent of the bleeding during surgery until that moment. I fixate on the color of my skin in disbelief. Bruises are usually a muted bluish-purple, but this is just a shockingly bright purple. And its not just my neck. Massive spots decorate my arms, stomach, thighs and hips. I blink repeatedly. I am glad the lights are dim. I reach for the faucet. I need to get out. Suddenly, I feel cold clean through.

I open the curtain. The nurse helps me dry, but after she leaves, I turn sideways in front of the mirror. Gutsy. And dumb. It is worse than I thought. I am still bent over like an extremely old woman, and I can't straighten out. I must find a way to get my posture back. If I live, once this breastbone heals, I will find some way to push my shoulders back, and I don't care how much it hurts to do it... *Scar me. Go ahead and scar me, but do not imagine me permanently walking around life like I have been beaten down by it.*

⁂

The voice warns that I have to climb from the pit. The voice warns me to do something quickly. Now! Okay...Okay, I'll call Jan. We've worked together before, exploring the physical and emotional effects of color, sound, and light. It's the "airy fairy" stuff, as William calls it. It is part of the mystery.

I need Jan to help me start my energy flowing. I am a dead battery. Lost from all power. Unable to give. Desperately hoping I can receive. Hoping I can hold a charge.

"I'll be there tonight," she tells me. I relax again. Jan is coming, I tell myself over and over again, until I doze at last without nightmares.

Jan arrives, coloring the space with fresh flowers once more. A huge bouquet, the scent of Lily of the Valley and beautiful pictures of angels her daughters have drawn for me. She offers me a medal from the Mother Cabrini shrine, a picture of Mary, and a cross.

She brings me tokens of faith. And I cling to them, knowing I will have to open a deeper faith to find myself again. There are levels of faith. Levels to faith and what each one will demand of you and what everyone provides. I understand only that I lay near the bottom rung. During the week, I'd told myself often that I was not afraid to die, for I believe in God's love and in the power of his forgiveness. I have learned a little of love and forgiveness during this life and I cannot conceive God capable of less. But I have lost faith in his plan.

Dear God, I do not wish to leave my little daughters all alone in this hard world. This dread haunts me night and day. Please, God, I do not wish to leave them all alone. This is why I imagine and fear arteries bursting. This is spreading infection.

Jan sits on the bed close beside me. I know she understands that I need her urgently, yet she holds my hand and tells me of her need for me. Jan's beautiful, dark hair is curling to her shoulders. It stands like a halo at her crown and is lightened there and the temples with a shimmering snow white. I always believe in angels looking at Jan. I always think their eyes must be clear and radiant, just like hers are. She is my green-eyed angel.

She talks of how much our friendship means to her life. She tells me of the heaviness she was feeling all day in her heart, and how she felt when she finally heard that I was in surgery. She understands at last why she felt that way. She tells me of the tears she cried.

And she tells me over and over how strong I am. How I am a strong and powerful woman. She has always admired my courage through all that has come my way. How each time, I make everything turn out more positive and come through stronger.

"I don't feel it now," I say simply. I see her strain to hear my lost voice. Her face grows determined and yet retains all its tenderness.

"Well it's still there. I see it. And you aren't going anywhere," she says with absolute conviction. "I'm not ready for you to go."

"I'm sorry I'm so needy," I say softly. Jan frowns at me. Then she shakes her head. "If you talk like that again, I'm going to be forced to hurt you. And you can't handle much more hurting, so cut it out."

We both laugh. A long look travels between us that tells me that she wants more than anything else to be here. My apologies aren't needed.

I nod. "Close the door," I say quietly. This is a part of my life that I'm not willing to share with people who most likely would not understand. And there is no way to understand fully or respect it unless you have personally experienced it.

Jan studies my body, head to toe, using a different seeing than most of us employ. Then she takes hold of my bare feet, and we pause, our breath deepening as minutes pass. And as time passes, I feel myself letting go of a thin wafer of worry. But the mountain weighs heavy below that first layer. A mountain that I will need to walk past to feel myself free. For fear has dug its mass in deep and only departs, when you're willing to ignore it, one little layer at a time.

"It's faint on the left side," Jan says.

"I know," I tell her. "I still can't find any pulse there."

"We'll bring the healing light down," she tells me confidently.

I hear Jan's voice, and I relax to visualizations I have done untold times. Until I can feel the first tingling of light again, and I move that energy through my body toward her hands, which feel like magnets, grounding me and pulling a force strongly toward them which my eyes cannot see. I can see nothing, yet I feel the heat in her hands, and the warmth reassures me. When faith wobbles, tangible proof steadies the tremble.

A healer's hands caress with warm, palpable, pulsating energy. Healer's hands hold the energy of life: they draw and transmit the energy of love, the core creative energy in me and in every living being. We forget it shines within us. We forget its healing power and its source. That night, when I need her most, Jan helps me remember. And when you remember who you are, when you remember you are God's child, in that instant, fear and its heavy net of illusions lose all power over you.

This knowledge is what I will struggle with in the days to come. I know this truth. I just have to keep trying to recall it, for darkness continually masks every truth we struggle to find. Living the truths you uncover is the biggest challenge. This is the fight.

We work for an hour before Jan leaves. "I'm right here with you, baby girl," she tells me as she leans in to kiss my cheek. And after she is gone, I am alone again in that small room. But not quite so alone, and then my fingers reach for the place that used to house the pulse in my left wrist. Please, please be there now.

One ... Two ... Three. ... Four ... Five ... Six ... Seven ... Strong and steady. I smile for myself for the first time since this all began. Then I stop counting the beat of my heart, and I lean way out for the little cross Jan brought me. My fingers curl tight around it, as my eyes close. I wobble less and don't bother wiping away the tears.

Chapter Ten

Will stops by to see me every day, but he is dealing with three kids and five pets and feeding everyone and running a business. He is twirling on high in the blender of life. I measure his level of stress by the distance he puts between us. He is all focus, all-business. Every ounce of his being in full "commando mode." And men have absolutely no spare time and no spare tenderness in commando mode. Tenderness or any emotions stand in the way of getting the job done.

I understand instantly from the tone of his voice when he phones me; from the rigid look on his face when he drops by.

The office computer crashed. It has never crashed before, but it does that week. Of course. These things must be expected when you are not making things go right. And neither of us is making anything go right. William is the only one who can work with the programmers over the phone and complete the endless series of commands to get the system back up and running. It will take untold hours to bring it back. "If you make one mistake," a programmer says, "you'll lose all your data. Impossible to believe, yet all the customer records, all the financial records, everything will be gone." Will makes the discovery that the backup tapes he thought were being dutifully run had not been run correctly.

It takes William days to run all the purges. The employees and business wait for him. One service technician is on vacation. Another one hurt his back and ended up in the emergency room. Customers are waiting. William goes out to fix the laser printers himself. This is life in a small business. And this business is still small with only fifteen employees. And he is replacing two key employees. Interviewing, hiring, starting training. I had been there and done all of it with him before. I understood completely, but that helped little. I don't want to understand

and be supportive. For the first time in my life, I know I want a man who can understand and occasionally support me.

I am thinking back on all our years together. In the early ones, when I was in college, we skied together three or four times a week. William worked at Eldora ski area, determined to escape the trap of office work. Odd jobs paid for his food and rent during the off-season; and when the snow fell, he always found work with a ski resort to get a free season pass.

I finished college. Will rode a Harley and played pool in the bars at night. I was a colonel's daughter, and my parents were not initially impressed with my selection, yet they had given me the nickname "Mulehead" as a child. And I was in love.

One morning, after five consecutive years of snow and full-time skiing, Will woke to a sunny day and a perfect powder slope and decided it could be just as tedious skiing every day as it would be going to an office. He told me then that being a ski bum was a different trap, one that would leave him with no money and little power over his life. There would always be someone else in control. And that he could not tolerate.

"I can't work for someone else," he said. A simple truth so simply said. I knew him too well to believe otherwise. So, life changed.

We started building our first business together, and we molded and nurtured it for fifteen years. Side-by-side. Up against a hundred walls, planning and pushing and willing our way around every one of them. Learning to trust our instincts and each other.

I went back to school and got a master's degree in business while I worked full time. I wanted the security of a graduate degree in my back pocket. William's entrepreneurial talent was his own security and the only one he ever needed. But he was never without a book in his hands and never without educational tapes echoing in his car; he never stopped working to improve himself. We logged endless hours at work, seven days a week, creating a strong, growing company with seventy employees, and financial success beyond even our expectations. Then we sold that business to an international corporation, and I retired pregnant with twins.

But that was seven years ago, before these heart attacks and surgery, I am mostly Mom. Busy with children, the house, and making countless meals. I never liked to cook. Liking the kitchen must be a godsend, yet I stir homemade soups, make fresh bread, and glance outside. But when I look into my daughters' eyes, I finally spot a clear chance to make a lasting difference. No one else will love them or care for them the way I can and in light of that basic reality, nothing else holds as much importance.

Business never made me feel that way; it shimmered ephemeral like last month's P&L statement. Trying to make it more tangible, I graphed rising sales and my rising income. I posted them month after month on a bulletin board in my office. I tacked up the projected future, well within range for easy viewing and reviewing. At month end, I'd take down the past. Page after page, year after year, scrutinized before filling the trash. I listened to financial statements. I charted and analyzed cycles of previous performance, predicting the probable future and implementing changes to improve numbers on future financials. The present always remained ungraspable, illusive.

I learned to master my emotions for they are noisy, time consuming and cumbersome. They'd offered nothing to the bottom line. I disciplined myself to shut them out and secured every vent where they briefly appeared. But I still couldn't widen my hands or my vision enough for the present or to connect with any fulfilling purpose for my life. Before children, it hadn't even occurred to me to try.

In these seven years away from office work, I never miss the business world. These days I watch my children; I see bright smiles and tumultuous tears. I have close friendships and flowers that bring me pleasure. But there are many times I've missed the closeness Will and I once had and what we'd shared, when we spoke one language. There are times I know he liked me far better when I wore a suit and talked marketing plans. But recently I've noticed that I am no longer able to silence capped feelings gushing up or my need to release them. It would make our life far easier if I could go back to mirroring William, yet I have caught new glimpses of myself and sense I like the stranger budding just beyond focus. At times I yearn to fully embrace this persistent stranger my husband does not welcome warmly in our home.

I know I could draw him back and draw back the mirage of closeness in an instant with a simple question about sales or service revenue. I know how to play this game well, but I don't *want* to play anymore, so instead I often stand silently, hoping he'll eventually notice I am no longer speaking...hoping most of all that he'll be interested enough in what excites me now to occasionally ask a few questions. Silence.

Sometime during the first month after the twins are born, William told me that he misses having a business. Ideas for a new one started swirling amid the constant feedings, diapers and care of two tiny babies. His need to work has nothing to do with the money: a constant burn flames inside him. And the challenges at work both feed and temporarily quench that fire at his core in a way being at home cannot. William is not a househusband, and I am not foolish enough to continue trying to make him one. You don't cage a tiger and see a happy tiger. You don't enter his den and live long beside a caged tiger. You sure don't exit whole. I tell Will I support whatever he wants to do.

And I mean every word. He wanted to start another business. I wanted it for him, yet as a result, our highly equitable and meticulously planned, totally unrealistic ideas of dividing childcare between us were quickly dissolved. Dead, buried but apparently not entirely forgotten. Conflicted desires trail a choppy wake kept ever in view.

The past and its memories ease away, and I look up to study William's face as he sits across from me in that hospital room. He appears cool and professionally preoccupied. In that moment, I could remind myself I need not read his detachment as if he were saying I don't care about you, but each day I have waited for him to talk about something more than the mechanics of daily life. I yearn for him to tell me that I mean something to him, that I am important to him, and yet I know, there is no way he will open up enough to give me anything. This man has walled himself off.

The distance between us grows steadily. We have hovered near this place before. We were hovering close when I took off my wedding ring. But I will say nothing of any of this to him. Talking to him now would make it worse. I would get hard looks and harder words, and I can't handle either. And I am tired of talking and trying to explain things I thought he should know.

My friends fill my needs. There is nothing I ever need to explain. Yet part of me wants to tell William there is danger in letting your wife go too long having her needs met by others. There is danger when a woman grows too quiet. Our marriage has survived on the times he's brought me forward into focus and when he brought his emotions forward too. But I am on his back burner now, simmering.

The young wife hidden within me wants desperately to be held, and she wants to say, "Hey, I almost died. Show me a little love." But I no longer dream a young wife's dreams. And I know exactly how a man's mind works in commando mode. I have done a long, lonely stretch in commando mode. Too long.

It is feeling like a desert. And I feel like I am sheltering the last remaining drop of water I need to get through a hot and barren land. I cannot linger much longer. Not if I wish to survive. For I have a new heart, and I intended to protect it.

⁂

It is dark outside my window when Dr. Davis drops by my room to check on me. It is my first truly conscious sight of him, but somehow, I feel as if I have known him years. We have earned mileage plus together. It is the same caring voice that comforted me in the ICU when his voice was the only hope I could cling to. When the respirator kept breathing. And I wished only to stop.

With a face that matches his voice, he pulls up a chair. Dr. Davis is too young to have deep lines in his face, but he runs his hand across his eyes briefly, the way I always do when I'm exhausted. He tells me he heard that I had a bad day on Tuesday. That was the day my blood pressure dropped so low, but I made light of it. I realize he is aware of what is going on with me. This man who performs two hundred open-heart surgeries a year manages to keep careful track of every patient. We visit a few minutes. And then he asks the question that floors me. I will think of that question over and over again. It will never leave me. Dr. Davis turns to look at me.

"What can I do to help you?" he asks slowly.

And I am thinking at first, from my years in sales, that it is an open question. It isn't designed for one-word responses. It isn't designed to get him in and out of a patient's room quickly. I tell myself there must be a part of him that is miles past tired of going into rooms, a part that would have very much liked to get in and get out quickly, so he could finally go home for some much-needed rest. But instead, he asks me that question. He asks it with the whole of his being. And in that moment, I know that I am staring face-to-face with compassion. And I see clearly when everything else melts away in a blistering bright sun, it merits standing.

I know nothing about Dr. Davis and feel suddenly I know everything. Everything that matters. What can I do to help you, he asks. His eyes and the lingering gentle quiet tell me if there is anything he can possibly do, he will willingly try to accomplish it.

But there is nothing I can tell him, for there are no simple answers for this mess I've gotten myself into. There are no easy answers. Dr. Davis patiently waits for my response, not realizing that he's made a friend for life if he ever needs one. But I can see plainly that my new friend needs sleep, and I am keeping him from it.

"I'm doing fine," I say simply. "But it would mean a lot if you could stop back, in a few days, when I'm feeling clearer, so I can ask a couple questions."

We shake hands, and I know he'll return for another talk. But I decide right then to keep it short, because I don't need him to do anything more. Asking me that question was gift enough. I will treasure it always.

⁂

One of the respiratory technicians arrives to give me another breathing treatment. This routine has been a constant since intensive care. I finish inhaling the medicine dutifully and show her I'm using my "incentive barometer" hourly to keep my lungs inflated and clear of pneumonia.

She is young and pretty with a soft and warming Georgia accent. She hesitates a moment from packing up her equipment and then smiles at me in a wistful way.

"I just have to tell you about your husband," she says. "I just feel I have to tell you that I've never seen anything like his devotion. He sat with you hour after hour in intensive care. He never even left your side the whole time I was on duty." Her eyes mists as she continues. "And I've just never seen anything like it. You know you see women do that sometimes. They sit right there, but you never see the husbands stay all night with their wives the way yours did."

"It was kind of you to tell me," I thank her. She closes the door as she leaves; yet her innocence lingers. And I'm wishing mine had too.

Oh, William why did we have to go sour on each other? There was never a lack of love.

The next morning includes another heparin shot in the stomach to reduce the risk of blood clots. They leave tiny marks, so you can count their number. Six bruises trail across my stomach in a line not far from my belly button. The nurse amazes me with the variations in their skill at giving these shots. Same needle size, same ingredient, but the level of discomfort was markedly different.

A nurse removes the huge IV in my neck today. I don't feel pain as it slips out of the artery, yet it's another thing I'd rather not watch.

After she removes it, she tells me she needs to put a new IV into the back of my left hand. For the first time, the job is botched badly. I've had a lot of IVs, and none of them feel delightful, but I expect it to go in the way they usually do. I now discover what a mess can be made of putting one in, and there isn't time to prepare myself for the repeated digging in my vein. Ouch! Lady, you have got to be kidding. I look at the nurse. The muscles in her jaw clamp tighter. She slowly works the needle into my skin yet again for another try.

"You have very difficult veins," she tells me.

And you have a very difficult time taking responsibility, I think. Everyone else seems to manage. After five additional minutes, I am ready to try it myself, because even having to keep my eyes shut, I can't possibly have done any worse. In exasperation the nurse calls for someone else to do it. Yes! Finally. Thank you.

Another nurse appears at the door, stares at my bloody hand, and says she doesn't want to do it. Coward! I call silently to her retreating back.

Another attempt begins by the nurse who is definitely not on a roll this morning with IVs. It takes two more gouging assaults; and by the final one, I'm thinking we'll both be bathed in sweat soon if this doesn't end.

"There. I think it *might* be in," she tells me. I glance uneasily at the wound because she appears to want me to assure her that it is actually in, but the needle hangs out farther than any I've ever seen.

"It looks okay," I lie. I cannot face another try. She nods brightly, and then with extreme care and precision, she mops up my crimson hand and secures the precarious IV with extra tape and a dressing. Glancing down I suspect she is trying to hide her work. Unclenching my jaw, I lean back hoping the rest of the day would be uneventful.

"I hate giving shots too," the nurse confides to me as she pauses near my bed. And she tells me that she doesn't think she could ever become a nurse because she hates needles so much. Why do people always share this kind of stuff with me?

Yet I make pleasant conversation because she's quite nice when she's unarmed, but I'm wishing she would consider career counseling before deciding to continue inflicting this suffering on countless more captives. I watch her leave, dreading her heparin shot in the morning. But it might be the last hurdle, because I may get to go home tomorrow.

I've been getting up by myself for days to use the bathroom. I walk the halls every morning and afternoon with a therapist, and I accomplish it with a slightly more purposeful shuffle than that trip with Terry from the ICU to the elevator. I'm sleeping at least four hours a night without nightmares. I'm off oxygen and my blood oxygen levels are holding up well. And most important to me, one circuit in my brain has turned back on. The TV is silent. I'm reading once more.

Dr. Davis returns for his promised visit. We talk a few minutes and then I ask him about the possibility of still making the trip to Hawaii that I planned for the last of August. He says I am doing well, and he doesn't see why not. And then I ask him what he thinks about me doing a triathlon someday. He can't know what the idea of completing one means to me. I'm not sure I understood it myself but being physically strong has always been important to me. It still seems important to this new me.

Before the heart attack, beginning training again invigorated me on more than just a physical level. Yet Dr. Davis talked about the elevated pulse and blood pressure that goes hand in hand with racing, and he thought it would not be prudent to do one. But he told me he saw no reason that I would not live to be an old woman.

"Really?" I say abruptly, and then as comprehension dawns, my question startles me. The sound of that massive, revealing doubt voiced for the first time shocked and then slowly embarrasses me. I'm revealing some new side of myself...a side I don't like. I have never been a pessimist before. I don't want to be one now, yet I sit mulling over my new negativity and again I come to know just how much I've lost in such a short time. Who am I? And as I sit there I know I need to learn to cultivate optimism again. I need it: I need it back quickly if I am to have any hope of living. Embarrassed now, trying to straighten and smooth down the wrinkled covers that drape me. Keeping busy a moment and knowing fully what Dr. Davis must have known before he made the comment about me living a long life.

"Yes," he says emphatically, and his eyes never waver. "You were in trouble when you came in. But you aren't now."

And long after Dr. Davis leaves me, I keep repeating his words. I keep trying to let them sink deeply inside my vacant core. Over and over I let them play into me. You were in trouble... but you aren't now.

⁂

William calls later in the day. I can hear the tension in his voice. He tells me the stuff with the kids and the house, and the animals and the yard, and the food is a full-time job. No kidding, I tell him. I know, I've been doing it every day and night for years. He says he doesn't think I have the house and kids well organized. All of it could be set up better and the girls aren't being expected to do enough.

No, I answer. They do plenty. At six years old, they make their bed, straighten their room, pick up after themselves, put away their folded clothes, empty the dishwasher, set the table for dinner, and clear it afterward. And they do it all with a smile most days and a big willingness to help and be part of our team. That's more than enough. Smiles are more than enough.

I don't like the sound of his voice and the start of the criticism. I've been told numerous times by people that I am extremely well organized. But my organizational skills are not really the point here. This is going nowhere I want it to be going. I'm not up for this, I think. But then, when has that ever mattered?

❧⁂❧

It's late afternoon July 11ᵗʰ. I should be leaving the hospital soon. A therapist verified that I could climb a small series of stairs, and I've set up appointments for follow-up visits with Dr. Jamisen and Dr. Davis. I've been assigned a home health care nurse and a visiting physical therapist.

The girls and William are due to pick me up. I feel excited to see the kids. I haven't wanted them to come here before now. I haven't wanted them to see me weak and all hooked up to tubes and leads. But I've made substantial progress and they will have to get used to this new me.

Beth Kelly and Dr. Jamisen arrive for my final checkout. Dr. Jamisen listens to my heart, and then he kneels on the floor as he looks at my leg incisions. The three of us begin talking, just making casual conversation and joking around a little. And then suddenly Dr. Jamisen makes an odd comment to me about the pain of losing your first love.

I glance at him, and awkwardly interrupt the flow of his sentence. Without thinking, I quickly say, "I don't know, I'm still married to him." For some reason I could scarcely breathe.

Dr. Jamisen pauses a second and then says, "Well, let me tell you about the pain of losing your first love. You think you'll never get over it. You think you'll die, and then you go to your twentieth reunion and you see her and she's ugly." The three of us laugh.

And then they leave, and I sit alone again. Baffled by Dr. Jamisen's comment, I begin thinking that I know about marrying your first love. And I can recall the agony of losing that love and the pain and joy of trying to rebuild it. I have tried desperately to forget, to put all this far, far behind me, yet do I wear this so plainly on my face for him to read? Silence surrounds me. My hand lifts protectively over my heart. And I move into memories again.

I remembered the morning I woke and knew I was in a trap. I was twenty-six and knew I needed out of it. And stepping out of that trap would be hard, but it was the best option in a bad situation.

I was ready to cut my losses. William and I had been together for eight years. I had never even kissed another man, not before I met him and certainly not after. I'd had more than my share of opportunities, for I worked with men; I spent most days in the offices of company presidents, bank officers, managers, and lawyers, yet I'd been immune to their charms because I had William. And although we never lived together, we'd spent many evenings in each other's apartments.

The truth was simple, and I felt its power. I hated its power and its antiquated inequity. But in truth, I had married him from the first night we made love, yet making love to me had not been any commitment to him. He had mentioned marriage and having kids in the first few years we were together, and I felt cemented to him and secure in the knowledge that he was in love with me and serious about me.

But the years went on, and I suffered through hoping he would propose and hoping he would surprise me with a ring on Valentine's Day or on Christmas, or maybe even on my birthday. And after a while, I found the holidays a little more painful than they had been in my childhood. Then I realized suddenly that it never even crossed his mind. I learned that playing house with a man is not making a home.

So at the age of twenty-six, I told him that I'd like to get married. He got a funny look on his face and said he'd think about it. His hesitation hurt. It hurt me deeply.

I hated the abrupt role reversal, for I had never initiated our relationship. I had been pursued with great passion and purpose, and I knew that I never wanted to be with any man who wasn't inspired enough to figure out how to call and ask me out. And, in the beginning, I never had to ask. I never arranged any dates. William did all the work, enthusiastically, and there was no doubting his desire for me. So I hated taking the lead in asking about marriage. But I knew exactly where I was heading, and I was more than willing to go there.

It didn't take William long to think about my proposal. The next night, he came over to have dinner at my apartment, and he casually told me that he loved me but wasn't ready to be married. He was thirty years old. I remember standing up from the table. I remember telling him that I loved him too, but that I knew myself well enough to know that I wanted a man who loved me enough to marry me, and I wanted children someday.

I remember pausing, and then I said, "I figure it'll take my heart about two or three years to get over you. And I'm starting now. If you need a friend to talk to on the phone, you can call me sometime, but we're done dating."

William stood up with a surprised look on his face, and he walked out my door. I closed it firmly. Suffering for weeks but never wondering if I'd made the right decision. My only regret was not making it about six years earlier.

Three weeks later William decided to marry me. He balked at the idea of a traditional wedding. He said he didn't want God in the ceremony. And I agreed to his request without even a second thought. We went to the County Courthouse to exchange our vows. I wore a plain beige dress and a pair of heels I'd walked in countless times. No family and no friends that cared for me stood by my side. There was no celebration that evening. I had dreamed it all so differently, the way all girls dream about their wedding day, but I loved him, and I married him. Yet it wasn't right. Nothing felt right or real about that day. The ceremony seemed all business. No flowers. No wasted time. No emotion. I felt somehow dishonored even though I'd conditioned myself long before to disconnect from the message of my feelings. But unlike business, hearts need the honoring of emotions to prosper.

God was most definitely absent from our wedding. It took me fifteen years to understand why nothing felt right on my wedding day, and it had little to do with the sterile ceremony sandwiched between our daily sales appointments. Reaching that understanding had nothing to do with using my mind or my analytical abilities, for the day I gained understanding I learned knowledge can arrive on a toe hold of pure intuition, and its dawning can usher as much devastation as a lightning strike from a seemingly clear sky.

Two years ago, just a few days before my forty-first birthday, I took my dog for a walk in the meadow. I tied up Tess outside our chicken coop, and went inside to feed the hens, but my mind wasn't on the animals. I was thinking about William and our marriage the way a woman dwells on such things sometimes. I remember standing there when a sudden and inexplicable knowing surged through me. I could not disconnect. And when that moment passed, I knew with certainty that William was right. He hadn't been ready for marriage. He was involved with someone else. He wasn't ready the day we got married, and he wasn't ready to begin our marriage until several years after it, when he finally gave her up. And the woman had spent all those years pretending with consummate skill to be my friend.

I'm not sure how I found the strength to leave that dark and dusty place, but I crossed the meadow back to our big, stone house. And I knew I would never be the same. Somehow, I finished the day. William came home, we ate dinner, and put our kids to bed. Later, we sat together in matching chairs in the family room, William's long legs stretched out on the ottoman in front of him. But I could not stretch out my legs. I turned toward him.

"Did you have an affair with her?"

His legs twitched as he lowered the book he was reading. But I did not need to see them for I knew. I knew cold, dead certain the answer to that question before I ever asked.

Then he hesitated. Hesitated longer than I had ever heard him pause in answering anything.

"Do not lie to me," I said as I watched him struggle.

"Yes," he answered finally. But then I knew William would not lie to me. He had never told me a direct lie. He deceived me, and made a total lie out of our life, yet he had never told me a lie. He never needed to for I did not ask. I was too trusting to even conceive asking the question.

We hung in total silence for a moment more, neither of us able to look at each other, and then he spoke again. He said, "I always knew you'd ask me someday."

It must have been agony having to wait fifteen years to answer that question, knowing all the while it would come. Yes, waiting would have been torture for me. Well, someday is here.

I could not draw one breath. It was nearly impossible to move, but I stood without knowing where I was going. All I knew was that I had to leave. I took a few steps away, and then he said quickly, too quickly, "It didn't mean the same thing to me that it would to you."

I remember my hand gripping my chest, trying to stop the pain in my heart. It was then I learned the pain of a broken heart is a physical thing. I never understood before. I never understood how it hurts, but wounds were first carved then. And it would take two years for others to find them. For others to try to mend them. But there is no one else who can do deep mending for you.

Tears streamed down my face as I stared at William. Hating the words he'd just told me. Hating him for thinking they could possibly make it better. So, it didn't mean the same to him. And does the same meaningless thing, when he does it with me mean nothing too? And if there's a difference, how am I to understand it? It's always been making love for me. Always. So, it's supposed to help knowing it's just sex to him.

His face was ghastly pale, and the tears kept flooding down my cheeks. How could he have done it? How could he have possibly done this for years and pretended it meant nothing. Betraying me and lying to himself. God, I hated him!

"Well, it should have meant the same to you!" I cried. "It should have meant the same." Slowly I turned and walked upstairs to a spare bedroom. Decades older, I closed the door on my life as I had known it. I closed the door on all that I had believed in with the heart that had loved him when I was just a young girl. I did not sleep once that night; questions pounded my head.

Come morning, I wanted answers. And I knew Will would be honest answering, because as odd as it seems now, honesty had formed our strongest link. So, I learned about the affair. The affair that began before our marriage and continued far too long after it. He told me that he was the one who ended it. And I knew this to be true. For I knew she had never wanted to end it. Never. She had been obsessed with trying to keep it alive, with trying to maintain any possible avenue of contact with him, even after the façade of her friendship with me had crumbled.

I remember shouting at him. Crying as words tumbled out almost incoherently. "Why didn't you marry her?" I sobbed. Another cavernous pause.

William answered my question. "Because I love you," he told me. And I hope no one ever does me the favor of loving me like this again.

During those days, I hated the exclusive bond I had with him. I hated it and I wanted to hurt William desperately the way he had hurt me. And I wished I'd had twenty lovers and that none of them meant anything to me. I wished he meant nothing to me. There were nights I thought I would go to a bar and stumble out with a stranger. And I'd come home just before dawn and smile sweetly and tell William that it didn't mean a thing.

But I did not go to a bar. That simple act would kill me. For it is no simple act for me and never could be.

Days dragged on as if in slow motion. Endless nights I stared at blank ceilings for hours, filling with horror at the deceit of our early marriage. Finally, I saw clearly. I listened again to my childlike laughter and my years of childish innocence. I looked anew at the ignorance that overlaid all of it, and I cried myself into exhausted oblivion.

I would never have thought such deceit or such blind trust possible. I would not have married William if I'd known the truth about that affair. I would have divorced him the instant I discovered it, if I'd discovered it while it was going on. And at the moment we were a decade and a half past it, we had three little girls who adored him, yet divorcing him was all that lingered on my mind. A moated wall had formed between us, and I had no wish to broach it. We were finished. This lie of a marriage was over.

But he broached it. He came to me one morning as I was going down to the gym, and he was shattered too. I saw it in his face. Wild Irish emotions float so close to the surface, run so close to the edge. This man who has always wept with me at sad movies. And I have loved that about him. That he can cry at movies that have anything sad happen to dogs, kids, people in love. And suddenly we are both crying. Oh, William, why, why did you do this? I think over and over. It does mean something. Do you not understand that now?

I tried to step far around him, but he pulled me down to sit on the basement floor, pulled me gently down in front of him.

"I got up this morning" he told me, "and I realized that I didn't even say I was sorry. I haven't even told you how much I've always loved you and that I'm sorry for what I did. What I did was wrong. I learned my lesson. And it has never happened again."

And I will never know if it was his trembling words or the tears wetting his face that touched me, but I looked into him. I saw him clearly. I saw him completely. And without further thought, I slowly opened my arms. And on that simple gesture, we began again. I tried to rebuild trust. We tried love again.

And most of all, I tried to forgive, for I still love him and because he asked it of me. But I could not forget. I learned it was near impossible for me to forget. Yet, I still played the fool, for I promised in those first days to never mention the affair again, and that was my intention, for I knew it was the right thing to do. But I had never ridden this train before, and I had badly misjudged the time it took to travel the tunnel. Trying to think and will my way through, I allowed myself far too little time, which only suppressed emotions and delayed the crossing.

So, I became a liar, for I had to ask more questions. William answered them all, painfully and patiently. I listened intently, alert for any signal that he wasn't telling the truth. In sadness, I remembered how safe it felt when I didn't need to evaluate any of his answers. I remembered how it felt to believe him and believe in him deep down to the core of my heart. And finally, the night we first made love, I wept inconsolably in his arms and I could not stop the great racking sobs that racked us both.

My life felt like the wrong page in the wrong book. I woke up. I went to sleep. I told myself it happened in a lot of marriages. Grow up. I made breakfast, lunch and then dinner for my family. I told myself not to think of it. I failed miserably. I was growing old.

And much later when I believed I'd vaulted over it, and I hoped I was finally free, some place, some innocent comment by a casual friend would awaken the darkness and the past would slam back into me once more. And the thickened scab ripped off the wound each time.

Vaulting over is not walking your way clear through. So, I looked again at all the mess inside. And I admitted it wasn't healed. I admitted there was more. And I wept again remembering what I'd thought of the woman. For years, she'd made certain I thought of her as a dear, close friend. And every time I thought she was seeing me, she was only seeing William. She was never my friend. Only his. I was used by her. Using me was once very convenient to them both.

And I learned there are limits to the pain you feel when you are betrayed by a man. There is a limit - it only takes your heart. But when you've been betrayed long by a woman who deftly mined you deep for confidences and given false ones; when you've been worked and manipulated and been lied to countless times with an easy smile, Dear God, it can take your soul.

I struggled with this second wound. Recalling all her lies, and it finally fit together. I understood all that she had done. I understood how flawlessly she did it. All the social get togethers and the couples trips she had initiated played out again for me. I stood back in awe at the bottomless depth of her deception and the callously smooth sound of those endless lies. Recalling how they never once caught in her throat. Not the ones she told me or the ones she told her own husband. She played us both. I stood back in awe within the fire of fury. I could never have imagined a force like this fury. And for the first time in my life I understood the rage burning behind a "crime of passion," for consumed by it, I felt close to committing one.

For in those days I wanted to destroy her for what she did to me and to my belief in the bonds of friendship and the bonds of marriage. I wanted to call her husband and shatter her phony life, the same way she'd shattered mine. I thought of it over and over, until I told myself finally, my God, Melissa, let it go! It happened long ago. Move on. I will not grant her any further power over my life. And I will not hurt anyone else. I will not hurt her husband. I will not spread this oozing darkness. Let it go! This isn't you, this isn't who you want to be.

I will not hand her my soul.

And the rage and shadow gradually eased. Very gradually. Only after I refused time after time to listen to its voice. But with that constant battle I gained more awareness of my thoughts, for I practiced deflecting infected ones from my mind the instant they appeared, before they had a chance to toy with or trigger negative emotions. Before they had a chance to lead me down places I did not want to go. I had known even from the first that I did not want to travel there, yet I did not know how to stop the daily freefall. But I learned.

I learned to keep her from my mind. I chose for her not to have any further impact on my life. I chose it. Are we not creatures given free will? I wanted to be completely free of her. Free of what I'd do to myself, if I did not give her up, if I did not give up all the hatred that I felt for her. There was a way out. I knew that. I'd known it all along.

I called her up one day. One day when I felt ready. I introduced myself, for I felt certain after all these years she would not remember my voice. I told her that I knew all about the affair. Then I swallowed hard and told her that I forgave her.

And she laughed and said, "see ya" and hung up the phone. And I was thinking, I hope not, for I have seen enough of you to last ten thousand lifetimes.

Click. With the receiver settled tight into the cradle, I learned in that instant that forgiveness is a daily choice. Made and remade with the light of each dawn. Just like living without fear. Living without hatred is a constant decision and the only one I knew I wanted to make. But it did not come instantly, and it certainly did not come easy.

One day animosity was gone. And just the sadness remained. A great sense of sadness and the thought that I would rather have a hole in my heart than her cavalier cruelty. No one on God's earth would believe who she is and what she can do. All with an easy smile. And you go to your twentieth reunion and you see her and she's ugly. Yes, it has been twenty years since we first met and became friends. And slowly you see yourself and you are ugly. You are human. It is okay...keep going...keep trying. No, I will not hand her my soul.

And then later, quite unexpectedly, I no longer needed to judge her. A layer of peace came to me then, as I could mentally wish her well. I wished her all the best, for I understood that I owed her thanks for what she offered me. And I discovered a gift when I reached toward forgiveness. And then in time, forgiveness too became unnecessary for there was no place else to travel with her except toward gratitude.

Without her, how could I have seen myself stripped to barest bone and seen the start of rebuilding stronger foundations. I have seen part of my wounds healed. They make steel, my girl, from beating on iron. Yes, Daddy. That they do. And a hot flame. It takes a burning, hot flame, but I'm thinking you knew that all along.

One night I lay awake wondering why with all my Celtic intuition, with my solid sixth sense that guides me clear in murky waters, why did I not know at the time? I was closed to it of course, for such a happening was not remotely part of my reality. But why? And why was I shielded from the truth for so long? There was that evening, when I was eight months pregnant and lying next to Will. I curled within his arm, when the question about the affair first came to my mind. But a voice inside told me not to ask. Not to ask such a silly question, and sleep found me instantly then.

The question evaporated from my mind. I'm glad I did not ask. I'm glad it was erased from my mind for a little longer, for I could not have handled the answer. Not with the heightened emotions of pregnancy and tears that stream at the simplest thing. This was not a simple thing. And there is perfect timing for each tick of the clock.

But I lay awake that night wondering why I did not know about the affair? Finally, I understood both my blindness and the protective shielding before pulling up the covers and closing my eyes to rest. I understood and made peace with that understanding, made peace, finally, with my ignorance. For faith covered me that night like a blanket.

Faith and peace told me that I was meant to be blind to it, knowing at the time would have ended my life with William. It would have meant my three daughters would never have been born. And it would have meant there'd be no chance to bring it all full circle. It's the full circle I want. It's the challenge and the promise of full healing and completion that lies before me. A sense of faith that somehow, I'll be guided to find it. Everything comes at the right time. Even lightning.

So, I learned about losing love and trust, Dr. Jamisen, though I did not allude to it when you came to discharge me from the hospital. You were right, losing that love was death and a slow agony that lived on.

And I'm sitting in this hard hospital chair, sitting all alone and waiting for my family to take me home wondering how to mend the rest of these wounds? It's fallacy to tell yourself that you can put your life back together and expect all the pieces to fit right when a part of your heart is missing.

"You think you'll never get over it," Dr. Jamisen said. "You think you'll die." Well, maybe sometimes you do.

Dear God, I want to be completely whole. I want to hear the whole of my laughter again. I want to hear laughter ringing rich with both wisdom and fresh found innocence. Help me. Teach me to understand whatever more I need to learn. There must be more, or I would not be sitting here lost and broken. There must be more work within the tunnel. Oh God, help me find the strength for honoring all my emotions. You can block them from your mind by force of will and training, but you can't shield your heart. A heart won't listen to lies long. My heart can no longer live with my lies.

How do I heal?

Chapter Eleven

William and the girls arrive to pick me up, and it takes nearly five minutes before we realize that William hasn't brought me any clothes. He offers to drive back up the mountain for them, but I tell him no. I'll probably need to walk about three feet from the wheelchair to my Jeep, and if anyone sees me, or if I offend someone, well, so be it. They'll just have to go about their day offended.

"I'll leave in the hospital gown," I tell William, "and we'll drop it off later."

It feels wonderful to see my daughters again. I've never been away from them for so long. They seem excited and cautious at the same time; I know they've been warned that they must not climb on me. I notice furtive glances. The cuts on my upper chest and legs are on full display, and I see no reason to hide them. William catches my eye and softly says that the scars might be a bit much for them this first meeting.

So, I laugh and ask out loud if my scars are grossing them out.

"No," they tell me, all talking at once. "Not too much."

"The scars will get lighter in time," I say. They'll always be there, but they'll fade to mostly white. "And I'll get stronger," I tell them. It'll take a while, but I'll do my best to get stronger every day.

They wear big smiles, but I know this has been hard. I glance at my littlest, my baby, Jacqueline. She stands off slightly to the left, listening to her family talk and watching me closely. I reach out toward her, and she slowly comes near, taking small tentative steps until she is next to the bed. A few minutes pass until she closes the gap between us and finally with a deep sigh, a sigh I will never forget, she gingerly leans her head against my hip. I smooth her golden hair. Savoring the wispy, soft silken touch.

Jacqueline looks up tentatively. I see my own face as a little girl;

she looks exactly like me except for those bright blue eyes. I caress her cheek. Oh sweetheart, I'm so sorry I rocked your world. Rocking mine is hard enough, rocking yours crumbles me to the core. A child needs her mother, and I am not the model structure of stability I want to be for you. I disappeared suddenly from your life. Failing you this way and seeing failure reflected in a little girl's less-trusting eyes hurts me worse than all the pain that has surrounded me for the past eleven days.

Jacqueline was still nursing when I had heart surgery. In my mind, before children and before nursing, I thought that nursing for one year was a long, long time. Nursing for two years was stretching the limit, and I firmly believed nursing for three indicated a mother's excessive neediness.

Meagan and Brenna weaned themselves by fourteen months and all seemed fine. But then Jacqueline came into my life so firmly attached to me, it would have been despicable to do anything but hold her close and let her nurse. My one-year mark quickly passed into two and then at two and a half I started telling her she was a big girl now and that when she was three years old, I would still hold her whenever she wanted, but she wouldn't nurse. Period.

So, we were all primed for that birthday. We'd gotten nursing down to just five minutes before bedtime, all comfort and little nourishment. But then the heart attacks came six weeks before her third birthday, and she was abruptly weaned from comfort overnight.

She reaches for my hand and clings tightly to my little finger. "Do you want to sit with me?" I ask. "I can scoot over and make room for you."

Jacqueline shakes her head emphatically, yet she does not let go of my finger. I close my eyes for a moment, knowing I'll have a few seconds before suspicion is raised. It'll be all right, I tell myself. Somehow this will be all right. Everyone is staring at me when I open my eyes, so I nod more eagerly than I feel, and I start sliding slowly off the bed.

It is hard to believe that I am leaving the hospital. William helps me into the passenger side of my silver Jeep. He closes the door and we start again. The seat belt pressing against my scar is a horror, so I move the shoulder strap away and use the lap belt. Thankful that there is no airbag on my side. The image of that deploying into my chest is my one remaining nightmare.

Everyone seems unusually quiet as we leave the parking lot. I glance at William. "Don't you think it was thoughtful of Dr. Lucas to stop by my room to tell me how sorry he was about what happened?" I begin.

Brenna interrupts. "Who's Dr. Lucas?"

"The doctor listed on my insurance card as my primary care physician," I tell her, turning slightly toward the backseat where she is sitting. "He was the one who refused to refer me to another cardiologist -- they're heart doctors. Anyway, he told me he realized he should have taken the time to listen to me better. It couldn't have been easy for him to do that, but it meant a lot to me." I turn forward gingerly again before continuing. "It takes a big person to do that. That was nice, don't you think?" I ask William.

"Yes, it was."

"He was the only one who ever admitted making an error, the only one who apologized," I add. "I guess doctors can't risk doing that too often."

"Why not?" Brenna asks.

"They're afraid of being sued," William tells her. We all fall quiet once more and the minutes and miles pass. I feel like a stranger again as we drove home, shades of the same surreal sentiment that I felt right after the first pain from the flap opening in the artery.

Driving back home that first time after surgery, I study scenery that is familiar when I am not. All here is known: the inside of this car, the way it smells of kids' left over snacks and my left over life, the road the Jeep travels is paved with memories of countless trips up and down, the passing trees: willows, crab apples, cottonwood, and higher up aspen and pines, the blur of houses and the people riding inside this car: all is well known. But I am not known, and it feels as if I am still emerging from a deep amnesia.

I glance at my family, and I manage a half smile I do not half feel. I know you all very well, but who am I supposed to be? I do not know myself. Yet something tells me I'm supposed to be happy to be out of the hospital. I'm supposed to be happy and laughing and making everyone's lives work. Well, they are expecting too much of me. I can see by the look on their faces. It is too much.

We pull into the drive, and I notice someone has tended my flowers. Red, purple, and pink petunias. Yellow pansies. Lilacs, lavender, painted daisies, lilies, and blue columbine all welcoming me. But I feel weak as we near the garage. I crack a window and take a couple deep breaths.

"Are you all right?" Will asks.

I nod.

William comes to my side of the car and opens the door. The kids pile out. The door to the house is unlocked, and I walk in. It's the altitude, I tell myself. It must be the altitude. We're up an additional 2,500 feet above Boulder, but I've lived at this level for nine years, so the logic of that idea quickly diminishes. No, I can't kid myself; I'm not feeling right. In fact, I am dizzy as I walk inside the house. Sara greets me with a big smile and a gentle hug.

"I need to sit down," I say almost inaudibly. I ease into my chair. William pushes in the ottoman, so it now serves as a bed, and then he shoos the kids out quickly. My head hurts suddenly. I've never had headaches. I close my eyes as the pain in my left temple grows stronger, and when I open my eyes a moment later, there are colored lights and odd geometric shapes in my eye. I blink. They do not leave. Oh please, I think, please let me be okay. I just told my kids I'd get stronger.

"I need a wet cloth," I whisper to Sara, and she hurries for one. I can't believe this. William sits close to me. I tell him then about the lights. About the sharp pain in the left side of my head. And I am thinking the worst without knowing anything about the medical conditions and what these symptoms might actually indicate.

I am thinking blood clots and strokes. And I am thinking I don't mind not looking good. I can live with that. But I do not think I will live well or happy without my brain. I've grown very fond of my mind and the way it moves around problems and the way it always brings back decent solutions. I make my living with my brain, and I do not wish its capacity diminished. I am afraid again. My heart is pounding hard again. Oh please, please God, help me be okay. I hate this; I hate all of this being sick stuff.

"I get lights like that when I get a migraine," William tells me gently. I appreciate his sharing, since he has never once dwelled on the migraines that he gets about once every ten years. But I don't get migraines. At least the person I used to be never got migraines.

"Will you call Beth Kelly?" I ask William. My voice shakes. "Can you call her and tell her I'm feeling very weak and seeing funny shapes and lights in one eye?"

William makes the call and reports back: Beth said to tell me to try to relax, breathe evenly, and to call back if the lights don't go away soon.

Good. Okay...so just breathe...Beth could make me pretend that these strange new symptoms were just normal. And that I am right on track with my recovery. I wonder what it would take to faze her... Beth, I just looked down and my heart has fallen outside my chest. Yes, completely outside my chest. And, I am breathing evenly...Well, I imagine that might ruffle her for an instant.

But thoughts do channel immense power. I know what she is trying to do, so I deliberately slow my breathing, trying to follow Beth's advice. I relax a little as I tell myself this is probably a migraine and not a stroke. Hey, Melissa give it your best shot, right here, right now, and if your best is death or a stroke, so be it. Go down with a smile on your face. Even if it's an uneven smile. I shut my eyes, aware only of sounds again. Aware of Will's breath as he bends close beside me, as he pushes back my hair and lightly turns the washcloth draped across my forehead.

About twenty minutes later, I return. Cautiously I open my eyes and notice the lights and shapes are gone. I straighten slightly in the chair. I hear the kids giggling in another room. Will and Sara look immensely relieved.

"I'm so sorry," I tell them softly. "I know I'm starting to be a major pain."

Hours later I still can't move from the chair. It is near the girls' bedtime, so I volunteer to read. We've read countless stories since they were little. It draws us together, our mutual love of books. But within minutes of beginning, I realize I can't do it. It hurts my chest, and I feel dizzy again because my breathing is interrupted by the sentences. I've come a long way but am still pretty pathetic. I can't even read a child's book aloud yet.

"I'm sorry, you guys. I'll try again later," I promise. But I see in their eyes that I am a far cry from the mom I used to be. The mom they were hoping was coming home.

I can't tuck them into bed because I don't want to tackle that long staircase but once that night. They give me kisses. We say a goodnight prayer together.

Meagan leans in to hug me and says, "It's like you're the baby now, Mom."

"Yes," I answer. "I know it seems like it."

Jacqueline turns toward me suspiciously. "You be right there," she tells me. "You be right in the chair when I wake up."

"I'll be here," I tell her, and I look at her squarely. The same way she is looking at me. Please God, I pray, after Jacqueline finally breaks eye contact, please do not make me a liar to my youngest daughter. Please let me be here for her.

William wants the kids to straighten up their things and get moving toward bed. It is not going well and spiraling down quickly. Quietly I monitor his tone and his expressions, reminding myself that the routine was consuming for me even when I wasn't sick. And he has the stress of business on top of playing Mr. Mom. But watching him I grow more uncomfortable. William can wilt most men when he chooses to. His effect on our little girls on my first night home is suddenly chilling.

He has lost his normal easy flow with them. I study their faces and see they've lost their joy in helping...in helping on their own, and in following their own "chore chart" and having me praise them for it.

William's behavior is a reaction to fatigue and monumental tension and yet, he would never admit to that, never. Oh William, cut it out, would you? Just cut it out and cut them and me a little slack here, please! No such luck. Usually he's great with the girls, spending more time with them than any father I've ever known. There are games and sports of all kinds, skiing, baseball, bikes, inline skating, and fishing. He makes up great stories in the car, and he reads to them, never missing a night, regardless of what is going on in his life, and I love him for all of it. I love him because I cannot think of anything a daughter needs more than a loving, attentive father. Except of course, tonight when it's obvious that they all need me. And I lay wasted in that chair, barely able to shift positions. I can't possibly shift what is going on.

I frown at William as they all go up to bed; I make sure he notices the frown because I don't want this to continue, and I can't go upstairs to make sure that it doesn't. But I can hear that it is not stopping. William doesn't appreciate my silent disapproval, and it obviously inspires him to become more dictatorial.

Listening I grow more irritated by him trampling on the home front.

I don't mind him filling in during the emergency, but this is my territory, and I don't like major changes instituted without my consent. I ease my head back on the pillow, understanding more about the comment he made a couple days earlier when he was telling me the kids weren't doing enough, and that I didn't have things well organized.

William comes down a short time later. The girls are crying loudly upstairs. He stops in front of my chair and stares down at me and my irritation.

"There need to be some changes made around here," he starts, and I sense battle lines being drawn. But I don't feel up for this. I feel like showing him the paragraph in my open-heart surgery book that says to avoid all people and all situations that are stressful. Many years of experience tells me this is going to become very stressful, very quickly. I am looking for a graceful way out because I'm no match for him tonight. At my best, I'm never any match for his ignited anger.

Let it go, I say to myself. Eat a little humble pie if you need to, but don't start up with him tonight. But I don't like the way he is talking to me, and I don't like the look on his face as he glares at me. William sits stiffly in the chair beside me. Facing me.

Back off, Melissa. Back down. But backing down never came easy to me. Not even now. It's hard to have conflicting goals and do them both well at the same time. I don't do it well. I just did it. And my only thought when I left the hospital such a short time ago was to enjoy every day left in my life. It was that thought that came to me first, that and the fact that for the past week and a half, I'd been surrounded by encouragement from strangers and loving expressions of support from my friends. William's anger is not what I want, and it is not what I need. Not ever again, and we might as well straighten that out right now.

"I can't do this," I tell him. "I can't watch you criticizing the kids and going around here like you hate that you've had to do any of this. That you hate having to help me. That I'm a bother and if you can just get back to working twelve-hour days, life would be great. It's the Gestapo around here tonight, and I want to be around happy people."

"Happy people are happy because they're getting their goals accomplished. And I can't get anything done."

"Happy people are happy because they decide to be. Period. Well, I want to be happy now. I'm not going to sit around thinking, when I get caught up, then I'll enjoy my life. It's time to figure it out now."

A vein rises in William's forehead. His eyes go cold and unflinching. "If I can get caught up at work," he tells me. "Then I'll die a happy man."

"You can't be serious. That's the only thing that matters?"

"The house is a mess. The kids are lazy, and you aren't handling anything I need you to handle."

I feel my stomach turning. I tell myself I should leave now. I should leave, except it would only make him angrier if I got up to leave. And it hurts when I try to even move. I am not up for standing. Finish it. You passed on the helping of humble pie, go ahead and have guts enough to finish this.

"I don't agree with you," I tell him. "The kids aren't lazy. And what's the big deal about the house right now? I don't care if it's a complete mess. I've been in the hospital for a week and a half and I can't do anything to straighten it up, so why don't you just let it go?"

He stands. "No," he says icily. "I'm not going to let it go. I expect there to be a few things done differently around here. And I don't want to do any of this anymore. If I have to spend all my money to hire people to do it for me, that's fine. I don't want to do any of this anymore."

"Your priorities are messed up."

"Well, I don't want your priorities. They aren't mine, and I hope someone shoots me in the head before they ever become mine."

I can't believe we were doing this. I can't believe we are this angry on my first night home. I'm upset to a degree that is making me extremely uncomfortable physically. I'd had nothing for days except people trying to encourage me and to help me. I feel none of that now. And I wish I could go back. I wish I could find my way back to someone's kindness.

"My mother would help me," I tell him quickly. "She wouldn't make me feel like I'm wasting her time and that she wants to be doing something else."

William picks up the phone between us and handed it to me. "Call her," he says. "Call her and I'll take you and the kids there tonight."

I take the phone. It weighs heavy in my hand. I want to leave. I wanted to leave him and his anger and mine, but I've never been more incapacitated in my life. Any activity requires colossal effort; my chest hurts constantly from the split sternum. I can't cook for myself, and

I still need five meals a day or I'll lose too much weight and energy. I can't drive a car. I can't put on my surgical stockings, and I can't even dress myself without considerable help. And I can't take care of any of the kids and their constant needs, because I can't even begin to take care of myself.

I'm holding the weight and the phone as the seconds tick. William watches me dangle. He watches me twist; I wish I had enough pride to walk out the door and die on the doorstep before I let him pull this on me, but I promised Jacqueline I'd be here.

Seconds keep ticking. I love my mother. But I have to face it; she wouldn't be thrilled if I showed up with the kids like this. And who could blame her. She wouldn't be thrilled because we're round-the-clock care she can't possibly provide. I'd be imposing on her life because I can't handle my own, and I can't ask it of her. She would try her best to help, but she wouldn't last more than a few days with this high maintenance outfit. And I wouldn't last nearly that long seeing the look on her face.

William calls my bluff before I even knew I was bluffing. I'm a slow player now. He is looking at me. I need time. Time to get stronger and time to figure my escape route.

"I'm not calling her tonight," I say finally as I hang up the phone. "I don't want to wake her. I'll call in the morning." But weak words said with conviction are still weak words. He won this round, and we both know it. But I am thinking too that he lost, big time, because I could never, ever have done to anyone what he just did to me. But just give me two weeks, two weeks to show him what he lost in trying so hard to win. Let me get my strength back, and I'm out of here. William sits down.

I struggle to my feet but find it's near impossible to get out of a deep, soft chair when you can't use your arms to push yourself up and when your abdominal muscles and legs are weak from lack of exercise. I'm used to the hospital bed where I could just swing my legs over. This fledgling effort hurts my chest, and I dig my short nails into my palms the last few inches up. A couple slow steps around the ottoman, and then I pause beside his chair before I start upstairs. I pause until he looks at me. I would have waited all night if I had to, but William has no trouble confronting trouble. When you're looking for trouble, turning to face it is no big deal. He meets my eyes quickly, and I'm surprised he doesn't stand again and let the five-inch difference in our height tell the story. But then standing wasn't really necessary tonight was it? His jaw settles into a hard, clean line.

I start toward the stairs. I turn away without tears because I don't feel any. I back away calmly, with intent, just like any good businessman. I hope he gets the full message.

My pulse is high. I don't have to take it. I know I need to calm down a few minutes before I attempt the stairs. I stand in the marble entry and look up. I've been dreading these stairs: they stretch on forever, and the last two times I walked up them, I had a heart attack.

An owl calls loudly behind me in the pine. I start up slowly. Very slowly. Still upset from the argument. I'm exhaling each time I lift my legs to take another step. I know how to exercise, and this is now major exercise for me. I'm halfway up. The grandfather clock chimes. Fifteen minutes has passed since I began the stairs. I glance at the top looming in the distance. Suddenly a sensation of pressure steps into my left arm. I still have numbness there from the heart attacks. I stop. *Relax.* I'm trying to take my attention off my left arm that definitely feels number. *Knock it off, you're just upset.* You're imagining it…

I glance down at my watch to take my pulse, but it is too dark on the stairs to see the numbers clearly, and I can't make myself believe it would be helpful to walk all the way back down to turn on a light. That was stupid, I tell myself. Think ahead. Plan what you're doing.

I will not call William for help. We're at our worst together whenever I need help. He likes me strong, competent, and independent. My independence eliminates any need for his involvement, except on his terms and his timing. He likes me when I succeed, and I'm succeeding at precious little now.

This evening reminds me of the night we first brought Meagan and Brenna home from the hospital a day and a half after their birth. I was exhausted and still aching from the changes in my body that delivering them had produced. They were healthy but six weeks premature. We'd been told to continue the hourly feedings we'd given them in the hospital. The feedings were to continue every hour around the clock. Day and night, around the clock.

Prior to their birth, William and I had set up the plan of dividing care of the babies between us. Our business had been sold and neither of us were working, and we had equal time to take care of the twins.

It all seemed equitable, and a division of labor would give each of us a little time to also do other things that we enjoyed.

So, we climbed these same stairs with the babies and set up operations in the babies' bedroom. Everything stood ready, as ready as it can be for two people who'd never taken care of infants. And we began. I was nursing both babies. I was pumping milk when they finished nursing, trying to get my milk production up. We were feeding them bottles of the milk I just pumped mixed with formula, then changing diapers and settling them back into bed, knowing the entire cycle would start again in about twenty minutes.

It started, again and again. Just when I realized I had to sleep or I would fall off the bed, William looked at me and said, "I can't do this. I need to get my sleep. I'm not going to do this at night."

And I thought why do you have that option? I'm the one who's been pregnant with twins when I'm thirty-six years old. I'm the one who just went through the pain of all this. But I looked into his eyes and I saw he was on edge. I saw there was no way I could force his cooperation. I saw that even if he agreed to help, which he plainly would not do, William angry was not who I wanted handling these babies.

So, our meticulously devised schedule for dividing childcare left with him. I looked at the babies who needed to be awakened and fed.

"I'm not going anywhere," I promised them.

And I didn't go anywhere, for about the next year. I was used to working long hours, but I was also used to getting six or seven hours of sleep. Not anymore. Everything I'd done in business seemed lightweight in comparison to the relentless needs of our infants. Sometime in those first few weeks, I told my mom, "If I can just get a full hour sleep. If I can just get one full hour, I'll be okay."

About five weeks after their birth, I logged three hours and knew I'd rounded the corner. At eight weeks, I slept a full five hours and felt near human again. I can do just about anything on five hours sleep.

And I did, but I knew the seeds for William's next business were born that first night, though he did not share that insight with me for another month. He helped during the day, but he was gone by 10:00 p.m. My mom kept telling me that he was a wonderful help. That she'd never seen any man help with babies the way he did. And I was thinking, why not? He isn't working. He never has to work again if he doesn't want to…

William was working again very soon. Building a brand-new business can fully fill any father's day.

I look up again and see I am getting closer to the top landing, but there are plenty more stairs to go. Then I hear the high whine of the blender. William is in the kitchen making a protein shake for himself. Perfect, I think. Let's be sure your unbelievably perfect, muscular body is getting exactly what it needs. Whenever it needs. I'm standing here trashed, and you have the nerve to tell me you'll take me to my mother's? You have the nerve to wear a look on your face that tells me plain and clear that you'd like nothing better. Another step.

Then without consciously inviting them, memories of Jacqueline's arrival descend upon me. Her birth had to be induced, and we went from no labor pains to her delivery in less than two hours, which challenged even my determination to do it without drugs, because there was no time to ease up to the intense pain. It was just there, and you deal with it. Like a shotgun blast.

I kept saying to William, "Please, just tell me I'm doing okay. I don't think I'm doing as well as before. Tell me I'm doing a great job." Will lay down beside me and kept talking to me, telling me I was doing great and that it was going just like before and it was almost over.

"Tell me I'm doing okay," I'd say again. But I never yelled or called him any choice names, so I figured some husbands suffer through worse.

I left the hospital two days later, holding that beautiful baby girl, thinking, this would be a piece of cake. It would be easy taking care of just one baby. And then Jacqueline developed severe colic. I'd done it to my parents, and now I got to experience the pleasure. Dear Lord! For five and a half months, I could not put the baby down. She slept at night, but only if we were pancaked together and she was latched onto my breast. During the day, she'd nurse and fall asleep in my arms for a minute. I'd try to ease her into her never-once-used crib, only to have her wake instantly, screaming hysterically.

I read everything. I talked to her pediatrician, and I tried anything she suggested that might comfort her. Nights were six hours straight of ear-splitting, ceaseless crying. I walked her, I patted her, I sang to her. And I was alone through every single night of it because William needed his sleep. As I walked my baby, I thought about how my Dad had helped Mom walk the floor with me. They told me that Mom took the first shift from eight until twelve and then Dad got up and walked me from midnight until four in the morning and then he showered, shaved, ate breakfast, and drove to work. They shared the load for five months straight. Why am I all alone in this while William is sleeping?

But I gathered everything I'd learned as a mother of twins; I stayed calm with the baby. Never once losing my temper. Never doing anything but trying my best to soothe her and to let her know that I loved her with all my heart. Somehow, we got through it.

And somehow, I'm going to get through this.

❧

There. I'm at the top of the stairs. I'm still furious thinking about these other times I needed William. But I'm furious most of all with myself. Why in the name of heaven have I let this go on. Why have I put up with this garbage? Because I love him? So what, I can get over it. I don't want to be treated like this. I am not going to be treated like this ever again.

I make my way to a spare bedroom with my quart bottle of water. I need to drink water, lots of water. Before the hospital, I needed at least four quarts of water a day. My need for fluids increased dramatically in the hospital. "May I have more water, please?" I asked the nurses several times a night. They pleasantly refilled the liter container every time I called. I wouldn't be able to get any refills tonight, but I definitely need this quart.

I look around the spare bedroom. There isn't any table near the bed to hold my water. I can't make it without the water, and I need a table close by, so when I reach for the bottle, it would be right there. Right there, so the pain of stretching too far won't make me groan.

William appears in the spare bedroom, his frothy protein shake in hand. "Are you sleeping in here?" he asks.

"Take a guess."

He lingers in the doorway. "I don't want you to sleep in here."

I'm cold silent, eyeing the room, still figuring there must be a way I can make this work.

"I don't want you in here," he repeats. "I want to be sure you're okay. I won't sleep well if you're here."

He has no idea what he's just triggered. "Well," I tell him coolly, "we certainly can't have that, can we?"

And without another word, he takes my precious water bottle toward our bedroom. Futilely I glance around the guest room one more time, and then I walk silently into our bathroom to scrub my teeth. William arrives, holding my quart in his hand. There is icy cold mountain water running steadily down the drain, making the only sound between us.

"I'm sorry," he says. His words are deliberately slow. His mood has mellowed considerably in the last twenty minutes. "I'm sorry that I lost my temper downstairs. I know you don't need this now."

I put down the toothbrush, turn to him, star at him, and say absolutely nothing. I figure that four seconds say absolutely everything.

I've never once in our life together not responded to one of his apologies. But not tonight. He can get down on his knees, he could prostrate himself along the cool, black and white Italian marble floor to beg forgiveness, but there is no way he's going to get it. And I wonder if he knows he is in trouble here. I doubt it. But I am done telling him. Done with even wanting to tell him. Figure it out for yourself buddy; take all the time you need. Just make my breakfast.

Chapter Twelve

The next afternoon, William is at work and Sara and the kids are upstairs. I'm lying stretched out on my chair and ottoman again. This has become home base. But during sleep my head falls off the pillow and I'm completely flat and lying as helpless as a turned turtle.

Suddenly I wake, realizing something is on my cut legs. I raise my head; four painful, pitiful inches and see my big, black cat standing on my calves, circling as if he's discovered a permanent nest.

"No, Tom!" I tell him, urgently. "You can't be serious. Not on my legs. Get down." He keeps circling. "I mean it, Tom, get down!"

But I've never been blessed with an obedient cat. Tom plops directly on my incisions. And it hurts, not only from the cuts, but my right ankle and swollen foot ache constantly from the missing vein and the lack of circulation. I can't pull myself up to move him. I might as well try a two-mile run.

"Sara!" I call loudly. "Please help me. Sara, Tom's on me!"

I have no idea where she is. I have no idea if she's remembered to turn on the monitor so she can hear me. But I'm pinned by my twelve-pound cat and can't rescue myself. Now I understand helpless. I only thought I did before. Now even my animals are turning on me. Don't cry. Don't cry over something like this.

Sara's voice sounds faint. "I'm on my way," she calls as she hurries down the stairs. She picks up the cat and props me back up on my pillows.

"Sara? You'll keep the monitor on?"

My plaintive sound stops her. "Of course. Are you hungry or thirsty?"

"No. Thanks though."

"Do you need anything?"

I sigh. "A new body."

As Sara leaves, I strain to follow her footsteps until I can't detect even the slightest sound, and then I glance around the room and sigh again. Worthless. I am completely worthless now. Just stop thinking about it and go to sleep.

⚜

Friends and neighbors continue sending flowers and cards, and they band together to provide dinner. Our fantastic neighbors bring dinner in shifts, and their loving support encourages me beyond my ability to express it. Dinner and their love delivered with it warm me nightly. Dinner each evening provides a monumental help.

All my women friends must understand this, because meals keep coming, and when I tell them we're doing fine and that William can cook, then my sister-in-law Tori starts bringing dinner too. And my four nieces come by to weed my garden. I feel continually warmed by their unsolicited help and attention. I tell them all that I'm doing better because the look on their faces makes me want to.

⚜

William's computer modems keep blowing out during the unusual lightning storms we have each afternoon. He goes through four modems in rapid succession. No, it has never happened before, not once in nine years. Now we blow out gates, doorbells, and modems. We're still not making things work right. We're still not getting the messages. William grows more hostile and hypercritical, and I'm counting the days until I'm strong enough to take care of the kids and myself. And then I take a step backwards.

Five days after leaving the hospital, I wake feeling strange, and I take a moment trying to access what is wrong. I'm weak, extremely weak again. Alone in our bedroom, I struggle to sit up. William is somewhere downstairs, and our friend Christine, who is still coming by to help, is somewhere with the kids. I reach for water and feel a warm wave tingling over my neck and head, similar to the feeling morphine had given me the time I asked Terry about it. But there is no Terry and no morphine, and then in the middle of the tingling weakness, I suddenly become aware of numbness on the left side of my head and face. I pinch my face hard. It is completely numb.

Oh dear God, not this, please not this. I try to stand; yet I stumble from bed and almost black out, but my right hand is clamped the bedpost and I reach the intercom to call for help.

Touch the bottom button. Hang in there. Push it. "William, I need help!" But I hear him on the phone talking to someone about the computer. He won't be able to hear me. I try again, shouting, "Christine, help me!"

"I'm coming!" she yells. I hear William then too, cursing, vaulting the steps. They are coming, I think as I weakly sink down. I lean limply toward the middle of the bed. Sweating, shaking and numb.

Oh, this is not good timing. Christine hurries to my side, smoothing back my hair. "What can I get you?" she asks tenderly.

"I'm just weak. I feel weak."

And I keep thinking that this is very poor timing. Dr. Davis is gone on a two-week vacation. William puts a call in to Dr. Jamisens' office, but he isn't on duty. The receptionist tells William if it is within two weeks of leaving the hospital after surgery, then Dr. Davis' office needs to handle it.

"But Dr. Davis's gone for two weeks," William explains before leaving a message for another physician to please call. But no one calls during the next fifteen minutes. William calls Beth Kelly, who returns the call immediately. She tells us we are to go to the emergency room right away if this doesn't clear up quickly.

Clear up, please clear up! I'm scared, and being scared doesn't help, I know it doesn't help, but I can't stop trembling.

William sits beside me, pulling the covers up around me. "I'll get you some food," he says apologetically. "I'm sorry I'm late with breakfast, I thought I could finish with the computer company first. I didn't realize it would take so long."

"It's okay, I can't eat right now anyway."

Another wave of weakness rolls over me, and I feel the numbness extend farther out. I rub my hand across my forehead. It is numb a little more than halfway across, and my face feels as if I'm prepped to have a cavity filled.

"Oh, William," I whisper and my voice crumbles. "It's getting worse. I have to go back to the hospital."

He helps me up gently and pulls on my jeans and a shirt. His arm moves around me securely as he walks me slowly down the stairs.

I call the girls over to me. I tell them that I love them. I tell them that I'll be home as soon as I can, but deep down, I'm not sure that I'm ever coming home. I've never been more scared in my life. I'm patting the kids and moving toward the Audi in the garage again.

William finally gets a call from another cardiologist on duty and he tells him that we are on our way to the emergency room. I lean lower into the car's leather seats, thinking that if I'm dying, it would have been a lot kinder just to let me go the first time. Trying to climb this slippery slope, trying to listen to everyone saying you can make it to the top no problem, trying to talk yourself into believing it and then sliding back down is torture. Why is all this happening to me? Why?

William and I walk arm in arm into the ER. When I left this place, I felt that I'd started some relationships that would see me through if something went wrong. But now I have to explain that I've just had open-heart surgery and that I'm a patient of Dr. Davis and Dr. Jamisen, "but they're gone."

They stick in another IV and hook up the EKG and watch my blood pressure, doing the basics, but it's clear they want to refer me quickly to the heart guys.

I hear the emergency room doctor putting a call into Dr. Jamisen's office. He talks to one of the doctors, the same one William talked to, and then he turns to the nurse and says, "He's not coming in. He said he doesn't know her or know anything about her."

With those words, I feel my lifeline sever with one swipe of a sharp machete. Do they think I am deaf? That I really can't hear someone talking eight feet away? I know it's the same cardiologist I saw the day before my Flight for Life helicopter ride and my open-heart surgery. The doctor who had told me to go home and put it all behind me, that it wasn't my heart. And I'm thinking he probably knows more about me than he'd like to admit right now. But I guess I can't blame him. Facing me probably isn't top on his list. Looking over patients who think you're wonderful probably feels a lot more satisfying than disrupting the rest of your scheduled appointments to meet one of your mistakes in the emergency room. And besides, it's within two weeks of leaving the hospital after surgery, so officially I don't have to be his problem anyway. I swallow, and the lump still doesn't go away. William pulls his chair up closer to my bedside, and I can't look at him. I feel like an orphaned, unwanted waif.

Beth Kelly comes to see me, and I can't even try to talk with her. I just nod and listen and hope somehow, she'll know how much seeing her means to me. But how could she, how could she really? All I want is to reach out and hold her hand. I want to reach out and cling to something, and I stop myself just in time before doing it. Beth pats my arm as she talks to me.

She tells me she'll send another doctor down after he finishes surgery. We wait awhile for the surgeon to arrive, and he sends me in for a CAT scan and an ultrasound scan on the arteries in my neck. Everything looks normal. No obvious clots or bleeding on the brain. The veins looks normal, but then, so did my heart.

The doctor meets with me for a few seconds, eyes me with cool, superbly detached suspicion, and tells me everything is fine. All my tests are normal. He doesn't have Dr. Davis's warm personality, and he doesn't bother to feign the slightest interest in me. He doesn't bother to even say good-bye, he just drifts from the cubicle, and the curtains drift behind him.

The nurse returns to tells me that the surgeon said my problems are all psychosomatic and all I really need is to see a good social worker. This news reduces me to a new, low level of disillusionment. My eyes well up as much from the nurse's eagerness to tell me this as being labeled a flake again by a doctor - a doctor who talked to me for less than ten seconds. But then he must figure more time is a luxury he can't afford and a luxury I don't need. He immediately understands everything about this case anyway.

And I'm sitting here wondering why this is happening again with this doctor? I'm sure diagnosing patients quickly is important, but I wish sometimes these myopic gods would take twenty seconds instead of ten and up their odds of success. Both impatience and disinterest can rapidly injure vulnerable people. This doctor has traveled a long, weary way from the healer he once wanted to be. There must be a part of him that knows it. I'm getting closer to believing I'd make a better diagnosis with a Ouija board. At least it wouldn't make me cry or lose hope in humanity.

Déjà vu hits as I dress to go home. Dismissed again as having mental problems, not physical ones. But the numbness that this social worker should supposedly help me with still invades the left side of my head and face. No one bothers to check my eyes, but the vision in my left eye is badly blurred and the images are somehow smaller than the images from my right eye. I've always had perfect vision, but nothing is clear to me anymore.

William takes me home in silence. I'm beyond discouraged. The little gains I thought I had made feel worthless now. Love seems long ago. I thought I was far past caring, but it hurts, it still hurts. And being alone with fear hurts too.

I say quietly, "Do you think I'll make it?" But I can't look at him as I ask that question.

"I don't know," he answers quickly. "You either will or you won't."

I keep blinking rapidly, staring out the window, thinking William once invested far more positive emotion in a stranger's dog than he's willing to do now with me. Don't show anybody any weakness. Don't say another word. Not to a doctor - not to anyone. Shifting slightly, I turn a little farther away, knowing he won't notice. Trees pass by in a blur. You'll either make it or you won't.

Brutal honesty always comes easy for him. At times he calls it kindness. At times I let this form of indifferent cruelty pass for kindness, and I sifted it through myself, trying to find ways to improve myself in light of his words. But I want far more consistent kindness than I settle for.

Dad, oh Dad, where are you? I never knew how lonely I could feel, and I can't find your love anywhere, because there isn't your kind of love anywhere. Two strong arms once held me up. Warm, safe smells of Old Spice, tobacco and Bay Rum cologne kept me close. But why did you raise me to believe men cherish you and take good care of you and protect you from the hardness of life and the hardness of other men? Oh Daddy, there aren't men like you anymore. There aren't men like you in my life anymore. And I'm stuck in this vacuum of your lost love, and I don't think I'm strong enough to pull myself out, for the world outside blows too hard.

It hits too hard for me, and I'm not thinking I want to stay much longer. Help me, Daddy, please help me stay somehow. You didn't raise me to be a quitter, but I can't do this anymore. I can't do this life anymore.

⚜

I no longer try to sleep without the hall lights on. I can't stand the darkness. No moon or stars shine on this cloudy night. I'm getting by with Tylenol for pain.

What do I take for fear? What do I take for this corrosive, boundless, black fear?

How do I harness these midnight thoughts? How did you do it, Dad? Men who fought beside you in three wars said there was no one like you in combat. That you lived without fear. They said you had once run laughing across a rice paddy while a sniper's bullets ricocheted water all around. They told me you saved men's lives without thought or concern for your own.

I'm thinking you were my Dad and I'm glad you didn't live to see the me I've become. "You'd be disappointed," I whisper. "For I'm afraid." I don't belong here, and yet I do not want to leave my daughters all alone. There's a dim light in the hall. And a faintly dim light flickering inside me. Neither one is bright enough for sleep or comfort.

⚜

Sadness shadows my next day. I can't hide it, and I can no longer fake it. My vision is still distorted. My head and face feel just as numb. I feel just as numb. Sara plays outside with the girls, but she surprises me, appearing suddenly in front of my chair. I look up slowly, trying to focus.

"I'll take your water and pillows," she tells me. "Come sit outside." Sara isn't asking; she is just moving my things, so I stand slowly, painfully. I will go outside to appease someone who obviously still cares deeply about me. I stand briefly in a summer I do not know while Sara arranges pillows on the back of the chaise lounge. I slowly lower myself into it. I look around as if in a daze. There are hummingbirds, and flowers, and laughing children. It is real on some level, but not for me. I don't feel part of this world anymore. I don't belong here with the bright colors and bright smiles. I'm detaching again. Detaching from a pain too great and a life too small.

❄

Friends start bringing videos to occupy my days, telling me they had fun picking them out because they know I haven't seen any of them. I watch for unmeasured hours. It is something to do. I know I'm an observer of life once again, not a participant. My own life feels too damaged to participate in. The watching goes on for days, and the nights again are the worst.

One evening after dinner William comes to stand beside my chair. I glance up.

"Take a little walk with me," he says. I shake my head. "Just a little one on the driveway."

"I don't want to."

He reaches down and takes my hand. "Come on, you're supposed to be walking three or four times a day."

I sigh and slowly stand. Acquiescing feels easier than arguing and he won't give up anyway. I don't want to argue anymore. Silently I walk beside him, out our front door, gingerly taking the stairs, moving down them on painful, swollen feet. I'm barefoot except for the thigh high white surgical stockings that reduce the chance of blood clots in my legs. I glance up and notice the girls watching me from their front bedroom window. I wave but I look away quickly, sorry they have to see me like this. It must hurt them, I think. I just can't move any faster.

I could never have imagined the difficulty recovering from the last heart attack and the surgery. I don't believe anyone who hasn't experienced it can. And I was fairly young and very strong going into it. William takes my arm and tries to look encouraging.

"I don't know how old people do this," I admit. "There was a man on my floor who looked to be about eighty who'd just had open heart surgery too. And I kept thinking maybe he felt so rotten before the operation that it wasn't such a big deal, but this seems big to me."

"It is big."

"Remember when I was twenty-two and had that abdominal surgery and was in the hospital for five days?" I glance at him and he nods.

"Well, the doctor told me then that I would feel like a truck hit me, but it never seemed like anything much. But now, now I feel like a truck hit me."

"Let's take your pulse," William says, so we pause, and he gives me the stop and start time. I quit wearing watches the day I quit business. He listens when I give him my heart rate.

"You need to start walking every day," he reminds me. I sigh again. I know I'm supposed to be walking. I just don't care anymore. I'm tired of trying so hard. I'm tired of failing. I'd rather just fail this time without expending all the effort.

We walk back to the house quietly. It seems like a long walk, but it's only ten minutes. William helps me back into my chair, and I'm sure this will be the last time I need to exercise because he's still trying to catch up at work.

But the next day, Will appears four times to take me for walks. He keeps track of my distance and records my heart rate. I go with him without arguing only because it's easier. He'll forget soon, I'm sure of it, and then I'll blow it off. But he doesn't forget.

"You're getting stronger," he tells me as he checks my statistics after one of our outings.

I don't return his smile. I just shrug. Leave me alone, I think. Just leave me alone and get on with your life. Marry some hot healthy babe twenty years younger than I am and a lot less trouble. Just leave me alone.

I don't call anyone when I have more nights of weakness, and increased numbness to add to the areas that have never regained feeling. I stop telling anyone anything anymore. I don't kid myself into thinking anyone cares or can help me.

I wake with my heart pounding at every noise the house makes. I lie beyond the bottom rung of faith. I keep waking over and over to darkness and the faint light that doesn't shield me from it. But I can't take a sleeping pill. If I start that, something tells me, I'll never quit. I flush the entire bottle of unused sleeping pills and untouched pain pills down the toilet the next morning.

That evening, I have no indication that something momentous is coming. I lie staring at shadows on walls and at a dimly lit clock that seems stuck too, thinking about arteries popping again. Reliving the unimaginable pain that comes when they go. I'm thinking about strokes again and about being helpless on the respirator. Remembering the respirator so intimately, it makes me gag. I quickly cover my mouth with my hand. Sweat sits damp under my arms.

I sit up to sip water and try to slow my frantic breathing and heartbeat. I try focusing on Dad. Thinking about him brings my only comfort. He was brave, I tell myself. He lived when many around him did not.

He told me once, in his slow western way of speaking, "They say when your number's up, it's up. And it's mighty true. It doesn't matter if you're hunkered down in a foxhole or wearing a flak jacket, if it's up, it's up. I've seen men die who had no business dying, and men live who had no business living. And there's no call worrying about either."

He reached out then and ruffled my hair and pulled me close in a bear hug. And it hurt a little, just like always because he was so strong. "Just think ahead, use your common sense, and the rest takes care of itself. How about some more hot tea?"

Dad's people were Scots. His grandfather immigrated to America and my grandfather still came out with expressions like, "bonnie lassie." The men stood unusually tall, black-haired, blue-eyed and proud of their scrappy Highland heritage, proud too that they were all "fighting men" who liked the feel of a raw steel blade in their hand. Dad told me of a relative long ago who had served in the Black Watch Regiment and was blinded by tribes in Afghanistan. He was left alive to wander the bleak, cold hills alone for days before he found his way out, back to his regiment, following the sound of bagpipes he imagined in the distance.

He found his way out and returned to his beloved Scotland, where he lived a full and useful life, dying one morning far past his hundredth birthday when he walked by himself to a springhouse to do chores for his granddaughter, but instead, he tripped on a raised flagstone.

I sigh. No, he never sat down and quit, he kept trying until he found his way out, and had he given up trying, none of us would be here. The pipes always move me, and we buried Dad to the sound of them. I guess you can't really lose the call of coming home in one generation.

I'm a Malcolm too, I tell myself and yet I'm sitting here quivering in a warm bed after a full meal. Dear Lord, the years have badly blighted our strong stock, but it seems the blight didn't strike until me. Well, I'm sorry I let everyone down.

Suddenly a line from Shakespeare comes to me, and in my mind I hear my dad's voice reciting his version of it. "A coward dies a thousand deaths, a brave man only once." His voice reaches me strong and true like a gong ringing out across a far and distant clearing.

And I hear those words and I hear dad's voice just as distinctly. I start repeating the line over and over in my own voice until I feel the weight of those words bring the depth of their meaning to my core. In that moment, I choose not to be a coward anymore. I don't want fear in my life, whatever little is left of it. I don't want fear inside me. I don't want this shade of evil. I sit up straighter in bed and stare hard at the dark gloom I've created around me. And I tell myself that I've already died more than my share this go around.

I'm not sure how to control all the things my body has been doing since the first dissection and heart attack, but somehow, I can learn to control this fear. Dad's blood still runs in my veins. And I'm not sitting here remembering him and hearing his voice for nothing. I'm making your words mine, Dad. *Semper Fi*, it will be. Always faithful.

And I recall right then how I "happened" to be right next to the hospital the day I nearly died, when it would have been far more probable that I'd be all alone in the mountains with three little kids. So, I figure Dad was right. God will take me when it comes my time to go and not a moment before.

I figure I can ruin every moment that has been given to me with the sort of thoughts that have been roaming wild and rooting up good ground in my head. Yet deciding is still a far cry from doing. I know that from experience. But it is a first step, and life is made of little decisions, and faint, first steps. Shaky steps you keep trying to take.

Fear doesn't just grow silent and it doesn't just go away. I know I'll have to put another and a louder thought in its place. I know I'll have to keep putting it there, and if I get tired of putting it there and tired of working on it before the work is done, then fear wins and I lose.

I lean back into the pillow with a mantra coming to mind and to my lips. I repeat it a hundred times or more. I'm not counting. It is the last thought I have before I fall asleep, and it is the first thought I make myself think when I wake in the morning.

"I choose not to be afraid. I trust in God."

And you can kill me dead, you can put me through any suffering you want, but I'm not changing my mind on this. Period. I want to hear the pipes again.

⚶

The next day when the visiting nurse comes, she checks my incisions, takes my blood pressure and talks with me. I look forward to her visits. But that day, as she leaves, she tells me there is a note that a doctor indicated I should see a social worker.

Yes, I got that comment already, I tell her. Hearing it hurts again, but it doesn't hurt nearly as much as it did the first time. And then she looks at me and tells me she was never the same after a car accident she had. She tried as hard as she could for a very long time to get back to where she was, but she never could. She tells me that I have to realize that I will never, ever be the same again.

I walk her the rest of the way to the door. I open it and politely say good-bye. And I close the door and lock it tightly. I stand there a moment more. No, I tell myself. I do not have to realize that.

That is her choice. It isn't mine. I have to believe I'll get better and that I can keep improving myself in all areas of my life. That somehow, I will be guided to come out of this better for having experienced it. I do not wish to stagnate on this hill, nor do I wish to roll farther backwards. I will choose the picture Dr. Jamisen is painting for me because it exactly matches the one I'll be painting for myself when my painting arm feels whole. But lady, I hope you have a very safe trip down the mountain.

⚶

William and I grow more distant. I've taken over tracking my own walks and am doing them by myself again. It's okay, he started me doing them, but he is back in his world and I am working my way up again through mine. Yet, his every contact seems increasingly harsh and more critical. I see myself pulling farther and farther away from him.

Somewhat similar, but very brief episodes of this have occurred on and off since we've married. And I try telling myself that the rest is good, and we normally have so much fun with each other, that I can deal with blustery, ragged periods for a few days out of the year. But this is not a few days. The storm stretches on.

I can't have this behavior around me anymore. His anger and personal attacks used to shock and sadden me, and after his temper cooled, he always said he was sorry. Then he would tell me that I should learn not to take it so seriously. They were just words.

But words pack power when delivered with even sharper intensity by one who claims to love you. I have often told him if I ever got to the point where what he says to me in anger didn't matter at all, then what he says to me in love would have no meaning either. I face that point now. I know it's not progress in our marriage that he can no longer reduce me to tears.

I do everything I can to not to ask for his help or to impose on him in any way. But one day, I can't stretch my arm up enough to get a bottle of olive oil from the upper shelf of the cupboard, and I don't think I should try climbing on the countertop.

"William," I call without thinking. "Can you help me?" And he answers in an irritated tone, "It depends on what it is."

That is all it takes. There have been so few times in my life that I've needed help or that I've actually asked for it. And I decide in that instant that I'll have a husband someday who is happy to help me when I ask. Maybe even before I ask. Or, I will be happy on my own. The truth is, I know that I can be perfectly happy all on my own. And that's where I'm heading.

It will be simple to move to another part of this house. I can't handle a move anywhere else yet. The idea of packers and house hunting is impossible, but this house is big enough for us to exist together without actually being together until we get the house sold, and our finances separated. I don't have any desire to work on it anymore. There is no middle ground we tread lightly on. I'm starting over.

William comes to the kitchen to see what I want and I'm already reaching for it. I look at him and say nothing. Will, I'm not angry at all with you now. I care about you and what happens to you. I always will care, for I'm cast from some antique mold that can't produce love too quickly or break it easily. And I do still love you. I just can't be married to you anymore. Your last unfeeling comment shines a spotlight on that decision.

Joshua 1:5, 1:9

...I will not leave you nor forsake you...
I command you: be firm and steadfast!
Do not fear nor be dismayed, for the Lord,
Your God, is with you wherever you go."

Chapter Thirteen

I continue practicing diverting fear from my life by consciously releasing it from every thought. And I continue the mantra, shortened after relentless use to, "I let go of fear. I trust in God." The numbness in my face is finally gone, though the vision is still off in my left eye, but it isn't a big problem. I still don't mention it to anyone.

After weeks of work, I realize I'm sleeping better at night, and sometimes when I wake, a warming wave of trust glitters through those cumulus clouds of fear still hovering near me. Trust feels true. I cling to it. Trust enables me to maintain and build a small place of peace inside, it enables me to endure constant physical discomfort and frustration, and it enables me to notice the summer season that will soon be gone.

Despite the shambles of my marriage, in the midst of its disintegration, I start coming alive again. And I feel happy to be alive again. I enjoy my friends, talking to them, sharing with them, and laughing with them. Suddenly, I find myself laughing more than I ever have before.

"I have a hummingbird heart," I tell Sara one new morning. "Filled with wild energy and wild joy."

I turn back to the window and watch the hummer as she flies from the sugary feeder. I hear her high vibration as she shoots skyward and I try inside to imitate it; I try to resonate with the timber and pitch of unseen yet sure-beating wings, and I discover, after some feeble efforts, that I can come close. My voice comes closer.

A cousin sends me a copy of *Chicken Soup for the Woman's Soul*. I hold it in my hand as I click off a video. I read it through without stopping one afternoon. And I cry. I allow myself to weep for all those strangers and all the moments of my life when I denied myself emotion. I cry all afternoon, not feeling any need to hide my tears. These are different tears, not born of anger or frustration or fear: my face embraces new healing tears.

William returns from work in the evening and leans down to give me a card from my friend Sister Maria Michael. I formally met her four years earlier when she taught me to milk a cow and drive a John Deere tractor at the Benedictine Abbey of Saint Walburga. I went back every week after the twins stopped nursing, so I could help milk the Brown Swiss cow because I thought fresh, farm milk would be the best substitute for the girls. And I went back to the friendship I felt with the young semi-cloistered nun and her laughing Irish eyes.

Joy lives in Sister Maria Michael. Overflowing joy and the uncanny wisdom to say the exact words I need to hear. One day, about three years ago, I was reading about Celtic crosses and trying to understand the full mystery of them and I thought, I'll ask Sister Maria Michael. She'll know something if anyone does. The next time I saw her at the barn, I casually mentioned it, and she got a surprised look on her face and said, "There's something I'd like you to have. I'll need to ask Mother Mary Thomas's permission, but I'll just be gone a few minutes."

She disappeared, and when she came back she was holding a twelve-inch sculpture of a beautiful black Celtic Cross. She explained that her father brought it back from Ireland, and she said she already had one cross in her room. She wanted me to have this one made from fired peat.

Sister Maria Michael has so few material things and so little contact with her much-loved family, and yet she parted with her father's gift easily. I reached for the cross with a sense of the same happiness she offered it in. And I took it home that day and put it on my desk and felt an odd sort of peace fill me just in looking at it. I told myself it must have something to do with the fact that Sister Maria Michael had spent hours praying near it. I decided that somehow, in some mysterious way that I could never hope to understand, my friend had embedded her peace deeply within it.

One day, not long after receiving the cross, I asked her about the rosary. I told her I enjoy learning about different religions, and I thought I'd buy one in the Abbey gift shop, and maybe someday, she could teach me a little about it.

Sister Maria Michael smiled and said, "I'll be right back."

I waited in the parking lot, just north of the monastery. She returned with a tiny, black leather pouch, and she held the pouch very gently in her small, work-worn hand. She stood close beside me and carefully unzipped it. Sister Maria Michael took out a delicate, mother of pearl rosary, with a silver cross. And she took out her brightest smile, pausing just an instant before she told me it was the rosary she was given the day she took her final vows to become a nun. She softly touched the small silver medallion and explained that it had been personally blessed by Pope John Paul. Then she told me she wanted me to have her rosary. I inhaled unexpectedly, breaking my rhythm.

"My own Mother's gone now, you know" she said, "and I have her rosary. And you can really only pray one rosary."

We hugged each other. I got in the car, tears filling my eyes, tenderness filling my heart. I drove about a mile to my folks' house, and I told my Protestant parents that my Catholic friend had just given me her treasured rosary. They smiled a little wanly and admitted that it was truly beautiful.

As I drove home, I kept wondering over and over, why would she do this? She has numerous sisters and brothers, nieces and nephews. I'm a near stranger, and I know nothing about the rosary. I don't even know enough to honor it the way it deserves to be honored. Why would she give me her special rosary? Why? It would take years to reach any understanding. Years showing the rippling effects of her generous gifts.

A few years ago, when I decided I wanted to find a church so my daughters could feel at home with God and with faith, none that I visited felt quite right, and in frustration at my failed efforts, as I was thumbing through the yellow pages, wondering what I had missed, I suddenly remembered Sister Maria Michael. I remembered her flawless wisdom and her contagious joy, and her giving so much when she owned so little. I turned to the listings under Catholic Church.

But I'm a Protestant, I told myself as I bit my lip. And then, before I closed the book and dismissed the idea entirely, I told myself that I was a Christian and that I owed enough to my friend to at least learn a bit more about the church that was the first, and one of the primary Christian Churches for the biggest part of these two thousand years.

So, I started learning, and I kept visiting churches, yet no one else could compete with Sister Maria Michael: no message ever arrived any clearer. Hers was a message in giving consummate, unconditional love. In seeing the best in one's fellow man. It's a love that always brings out our best. It's the love that brings us to our best. And I believe it's the message that Christ lived and fully delivered.

Sister Maria Michael seemed surprised when I told her I was joining the church, since she'd never mentioned it in any of our talks. The Easter I joined happened to be my birthday, and I had a Celtic Cross necklace made for myself, one that's a smaller replica of the cross Sister Maria Michael had given me. It's the necklace I removed just before the massive heart attack. I wear it every day, and I think of her every day.

After that first year of going to the Abbey, I stopped milking cows, and then I saw my friend for only a few minutes every year when I took flowers to the Abbey on her birthday. I never knew her schedule or the hours she was in church or in prayer, I'd just drop off the arrangements of bright yellow daffodils to be delivered to her by one of the other sisters. Then I'd start to leave, and she'd be there suddenly, by coincidence, just coming across the parking lot, or coming in from a barn, or walking toward me from across a hayfield.

I don't believe in coincidence anymore. I just can't. Meeting Sister Maria Michael each year by coincidence at the Abbey has cured me of it. We always meet and we talk for a moment as close as sisters could ever be. Then we hug each other and say good-bye again for another year. Yet, I know our paths will cross once more if it is meant to be. For it was always meant to be. Something deep and strong lives between us, an eternal bond. I'm sure she doesn't believe in reincarnation, but our connection feels ancient to me, as if forged by countless knowings.

I'd thought of her numerous times when I was in the hospital, and I'd wanted her to be aware that I was ill. I'd asked William and a couple friends to please call her, but with everything going on, no one remembered to do it. And I realize I still need her and although I know I won't be able to see her, somehow her thoughts will be with me and somehow, that will help immensely.

So, I put a call in to the Abbey a few days earlier, and I'd talked with her briefly and told her what happened. And when we hung up, I breathed a sigh of relief.

A couple days have passed, and Will bends down, handing me the get-well card she sent. I open it and unconsciously reach for the cross, "our Celtic cross," at my neck, touching it gently as I begin to read.

"It is times like these," she writes, "that bring to the surface how much one cares for another person. You are in my every prayer."

My eyes brim suddenly. She's a contemplative nun and prayer is her life. God is her life. That I would mean so much to her that she would include me in all her prayers breaks loose some great barrier hidden deep within me.

"She prays ten hours a day," I say to William as I weep. "And I am in her every prayer." William watches me closely but says nothing.

I am in her every prayer, I tell myself over and over again. "I let go of fear," I whisper endlessly. "I trust in God." And I smile through the tears.

⁓⊰§⊱⁓

Later that night I begin my still-laborious way up the staircase. It takes only five minutes now, not twenty, and although it still feels agonizingly slow, I know it is much better. I am near the top when I hear the kitchen door open, and I look down to see Will peek his head out, obviously checking my progress.

I turn away and keep going up, and then, when I am five steps from the top, he leaps clear of the door and starts racing up the stairs, bounding up three at a time. Fiend, I think. You fiend. And then I can't stop myself from laughing.

"No you don't," I say grinning while trying to ignore him, trying desperately to concentrate on hurrying the last two stairs. But hurrying is impossible, and he is charging the top like a crazed wild water buffalo.

"Let me win!" I shout.

Will freezes at the last possible moment, so I can finish first. Finishing first and laughing like this feels good. I go to bed knowing joy is a powerful medicine. And anything except laughter is pure illusion.

⁓⊰§⊱⁓

The next morning, William begins putting on my thick, anti-embolism hose. It's not an easy task, but he has to do it before I can get out of bed. He struggled with them the first day, saying through clenched teeth as he tried to get them stretched enough to go over my foot that he'd like to see the nurse who can get these on. I told him the truth. They all get them all on pretty smoothly.

William has mastered them now, and they're quickly on my legs, going up mid-thigh. My right foot is still puffy and looks like a stuffed sausage. He finishes getting the stockings on, but one feels way too tight and is bending my toes. And I realize he needs to pull the stocking out from the toes a couple inches, so it doesn't force my toes into a curling ball.

"Wait," I tell him, as he's turning to leave, "Pull out the toes. Pull them hard."

And that is exactly what he does. William takes hold of my swollen, very painful toes and pulls them. Very hard. I scream. And his eyes go wide in horror as he realizes his mistake and he instantly yells twice as loud as I did.

Then looking at his frozen, gapping face, I forget the pain and start giggling and it soon turns to hysteria, and I'm helplessly tossing side to side on the bed, holding my chest, desperately trying to stop because this raucous laughter hurts badly. But I can't. Will totters onto the bed laughing too, and I turn away so I don't have to see him convulsing, but every time, when I finally manage a normal breath, his ceaseless snickering grabs me again. Stuffing a pillow around my head, doesn't help, I still hear him. Stop, please, you have to stop. I try waving him away frantically. And then at last, it seems quiet and I cautiously take the pillow down. I take my first full breath and manage mumbling, "I meant to say...pull...pull..the...nylons."

And we both collapse in hopeless hysterics again. Despite being able to laugh with each other again, William and I still live in different worlds. I'm not kidding myself any longer. Wishing it weren't true doesn't change anything. Laughing doesn't change anything; we've always been able to laugh, and it has seen us through rough waters but that doesn't change the fact that we're drifting through ice floes.

The following day, as we're driving to my follow-up appointment with Dr. Jamisen, I glance at Will and look away just as quickly. My decision to go my own way is the right one. I'm just not certain how to tell him. But it has been on my mind a couple weeks, and I know it isn't honest to keep it from him. Even though my survival seems dependent on gaining a little strength and keeping all turmoil to a minimum, not communicating how I feel isn't right, and imagining he is going to figure out something is seriously wrong between us or imagining he should know without me spelling it out, is not just imagining, it is sophomoric.

He looks all male, all focus behind the steering wheel. There is not going to be a better time, and it isn't ever going to be easy. I decide I'll tell him that I want to separate. I take a breath and tell him that I'll move to a new bedroom so I can have my own area for as long as we are together. Until we have everything divided up.

William instantly cuts me off. "I don't want this 'for as long as we're together.' If that's what you want, let's do it. Let's do it now. Call the realtor and the movers. Let's go."

Great... So much for honesty and open communication. I still can't physically handle a move now, but William would push this through at lightning speed, because lightning speed is all he knows. I turn to him again.

"Can't you give me a little space?" I ask. "Can't you just give me a little more time until I'm stronger?"

He says nothing. His chiseled profile looks hard and cold. William always answers, but not then.

"I see no kindness in you," I tell him, finally. He drives on. Completely quiet. This is the first time I've seen him quiet when he is angry.

And it is kindness I know that I need. It is simple kindness I crave. I've responded to even the smallest of kindnesses from others lately- Beth Kelly, Sister Maria Michael, Dr. Davis and Dr. Jamisen-everyone except the man I married. I stop that thought, because the truth is William could be kind. Despite my childish comment to William, which was meant to wound, those tender times have kept me here. They've kept me married.

We pull into the parking lot of Dr. Jamisen's office. I get out of the car to a light drizzle and hurry to get under cover. William calls out a comment about me not even waiting for him, and I look back to see Dr. Jamisen has just arrived and is crossing the parking lot too. He claps William on the shoulder; they laugh together about something, and I look away and walk the rest of the way to the door. But they quickly catch up. William opens the door while I walk in, and Dr. Jamisen follows behind me.

I turn to look up as Dr. Jamisen asks me if any of the women he's asked to call, any of the young women who are doing well after having serious heart problems have called yet. I tell him no, not yet. He says he'll make sure they call, and then he disappears into his office to start seeing patients.

I sit waiting briefly for my appointment, realizing again that Dr. Jamisen wants me to focus on the possibility of a full recovery, and I know he cares enough about me to bother trying to spearhead a pep talk. His concern and timing help more than he can possibly realize.

During the appointment, Dr. Jamisen says I'm doing well, and the incisions look good and my lungs sound fine. "There's no sign of congestive heart failure," he tells me. "You don't want to have that," he says before abruptly changing the subject. I wonder what congestive heart failure is for a moment, and then he asks me another question.

I feel safe with Dr. Jamisen in the room. There won't be any arguments or unpredictable anger or feeling like I've failed at something terribly important for at least a few more minutes.

I ask him about the planned trip to Hawaii again. He says he thinks it would be fine, and when I leave his office, I feel better and stronger than I felt before. Talking to him is like that, and I'm confident he has the same effect on other patients. I glance overhead and notice the light rain is over; the sky calmed to Colorado blue.

⋰⋱

I spend hours sending thank you notes. I've never felt so loved by so many people. Friends, neighbors, and family members astound me with their thoughtfulness and their expressions of concern. I breeze through a note to Beth Kelly and Lori, the nurse with Flight for Life, thanking them for doing their job and so much more. But I labor with the note to Dr. Jamisen and one to Dr. Davis.

I struggle trying to express what I feel for the two men who gave me another chance at life. I don't know how to explain to them how much their caring and concern mean to me. How can I explain that it felt like the very gentleness I knew in my dad and it is vitally important for me to see that some men can still offer it from time to time. But I can't tell them these things; at least there is no way to attempt it in a note.

And I remind myself men aren't usually much for thank you notes anyway, unless they're trying to sell you something. But I decide to send them one; the last time I negated my voice, it nearly cost me my life. Still I hesitate again a moment before I mail the notes, telling myself the doctors would probably decide that I've gone completely off the deep end. And I have. Dear God, I know I have, but I have no desire to languish in shallow waters.

William brings breakfast while I'm in bed the next morning just as he's been doing ever since I got home. I thank him and reach for the plate. He hasn't pushed the separation by calling for movers or realtors or lawyers. I appreciate the breathing room and the effort he is making.

I lay stretched out in nothing but white panties and a silk, burgundy kimono that half covered my chest while vitamin E soaked on my scars. I've lost eight pounds that I did not need to lose: my muscles have lost their definition from a lack of hard exercise, and my breasts have lost their round softness. But I am sleek, with hints of strength beneath my frailty. I stretch slowly, like a battled mountain lion basking in the sun after a hard hunt, and then, quite unexpectedly, I feel sexier than I have ever felt in my entire life.

William lingers in the room and then on some impulse, sprawls across the bottom of the bed to watch me eat. To watch me and the smile on my face. The tension between us seems lifted since our discussion yesterday, and there is an odd sense that I can talk to him suddenly like I'd talk to an old friend: like I'd talk to one of my girlfriends. He doesn't act busy or preoccupied and obviously has little interest in leaving or doing any of the critically important things on his ever-long list.

"I'm thinking of dating," I tell him lightly, the instant the thought comes to me. And the truth is, I'm not playing games. I'm thinking seriously about dating. Because I'm thinking about the attention a man gives you when he pursues you, when he wants you in his bed. There is nothing quite like it. And I know it now for exactly what it is, but still, I want it.

"Dating?" I can hear the surprise in his voice. "What do you mean by dating?"

"I want someone to pay attention to me. Someone I can have fun with. I need some fun."

Will is quiet for a moment, studying me again. And then he says, "They're only interested in sex, you know." I smile, thinking he sounds more like a father than a husband, but he's hanging in there pretty well; in less than a day he's had to process a separation and a wife who wants to start dating. And he's calmly telling me they're only interested in sex. Well, that's news.

I laugh. "I can handle it." I fluff the pillow behind me, before I lean back leisurely into it again. "I know I look pathetic, but in three or four months, I can get my body part-way back. And I bet I could look good. I could be pretty if I worked at it the way some people do."

"You look really good now," he insists.

I stare at him, searching for signs of sincerity. "Thanks," I tell him, genuinely pleased with the compliment. I smile. "And you know I'll never be able to sleep with someone I'm not in love with," I reassure him, "but I want to be in love again. I want someone to be in love with me."

William is listening, actually listening to me. He hasn't interrupted or advised me or corrected me. He's suddenly doing everything that keeps me talking.

"Any successful man has drive," he offers finally. "He isn't a noodle or a wimp, you know."

I laugh again. "I don't need a successful man. I already made my own money."

William grins at me. "You need a successful man, or you'd make mincemeat out of him in seconds."

"That's not true. I'm very easy to get along with. Don't look at me like that, you know I get along well with almost everyone." I pause a second. "And besides, think about someone like Dr. Davis. I bet a man who does heart surgery can probably pay the bills. Even my bills," I add with a touch of sarcasm since spending is always an issue. "Come on. Just think about it. Dr. Davis' successful, he's clearly focused, and I'll bet he's kind. At least most of the time."

There's a very, very long pause. I keep watching him. Watching for the inconvenient honesty that first drew me to him.

William nods at last. I know he has to. "You're probably right," he admits. "But Dr. Davis' married."

"Oh, William, for heaven sake. I know Dr. Davis' married. I don't mean him specifically; what kind of person do you think I am?"

"I said there must be at least a couple kind men alive in the world. And you know my Dad was successful and intense in his career, but he was always respectful to my mother. I don't think anger and criticism have any part in being successful. It's just a waste of energy and it takes people backward, not forward."

At that moment, I think of one of my good friends, Molly. A few days ago, her boyfriend arrived unexpectedly with the car to pick her up at work. She'd ridden her bicycle, and it had started raining heavily. He'd told her that he didn't want her to have to ride home in the rain.

"That's so sweet." I'd said to her with a sigh.

And then she added, "Kindness is an aphrodisiac." I laughed with her and said, "I wish they'd figure it out. But I was thinking some of them probably have and I'd like the chance to meet just one. For the first time in my life, an attentive, understanding man shimmered like a novel, brass ring I imagined reaching. And I'm definitely thinking about dating.

⊰❀⊱

The next morning, I walk down to the breakfast table for the first time and surprise everyone by my arrival. And I surprise everyone also because I'm not wearing anything on top but a thin layer of cream on my scars.

"Hey, Mom," Brenna announces helpfully, "Your shirt isn't on."

"I know," I say smiling. "This feels good. It feels free. It's kinda silly we have to go around covered up all the time." William's scrambled eggs are congealing quickly in the pan while he observes me quizzically.

"And your posture looks so much better," Brenna continues exuberantly. All three girls beam at me.

"Thanks honey," I beam back. "I'm just starting."

⊰❀⊱

I've begun reading one of the *Chicken Soup for the Soul* stories nightly at the dinner table over dessert. These stories produce a strong and predictable effect. Meagan and Brenna are old enough to understand most of them completely, and Jacqueline follows the gist occasionally and questions constantly. We patiently explain the stories to her, but I never make it through one without my voice breaking.

I dab at tears and look over at William, who always cries too. He clears his throat, blinks hard, and tries to pretend he isn't choked up. I've learned a lot about men's techniques watching Will try not to tear up throughout the years. Long ago, I practiced every well-placed cough and every maneuver with a vengeance until I could justly call it my own. But I don't bother anymore. It's like taking off my shirt. It feels free and it's completely me without need of cover or camouflage.

Will loads another dish into the dishwasher and eyes me steadily. "Just don't read the Wilma Rudolph story again," he tells me. "I'm not kidding. I can't take it a second time."

❦

There are things I wonder about during the time I spent in the Cath Lab and during the surgeries. Things I can't remember about intensive care. William is able to fill in small parts of it, but there are still huge holes.

One day when we're talking about it, I ask, "Were you worried when I went into surgery?"

"Not too much," he answers after a moment's consideration. "Not until after the first surgery when Dr. Davis kept talking about the way you were bleeding. I thought he was foreshadowing too much and that he must not have a good feeling about it, if he needed to repeatedly call attention to it."

I'm waiting, wanting him to tell me more, to fill in every possible detail and emotion that accompanied it, the way a woman would, but he isn't saying anything. So, I finally ask the question I most need answered, "Did you ever cry?"

He hesitates before he bobs his head. And I wait expectantly until the pause is so awkward that he has to continue. "When you had to have the second surgery, I was sitting in ICU, thinking how much the kids would miss not having you. How hard it would be for them to lose you."

Another long pause.

"So, you cried then?"

He nods again, reluctantly. And I know he's not going to say anymore, but I'm glad that ranked up there with Wilma Rudoph. And Bambi. Will always loses it over Bambi. Just show him the cover of the book and he turns away quickly. And the kids can beg, he can't read it.

"Oh, I'll read it," I tell them, as I take over, turning pages. It's a bummer book, why did I buy it for them, I always wonder. A grandparent shouldn't have to shoulder Bambi's Mom getting shot, why do we inflict it on children? We tell ourselves they have to learn life can be hard. But I'm telling myself now the truth is that misery loves a little company. Maybe kids someday will be wise enough to make their life a little less hard, if we can just discipline ourselves to stop passing around Bambi and all the other classic hankies. Life is meant to be enjoyed sometimes even more so in the midst of trials.

❧

I don't move out of our bedroom. William offers me plenty of space and no pressure. It's a big room, and we can't have sex because it, like most physical things, is still impossible for me. One day he casually mentions it.

"You're kidding, right?" I can see he isn't kidding.

"The heart book says four to six weeks after a heart attack," he says.

"You're dreaming," I tell him. "A man must have written that. A man who'd never had a heart attack and open-heart surgery. If things were perfect between us, I still couldn't. And they aren't perfect. I don't want to have sex." I stare at him open mouthed. "Please tell me you're not actually thinking it would be fun for me?"

"I could figure it out."

"I'm sure you could. And it's very considerate of you, but don't bother."

Then I recall the only other time in our life together we'd gone so long without sex is after the kids were born. That was unthinkable for me. This feels even more unthinkable.

But back then, one night, a month and a half after the twins were delivered, he turned to me and said, "It's been six weeks."

I stare at him in exhausted disbelief. "Six Weeks? No kidding? What, to the hour?"

I hadn't been paying attention. Or counting the days like he's obviously been. His mentioning it feels like just one more thing I'm suddenly supposed to start doing. Volunteer to give me a couple nights of decent sleep, then try suggesting it again. And I promise I'll try remembering how much I used to like doing it. I promise I'll try forgetting that's exactly how I got myself into this mess to begin with. No, I can understand why you're counting the days, and precisely why I'm not.

But those times were different. Now, I have no intention of making love with him again because I know I have to move on or move right back into the same routine. And that I cannot do. I want to live.

⊰3⊱

One morning, William is dressing for work. I've seen the sun rise, taken a shower, and I am now getting dressed too. I place a couple curlers in my hair and turn the blow drier on for a few minutes. Will stops cold and turns toward me. I've never put curlers in my hair before.

"Sara taught me," I explain smiling. "I feel like a teenager."

Then I put on lipstick. It's the first I've ever owned. It arrived as a sample in the mailbox. The color's great, close to my natural lip color.

I keep dressing, slipping into a bright red silk blouse, leggings, a short skirt, and black suede heels. I stroll downstairs humming and telling myself no one would guess that I'd just had a heart attack and a triple bypass.

William is downstairs almost ready to leave for work. He stops loading paperwork into his arms the minute I appear in the kitchen. He just stares at me. I stare back, pretty brazenly, with a big smile.

"You look great," he tells me. "Where are you going?" He asks a moment later, not sounding as casual as I know he intended.

I reach for the egg pan. "Oh, probably nowhere. I just wanted to get dressed up."

⊰3⊱

A short time later, William suggests we try seeing a marriage counselor. We've done this a couple times before, and for months we rehashed all our personal issues, spent a lot of money, and had no noticeable, lasting results. I don't want to run along the same old ditch all over again, yet I tell him I'll think about it. He's been unusually mellow and easy to get along with. He's trying hard, and life flows smoothly when he makes any consistent effort. There's nothing like a man who's motivated.

One day he asks, "What do you like about me?"

The question startles me because I've asked him that question many times during our marriage, but he's never once asked me. But he is now, and it seems like he's hanging on my answer. And I know it's very important when answering this question to list a few things pretty quickly. I like to think things over completely and then comment, but long delays are not appropriate here, I remind myself. Seconds become exceptionally painful for the person who's waiting.

"What do I like about you?" I ask, repeating his question the way I always do when I'm surprised and unprepared and trying to buy a few seconds for my plodder brain to speed up.

"Yes."

"There are lots of things. I like that you're hardworking. I don't admire lazy people. And you never give up or quit. Once you set a goal, I've never seen you not achieve it. And you're honest and have strong principles - except that one phase during our early marriage," I add with a wry smile. "Let's see," I continue quickly. "You make me laugh. You have fun with the kids, and that's important to me. You bring me flowers, and I never have to hint about it. And I like that you planned that big surprise 40th birthday party for me. You cry at movies more than I do. I don't think I could ever trust a man who can't cry at a really sad movie. You also have an impressive body, and you're really good in bed."

He is smiling broadly, and I relax knowing I did fairly well under pressure with no time to prepare. I'm big on preparation.

"I sound pretty perfect," he says brightly.

And I laugh, thinking to myself that as long as I had the part about being good in bed in there, the rest, for a man's mind, is superfluous.

"Well, pretty perfect," I answer. "It's just that one thing. That explosive temper, and the being critical thing I have a problem with. I don't like your atom bomb anger, and you'd need to find some way to defuse it other than dropping it on me."

"That's all?"

I hesitate, my mood suddenly shifting because I can see William is very serious and I don't want to mislead him or myself.

"Yes, I guess that's all. I really wouldn't care how you do it. Leave the house. You can stay gone for days or weeks until the destructive mood leaves you. And I also don't want someone constantly telling me all the things I'm supposedly doing wrong, at least not as often as you like to. I don't expect us to agree all the time, but I want to be able to talk about problems without it turning into a furious personal attack. I want to be treated respectfully, the way a man should treat his wife, and I don't want every little thing turned into a big issue. Life can be a little more fun."

"What about work?"

I realize then that we're negotiating for high stakes here. And I can see also that William knows all along that he's negotiating, which puts him one full step ahead of me. Okay, I'm up to speed now. He saved work for the last issue. You get understanding on the little issues, get things rolling smoothly, I understand, but I'm still not negotiating well, not even now, because I'm just shaking it out as straight as I can. And it's all going to fall out and end up wherever it lays. So be it. I can't do anything but shake it straight. I frown briefly.

"I really don't care how many hours you work, you should know that. I can keep myself happy and entertained. Start another business if you want. Slay the dragons," I say slowly, "just remember to check your weapons each night at the door."

He pauses about five seconds, appearing deep in thought. "I can do that," he says finally.

"That's great," I tell him lightly as I walk into my closet. "If you can," I call to him, "then we've got something to talk about. Let's see how it goes."

I'm looking for a skirt, but I know Will is still standing just outside the door. I smile. "And we can pretend that we're just dating." I've never paid any attention to clothes. I detest shopping. I'm sure I spend less in a year than the average woman spends per month.

"I think I need some new clothes," I say after a thorough look. "But I could probably have some of these old dresses altered."

"What about the suits," he offers, sticking his head in.

"I'm not wearing them. Not ever again. I'm not a businessman anymore."

Will laughs. He loves to shop, and he loves going out with me when he can manage talking me into it. He'll park me in a dressing room and bring me things to try on. Everything he brings fits perfectly. And he looks like a little kid smiling when I walk out modeling for him.

"I'll take you shopping," he suggests eagerly. I have to smile at the look in his eyes. I know it now for exactly what it is. And still I want it.

Chapter Fourteen

Sara just returned from her grandfather's funeral in Illinois. She and her husband Mark, William and I are sitting on our back patio while our kids play together in the backyard. I haven't seen Sara the past four days and we've missed each other. We catch up while we're both keeping one eye on the swing set.

She tells me about discovering poems her grandfather wrote to her grandmother. She tells me how they made her weep because they were so tender and romantic.

"It's like a woman wrote them," she says with a sense of awe and I understand her immediately. She tells another story about her grandfather once taking lipstick and writing how much he loved his wife and how beautiful she was, and he wrote it in huge letters all over every mirror in the house.

"And lipstick is almost impossible to get off," Sara explains knowing I have little experience with it. "But my grandmother didn't care. She left it on there for days, and she couldn't stop telling everyone about it."

"Oh," I say, instantly near tears. "Oh, Sara."

She sighs deeply. "I know," she says. "I know."

Mark and William burst out laughing. But they're watching us closely, like we're speaking a foreign language they're partially trying to understand, because at least part of the time, it would be highly beneficial to understand it. Sara stops frowning at Mark and turns to me.

"They haven't got a clue," she tells me.

"Completely clueless," I add, agreeing with her.

☙❧

Later that night William and I are cleaning up kitchen debris and discussing relationships and the profound, yet socially camouflaged differences between men and women. Something's puzzling me, something that seems so basic, but so obviously ignored. I pause while loading the dishwasher as I'm pondering this problem, and I'm hoping William can enlighten me on the working of a man's mind. This puzzle makes absolutely no sense to me, and men think themselves very logical creatures. I'll give him a try.

"So, if men are primarily interested in sex, and kindness is an aphrodisiac to women, why don't men just consistently try being kinder?"

William pauses instantly, and I have his rapt attention as I continue, "I'd bet any man who understands has a hard time getting dressed in the morning," I chuckle.

His eyes light up as if some original revelation has just dawned on him and he's speechless for a few seconds, as it continues washing over him. The faraway look on his face intrigues me. What in the world is he thinking?

"I think some guys have this figured out," he says slowly and then he speeds up as he continues, obviously excited, his voice brightening eagerly.

"You know," he tells me, "like some of these European men that are supposed to be so charming and attentive."

"They must, I agree," I say thoughtfully.

William strides to me suddenly, bending on one knee, picking up my hand, then rising and easing me backwards, brushing his lips romantically with mine.

"You look mahvelous," he intones, doing a perfect Billy Crystal imitation. "Absolutely mahvelous."

I crack up, but he hasn't released my hand, and I don't like the new look on his face. It's devilish. His smile is devilish. And I feel as if I've offered clues for a priceless treasure to a pillaging pirate. I retrieve my hand and stand up.

"But if you use the information selfishly," I caution, "then you're nothing but manipulative. You'd be nothing but a playboy, Casanova type." I cringe. "You have to use it because you love the woman and you truly want to make her happy. Otherwise, you'll never know the deepest love."

He laughs. And I know he's thinking, Big deal, baby. Try me.

A week later I admit to myself that we're doing better, like we used to do many months before the heart attack and long before the Gestapo started hanging out behind our door. It's easy, frequent laughter and feeling like we want to be together again. One day we successfully talk through some tough issues, like budgets that usually blast all our buttons.

William has one driving, dominating principle concerning finances. Take it in fast and let it out slow. Real slow. I've always believed in saving, and living within your means, and not going into debt, but his idea of letting it out slow, sounded like a loud, shrill squeak to me.

But for the first time, we talk about money, and some of it that has actually been spent, and no one loses their temper. This seems nicer, I think. Considerably more mature and civilized.

William is reading constantly, studying everything he can, trying to master his temper and critical comments. And he's working with a counselor, Charnie, who comes by the house almost daily. In fact, she's becoming a fixture at our house. A friendly yet determined shining fixture who stands barely five foot two.

I like chatting with her before they started their sessions, and William seems to have met his match in this little dynamo. Whatever they are doing definitely helps. He hasn't lost his temper once. He gets quiet and leaves the room occasionally, and William has never been one to leave a room. The infrequent hints of irritation he shows doesn't amount to much. It's real life in a busy household, and I've bested that numerous times. We'll just see how it goes. I want to keep healing.

A week later I admit to myself that we're doing better, like we used to do many months before the heart attack and long before the Gestapo started hanging out behind our door.

Friends continue bringing me videos. Will sits beside me one night after the kids are in bed, and we watch Bill Murray in *Groundhog Day*.

It's the perfect movie for us. We roar with laughter; we keep glancing over at each other, glancing back to the show. No, I think. No, it can't be this simple. But life's meaning seems so cleanly woven within the scenes and the contrasting warp is clearly visible.

Watching Murray relive "Groundhog Day" over and over and over, sharing his growing frustration, felt like where we've been. Seeing him finally get it right is where we'd both like to go. Life's too important not to get some of it right some of the time. And neither of us is a quitter.

We turn off the video and the lights. "Goodnight," William says pulling up the covers around me. "I love you," he adds tenderly.

"I love you, too."

William is still giving plenty of space and abundant kindness, and the sense of freedom I feel grows more tangible each day. But there will be a choice to make soon, and I know it, but knowing it lies ahead isn't daunting. I understand some of the things that I desire in a relationship, and if I make a wrong choice, I know I'll keep gravitating back toward the pull of a better one.

A homing device for happiness is activated within me now. Once awareness sparked, it cannot long be ignored. It'll be okay, I tell myself, I've made a lot of decisions in my life. I've made a lot of mistakes, and I've learned something from every one of them. I fall asleep easily that night, with well-practiced mantras and a nearly dark room that feels safer and warmer than darkness has ever felt before.

❧

William stands in front of me a few days later and he tells me he wants to recommit to our marriage.

"If you'll have me," he adds gently.

He has a look on his face that I am sure I've waited all twenty-five years to see, but I can't answer him now. It's too soon.

I know he's been working hard, and there is something very different about him, and I like the difference. But it seems too easy. I'm conditioned to be wary, yet part of me wonders why I always make it hard. What's wrong with easy for a change?

❧

William calls on his way to work the next day, barely five minutes after he leaves the house. He calls just to tell me that he loves me. He says that we've grown up together and he never wants to lose me.

He tells me that everything he's ever done, he's done for me. A taste of heavy emotion hangs in his words, and I know he believes everything he's just said. I wish desperately I could too.

⚜

The next morning in bed, he leans over to kiss me. It's a tender kiss that grows in passion. We kiss for a long, long time, the way couples do before they've ever made love. When kissing can create exquisite passion. The way we haven't kissed in a very long time.

Then I shift my lips and move away.

"We shouldn't take this further," I tell him. "If we start having sex again, you'll lose your need to work on this stuff. The changes between us have to grow permanent or it won't work."

Suddenly, I think of the line from the movie *Parenthood* with Steve Martin. A young girl has been abandoned. "He told me he loved me," she sobbed to her mother with palpable disillusionment. "Sweetie--oh--they say that," the mother tells her daughter knowingly, "then they come."

I remember loud laughter from the movie audience after that line. I remember a lingering of shared pain hidden behind it too.

William leans up on his elbow. "I understand exactly what you're saying," he tells me as his eyes fix to mine.

"That's good. Because I won't do it the other way anymore."

I study him, like I'd study a stranger. He's forty-seven years old yet still strikingly handsome. Most women would believe they'd tasted heaven to lie in his arms and know the pleasure of his touch. But this has always been easy for us. I know there must be plenty of men who share his skill and his understanding of a woman's body, but I'd never once had cause to wonder what I was missing. And that was nice, very nice, but it isn't enough and was never meant to be.

William is watching me, while I watch myself through his eyes. I've experienced love's joy, and its deepest pain, and I'm lying beside him thin and suddenly a little more vulnerable. But then I realize there is no greater gift on God's earth than the love that I have brought this man. The love that I could bring to another man. And I'm wondering if he finally knows it. And I'm wondering then if William feels a little vulnerable too.

"You'll have to risk it," he tells me finally. "You'll have to risk that I can be just as attentive afterward."

We both laugh knowing this is like asking him to walk on water. Backwards. Yet he pursues every goal with bulldog persistence until it is his. And he's a great salesman.

Oh, life is interesting. I stretch out, feeling like that lion again. I look long and hard at him. "You'll have to risk it too."

ᢀᢄᢀ

The next morning before the kids come down, I tell William that I need to talk to him, remembering an instant too late that he always hates it when I say that. He prefers I just start talking. The buildup makes him nervous.

"I don't want to celebrate our wedding anniversary on the day we got married," I tell him, and I feel as if I'm making perfect sense because I've been thinking about this for hours. But of course, he has no idea where I'm going with this one.

"I need a new day," I explain. "The old one just reminds me of all the stuff that was going on when we got married. I need a new day, something special to both of us. I need a new marriage."

"Just tell me the day," he says nodding "That's fine."

I leave him, but a minute later I stop suddenly. I have to laugh at myself. Good grief. Same girl, different decade. Make love to me, and I think about marriage. Decidedly old-fashioned to the core, yet I'm not completely convinced it suits me anymore. We'll have to wait to see how well it plays out this time around.

ᢀᢄᢀ

About six weeks after my surgery, William comes home for dinner on time; his arrival surprises me, but the girls and I call out a cheery welcome. I study him a little suspiciously as he sits down. Disagreements about our dinner hour have been as constant as the setting of the sun, because I believe in the importance of a family sitting down together and talking with each other at dinner.

I discovered early on, this plan proceeds most smoothly, if every member of the family arrives at the table at the same time. I could manage the girls, but I had never been able to convince Will of the benefits of this arrangement. I had only been able to inspire him to consistently sabotage it.

He owns the company, I'd thought in anger, he can leave whenever he wants to. All the employees bolt at 5:00pm, so it's not like there's anyone to talk to at that hour. He has a thirty-minute drive with no traffic to reach our door. And I'd suggested countless times that he could work another three or four hours if he wanted to in his office at home, after dinner.

"Please, it's important to me," I'd pleaded. If he cared at all, I used to tell myself, you'd think he'd at least make an effort. But he rarely arrived on time. Ten to forty minutes late each and every night. Making his point each and every one of them.

And then, this afternoon, enjoying the day and determined to enjoy the evening, I figured that I was finished making an issue out of his tardy arrivals. I was finished with ruined dinners and faulting anyone except myself for them. A family dinner will always be important to me. I'll have dinner, just the way I like it, and the girls and I can have a fun time together. If he chooses not to be with us, he'll miss out. But I choose not to upset myself.

I realized right then that I was responsible for my own reactions and emotions. It's an easy habit to point the blame at others, but then you give away your ability to determine your own mood and behavior. As of that night, I felt done with playing the victim role to my husband. I'd overheated my last dinner.

I hum my favorite songs as I make a special meal, realizing he'll probably eat it cold, but it will still be special. And then suddenly I hear the garage door open. He's here, early, and asking if he can do anything to help. Pretty smooth. The man has more intuition than I give him credit for.

I ponder his enthusiastic smile, deciding then that I'm an arthritically slow learner. Little interior changes can indeed shift the exterior. I knew all along if he wanted to be on time for dinner he would be. I knew it wasn't the money or the need to keep working long hours or the need to keep making more of it.

For the greatest gift money ever gives is the gift of knowing you need to look elsewhere for permanent peace and pleasure. You need to look within. We both learned long ago that if every business or money problem was solved, other problems can instantly gather to fill the void. Yet despite of that basic fact, for a man with drive, the challenge of the game is pure inspiration. William still needs to play the game. And he wants to succeed at whatever game he plays, to accomplish what he sets out to accomplish on his own terms and on his own timetable. Who can blame him?

William grins bright azure eyes at me as he puts down his fork and tells me dinner tastes delicious. And I know that it's now part of his game and being home for dinner on time is one way he chooses to eliminate problems and win. I smile too and tell him sweetly that I'm glad he likes it.

Within a few days, I realize something is bothering me. I scour my mind several moments before I hone in on outer edges. Then I'm ready to talk to William.

"Do you have a couple minutes?" I ask as I stand inside the door to his office. He looks up from the computer terminal.

"Sure," he says, and I walk in. He has one of these, have I done something wrong I don't know about looks, on his face.

I sit down with my confused frustration and notice his fingers easing off the keyboard.

"I don't want to be the one to pick the new date for our new marriage," I tell him quickly. "I want you to do it. Pick someday that means something. I don't care if it's in six days or six months, you plan it. You take the initiative. And if you don't plan anything, that's okay too," I said relaxing finally. "Because then I'm going to figure we're still just dating for awhile."

This whole new marriage talk feels way too premature. But I'm finally breathing normally again. A broad smile breaks out on Will's face. I see him make a quick note in his schedule. And I'm watching him, realizing any woman would think of nothing else. She would never, ever need to make a note. But hey, at least he wrote it down. So next week, he will have a reminder about a new marriage. And the labor I'm going through attempting to erase and rewrite on the chalkboard of life does not escape me.

Jacqueline calls me from upstairs, sounding like she's in a cave. Probably another fort she's created which means I'll need to remake two beds and hang up at least five towels.

"I'll be right there, honey." I answer.

I start up the stairs and smile again. I want to heal. Having fun, fooling around and laughing way too much and too loud, plays a part in healing. But if he never plans a new marriage date can I just sleep with him?

There'd be so many advantages in being able to think of sex as nothing more than a fun activity the way men can. Surely some women do it and if they can, why can't I? Relationships can't hurt as much if you don't love as much. If you never really give fully of yourself. And I don't ever want to hurt as much again.

I'm dating my husband, and any marriage plans are left up to him. And I'm wondering if he'll pay any attention to that note when it surfaces again in his schedule and how far he'll advance it when it does.

A nearly perfect 2.5 carat marquise cut diamond still waits in my jewelry box. A side of me sometimes feels nearly ready to slide it back on. But he'll have to ask me this time. He'll have to ask. And depending how long he takes and how things are going, I'll make up my mind right then what to say. This time, I'm not forcing things that don't feel quite right. I'm taking my new heart down off my sleeve and tucking it tight in a far safer place.

Whenever William drives away from the house, I always take a moment and walk to the glass side door. He stops the car as we wave to each other before he leaves. We've done it for years, and the kids usually join me as we sing, "Make a good day, Dad, Make a good day."

Today the kids are busy coloring as Will leaves the house; I stand alone at the window waiting for his car to pull around. He stops the car and glances over to see if I'm at the window.

I am. And I'm wearing the same long white robe that I wore on that second trip to the ER. Still naked underneath. William watches as

I slowly undo the belt and hold the robe open wide. I see his face and his instant thumbs up. He drives away laughing. I laugh too. This is the stuff a man's dreams are made of.

William calls me in his car, and the guy is still laughing. "Hey, that was great," he says, "but please don't do that when I'm going to work. I might have to attack some poor woman on the street. How about when I'm coming home?"

"I'm never at the window when you're coming home."

"What if I call and tell you I'm coming home."

"Oh stop, just enjoy it."

"I did, trust me, I did."

"The scars aren't too bad?"

"You look beautiful."

Later that week, after a nap, I'm in the kitchen making a salad. Sunlight shoots through tall windows as I work. I'm suddenly drawn like a moth to the light and the air of the open screen door. I linger there, staring across the fertile, green fields for a few minutes before hunger reminds me what I've been doing.

I take a couple bites, guzzle water, and then glance at the clock. An impish grin seizes me the same time the impish thought does. Yes, this is perfect. Jacqueline's just begun her two-hour nap, and William won't leave to pick up Meagan and Brenna from my mom's house for another hour and a half.

Being back in my body is finally starting to feel safe again. Safe and a whole lot of fun. I pulled off my shirt and the lacy, white camisole underneath. Unhooking my bra, it drop into the soft pile growing at my feet. I ease off my jeans and my panties, stand up tall, completely naked and free in bright sunlight. I feel wonderful. Why haven't I ever done this before? Why haven't I even thought of it. Now I'm like a baby… naked and brand new.

I walk toward William's office, hoping he is on the phone. Chances are that he'll be on the phone, and I just want to see his face; I just want to hear his voice fumble while he's talking with his CPA or some lawyer or a customer when I walk into the room. Please, please, I haven't had a really good laugh yet today.

Will isn't on the phone. He sees me.

"Oh!" He stands, seemingly unable to finish a sentence. Two jabs at the computer keyboard and he crosses the room, gathering me into his arms. Then lean back leisurely to look down at me, he sighs deeply.

William exhales and shakes his head. "Oh, the trials and tribulations of working at home."

Together we walk past a broad bank of south-facing windows, and then William pauses at the bottom of the stairs. Four people could comfortably walk abreast up these stairs, but he stops to let me go up first. I know what he is doing, but I humor him and continue walking up a couple more steps until for a moment, it is too much, too much close scrutiny under too bright sunlight. I stop, but then I have to smile again as I look back at him.

"You're such a gentleman," I say slowly with a southern accent. "Letting me go first and all that." I reach for his hand; he lets me pull him up easily.

And I feel like a little kid, doing things a little kid should never be doing. A little kid with lots of time, running toward a favorite playground.

"Let's not rush," I tell Will eagerly. "Let's stop when we think we can't stand it, and then we'll just talk or something for a few minutes."

"Sure."

"Promise?"

He smiles. "I promise. It's called "Chinese style."

"What do you mean?"

"Nothing," he says laughing at me. "It's an old joke."

"Well, it certainly doesn't sound like a very nice one, or one you could share with many people . . . but why don't you teach me."

By the middle of round two, I can barely get my breath, but I ask again. "Promise?" Will just laughs. He loves any challenge, and I know I can play for as long as I like. I lose it early in round three, and then we're untangling ourselves when I start giggling.

"Was that my idea?"

"You mean sex in the afternoon or not coming soon?"

I smile at him. "Don't be crude." I yawn sleepily. "I think I'll take another nap."

William was out of bed, pulling on clothes. He walks to my side, leans down to kiss me softly. "Must be tough," he says. "Nap, sex, nap."

"Well, I wouldn't say you've suffered either. You'll probably start asking if I've taken my nap yet every afternoon."

"No," he says, amused. "I'm not suffering. Drop by my office anytime you want."

"Not a bad date, huh?"

He laughs. "Not bad."

"I'm thinking I could be pretty popular."

"No doubt. If they only knew." He starts to leave.

"Will?" I call and he comes back from the bathroom.

"If I ever have a heart attack when we're making love, would you lie, would you tell the doctors I was just working out or something?"

He has a puzzled look.

"I mean, if the heart attack didn't kill me, I know I'd die from embarrassment."

"What, you think they don't know you do it?"

"Well, of course they know I do it." I grin. "But I don't ever want to have to go to a hospital and have everybody talking about me just doing it. I mean guys don't mind that sort of talk, they'd probably be proud to be caught in the act, but it would really bother me. So would you lie, please, I know it's wrong, but it's kinda like working out, so it wouldn't be totally wrong."

He shakes his head slowly. "Now you want me to be immoral and lie for you."

I frown.

"Okay," he says, feigning duress. "Okay, I'll do it, just remind me in case I forget."

"I can't remind you if I'm dead."

"If you're dead, does it really matter?"

"It certainly does! I don't want the undertaker snickering. I know his entire family."

William chuckles as he leaves me, and I settle in around the foam tube of my neck pillow. Another big sigh and another yawn. Still plenty of time before Miss Jacqueline wakes up.

Before I fall asleep, I start thinking that sex is definitely a man's game, because it's completely up to him if a woman feels pleasure or pain, but it's pretty well anatomically guaranteed he'll enjoy himself. Another basic inequity that irks me.

There was one time I remember William reaching for me, and his mood was very different, more intense than tender, more urgent. I remember the feel of his body and muscles like hard bands wrapping all around me, and it scared me. It completely shook me because in that moment I knew I was completely powerless beneath him.

It was then I understood that this act of passion between a man and a woman could be something far different, if he chooses it to be. I will never forget that moment. I had to keep telling myself, it's Will, just relax, it's Will. But I know the feel of raw male power consuming me. And I will never forget it's a type of power and strength that I will never possess no matter how hard I work out.

And then he had whispered with a funny sound to his voice, "Did I hurt you? I'm sorry if I hurt you."

"No," I answered quickly. "You didn't." He seemed immensely relieved. But I was thinking, no you didn't hurt me. I just know now that you can.

⛧

It's the first trip down the mountain by myself. I've calmed fluttering of anxiety and started the car telling myself, it's no big deal. We're out of milk and bread, and I've driven away from the house thinking it's just a quick stop at the little store near the bottom of the hill. But that trip is meant to be far more. And all that it is meant to be I may never know, but it has continued to provide me with far more nourishment than a bag of groceries.

Throughout the following years, the memory of this trip will never stop feeding me. And it is telling and perhaps a bit sad that some of the more potent moments of our life can pass us by completely unseen, or in this case, nearly unnoticed. It is the strength of the illusion perhaps, blinding us to what is real. But less than seven seconds after I find a convenient parking space and close the car door, I step out of the illusion for the briefest of moments.

I glance up and notice a group of bicycle riders standing together, off their bikes, just talking with each other in a friendly way, near the entrance to the store. Suddenly one of them is coming toward me, and I only need to take a step or two and we are standing face to face with each another. His are the bluest eyes I have ever seen. And we smile brightly. His hair is pure white and then he speaks kindly to me.

"It's so good to have you back with us!"

"Thank you," I answer cheerfully, yet robotically, I just keep walking into the store. I believe I'm half way down the first aisle before I stop. His greeting to me plays again in my ears. Then, completely confused, I walk back toward the entrance to briefly stare at the small group still standing and conversing with each other.

They all have bright white hair. They all have bikes and every one of them appear leanly muscular and fit with erect and perfect posture. Their every movement and gesture exude youthful energy.

It's Boulder, home of world-class athletes and good fitness, and yet still the picture feels strangely incongruent. I stare just a moment more, still not understanding before I turn away and begin shopping. The man's eyes just would not leave me and so, I walk back one more time. This time as I walk outside, they're gone.

I have shopped at that store for years, but I have never once in my life met that man. It would have been impossible to forget the brilliance of his eyes. And I have never before seen a group of ancient riders.

And yet he had clearly approached me within moments of me getting out of my car simply to say it was good to have me back with them…How did he know me, I wonder. How did he know that I'd been gone? And how is it possible for him to know it is my very first venture out by myself since the heart attacks and surgery?

I will never logically answer these questions. His words will encourage me through countless times that feel dark.

Yet his eyes warm me. They are glad to have me back with them. I am back…And I would never want to disappoint any one of them.

I drive back home that day and tell William and the girls I have just met an angel. They do minister to us. We are always within sight and even our simplest travels are well known and duly noted. Sometimes they appear on bicycles maybe just to help us laugh at life and at ourselves.

One of the ancient riders will appear again to me another time, years later, perhaps to help cement my knowledge of God's watchful presence. One day when I was feeling unusually discouraged and overwhelmed with life and busyness, I was out again doing errands. Alone in my car, I stopped a moment before leaving a shopping mall parking lot to return home. And I'd said a simple, heartfelt prayer.

"Dear Lord, help me. Please send me some help."

I started the car and drove to the exit. An instant before I would have turned right to merge into the traffic, he was suddenly in front of me, on a bicycle crossing directly in front of my path. I stopped the car abruptly and our eyes met. I could not ignore the blue in his eyes. He nodded to me and then smiled. And I could almost imagine him doffing a cap on his pure white hair, yet he kept both hands on the handlebars.

"Good day to you," he said in a bright greeting.

"Good day," I answered smiling back.

And I had not driven even a few yards away before it dawned on me. I was moments quicker that time.

"Thank you, Lord," I said softly as tears came to my eyes.

Help had arrived. For He hears our prayers. He does send us assistance, whether or not we are even aware of it. Whether or not we feel gratitude and gather the gift. His angels are always near to do His will. And perhaps once or even twice in time, you may wake just enough to know one has crossed your path and spoken to you.

⇥✥⇤

The cut-off time for the trip to Hawaii has arrived. I feel stronger and the doctors still seem to think it is doable. I want to attend a writing convention there. Exactly one year after Dad passed away, I'd sat at my desk weeping with memories of him. Weeping that there would be no more. Trying to cope with never seeing him again, or hearing the sound of his calming voice, I'd written a short story about his illness and his funeral. Most of all I wrote about parts of his life that had mingled with mine and left me forever altered.

A couple months before the heart attack, wanting to learn if there was a way to get the story in print, I'd sent the manuscript to the writing convention judges for consideration. I'd been accepted into their seminar with good instructors, and though I told myself I should go some other time, that there was no real rush, no real reason to push it so soon after surgery, something pushed and drove me.

"I really want to go," I tell William now as he sorts through mail on the kitchen counter. He is home early again, just like every night.

"I know you do," he says, but he pauses, and I can see then he is clearly questioning the wisdom of my making the trip.

"I'll only be gone a little over a week. Sara can come over to keep an eye on the kids, so they wouldn't be any extra work for you." I wait. Still he sorts mail.

"I can handle it," I insist. "You know I've traveled all over everywhere by myself. I want to go," I repeat again.

He nods, throwing out catalogues and junk mail, but he frowns slightly.

"Everyone says I'm doing great."

Then he looks up. "You are doing great. But it might not be smart to rush it. It's a long way, and if something happened, I'd want to be with you."

"If it does, you could fly out. And besides, nothing will happen. I really am doing great." And then I smile very enthusiastically. "Just today, when I was leaving cardiac rehab at Mapleton, I was walking across the parking lot to my car, and I had my running shorts on 'cause it was so hot, but I was getting close to my car when this pickup drove by and..."

Will ignores the rest of the mail and is suddenly paying close attention.

"The truck seemed to be coming pretty close, so I stepped between two parked cars to let it pass, and then I looked at the truck and noticed it was going unusually slow and the two guys in it kept staring at me. Well, then the guy closest to me whistled. You know what I mean," I add a little embarrassed.

William nods.

"But I felt good. Not like a cardiac patient or anything. And it made me start thinking how great I feel and how I've made a lot of progress. So, I'm sure the trip won't be any problem."

"That's fine if you want to go," he says then, turning back to the remaining mail. "But I'm coming with you."

He's caught me off guard again. Before the heart problems, I'd been looking forward to an extraordinary week of reading and study and quiet time to walk along the beach by myself.

"But then I wouldn't want to leave the kids..."

"The kids can come too, and I'll take care of them while you're in the seminar."

"Oh, come on. That's too much work for you. It would be a big hassle. I just want to go by myself."

"The kids and I can have fun, and in case you need help, I want to be there." A determined look locks on his face. "I'm going," he repeats, but he doesn't really need to.

I turn back to dinner and the ground turkey in the pan. That was dumb. If I wanted to go alone, bringing up that story about the wolf whistle was exceedingly dumb. Dad always taught me to take a few seconds to think before I speak. Rambling on like that was careless. It was not the kind of thing to tell a man like William. I stand quietly, wondering if there is some reason I don't really want to go alone. No... I dismiss the thought. I haven't made any time for myself in five years. I crave a few days of quiet. What is it then?

The meat browns quickly, recalling my attention; it sizzles in a thin coating of olive oil as I wonder if there is not some reason William is meant to be with me on this trip. I do not believe in coincidences. And I am about to become eternally grateful they do not exist.

⁂

Plans for the trip progress quickly; we've lengthened the stay an extra week in order to make a family vacation after my seminar finishes. Mom decides to come. She loves beaches. We enjoy spending time together, and most of all, she tells me, she wants to help with the children. And then right before the trip, Mom calls. Her voice sounds a little less cheerful than usual.

"What's wrong?" I ask.

"Oh, nothing, I just fell."

"What do you mean you just fell?"

"Well, I didn't see a wet spot on the linoleum floor, and my foot hit it and I went down bang, real fast."

"Are you hurt?"

"Oh, not badly, I just broke my arm."

"You broke your arm?"

"Or my wrist, I'm not sure. I'm going to a doctor now."

Going to a doctor, this must be bad. Mom flourishes thirty-five years between medical appointments. You could count her entire history of doctor visits on one hand.

"Are you in a lot of pain?"

"Not so much now. I almost blacked out right after it happened, but I got up and after I cleaned up the mess on the floor, I got dressed and I'm ready to go now."

"Mom," I say, exasperated, "I wished you'd have called me right away. Just wait, I'll be right there so I can drive you."

"No, I want you to rest and just take care of yourself. I'm fine, and I don't want you to have to drive down that mountain."

"I've been driving again for almost a week."

"Well, you shouldn't be. It's probably tiring making all those turns, isn't it?"

"It's not bad," I lie. "I'll be there. Just wait for me. Please, I want to go with you."

But Mom's emphatic "No" is accompanied by a promise to call with a doctor's report the minute she gets back.

⁂

The news is discouraging. Her arm is so badly broken that she can't possibly go on the trip. She might need surgery and the physician needs to see her in ten days so he can determine if it is healing properly.

"I really wanted to go," she laments.

"Then go," I tell her.

"He says I can't. But it might be my last chance." Her voice breaks a little. My mother's voice rarely breaks.

"There are competent doctors in Hawaii. Just have this doctor X-ray it one more time before we leave, and then if it looks like it's healing fine, we'll have it checked the following week in Hawaii. Okay?"

"Well if it's hurting badly and you don't want to go, that's one thing. If you aren't going because some doctor tells you that you can't, that's another. You can do whatever you want. It is always your decision. Always. Okay? Mom?"

"Ok." She still doesn't sound like Mom.

"Is the pain very bad?"

"Well, yes." This definitely isn't Mom.

"Didn't he give you a prescription for the pain?

"I don't really want to take anything. I'm sure it'll get better."

"I'm sure it will too but let me come down and get it filled. Then you can sleep tonight. Just take it at night, and you'll only need it for a couple days," I add, hoping that will convince her.

"No, you don't need to come down. Joe said he'd get it filled if I need to."

"Well, you need to."

"Well, I don't know. Maybe. I'll let you know how I'm doing in the morning."

Oh, Lord.

And so seven weeks after heart surgery, the suitcases lie open before me. Mom is coming after much prodding from me and the rest of the family. The doctor takes another X-ray and says her arm looks fine, and Mom assures him she'll have another doctor in Hawaii to monitor it.

Packing for five people for fifteen days proves challenging. This duty would usually be my total responsibility, but Will does everything he can to make it easier. "Just do the lists," he says helpfully, "and I'll get everything you need. I want you to sit there and take it easy." He completes endless trips up and down the hall, bringing me piles of clean clothes, which I transfer into the right suitcases.

"We have to go light," I inform everyone, as they attempt to smuggle more. "Dad doesn't need a lot of luggage to handle, and I can't carry anything." I turn from the girls to William as he arrives with another load.

"I'm sorry I can't help much," I tell him.

"It's okay," he says. "We're doing fine. Do you need more water?"

"No, thanks. Thank goodness this isn't a ski trip."

But even a meager wardrobe results in two big suitcases. And two carry-ons for books and the laptops we feel we couldn't survive without. I need mine for the seminar. William needs his for work.

"Mom will have luggage too," I say anxiously. "And you know she can't carry anything with her broken arm." I catch his eye. "William, we've got to keep insisting she doesn't carry anything, or she will."

He nods knowingly. "It'll be all right."

"We'll just get a porter everywhere we go," I suggest. "And we should allow plenty of time to make our planes. I can't do the racing through airports routine anymore."

"We'll leave in plenty of time. I'll take care of everything. Stop worrying."

I stop worrying. We make it to our first plane with ample time and settle into our seats. Mom begins reading to the two grandkids beside her, and I start relaxing. Ignorance is bliss. But it is still ignorance.

Chapter Fifteen

We arrive in Hawaii late in the evening after fourteen hours of traveling. I step off the plane and follow the rest of my family into the open airport terminal. Jacqueline has fallen asleep into one of those near-comatose states only a two-year-old can create. William and I quickly decide that I'll wait with her, so he doesn't have to carry her while he is gathering luggage.

I sit down with my little girl asleep beside me. I glance around at pretty potted flowers and an assortment of not so pretty people. Airports late at night offer little comfort for weary travelers. There is a group of five guys wandering around who don't look like they're flying, and they sure don't look like they're there to pick up a passenger, and I'm suddenly feeling apprehensive without William.

I hate this hot, sticky, sweaty weather. I wipe the bridge of my nose and fan Jacqueline's damp hair, but I stop abruptly. I sit very still.

Something is happening. Something is going wrong. I lean back gingerly in the hard, plastic, ugly orange chair, feeling weak. My feet and legs are tingling all over with tiny electric shocks. I stretch out, shaking them slightly. Maybe they are just cramped. Breathe. It's okay. Just relax.

At that moment, my left arm goes numb. No pain, just a sudden sure numbness. And the left arm thing hits me right in the gut. I don't ever want to do the left arm thing again. I don't ever want to be numb again. There's no pain, I tell myself, over and over. Relax! It's okay. Okay. But I don't feel okay.

Oh, Will, please come back. I can't even stand up to try to find you. And there is no way I can pick up Jacqueline. No way I would ever leave my girl. I glance down at her and at the strangers milling around. If I pass out, someone could take Jac. And William would never find her or know where she was. I drape my good, right arm across her. My heart is beating too fast, too erratically, and the blouse I'm wearing jerks with the force of it.

I lift my right hand from Jac briefly to touch the wild pulse at my left wrist. No, forget it, I don't want to feel it anymore. It's a shrill scream in my ear. Yeah, I hear you. I know something is wrong again. But it won't be right now.

No one is working the ticket counter. There isn't one official, or even one near-normal looking person anywhere I can ask for help. Some woman is sitting about ten feet away, and I'm trying to figure out if I could time it so I could call to her before I pass out. But she doesn't look at all friendly or helpful. I dread asking for her help unless I absolutely have to, but when I absolutely have to it might be too late.

What have I done? I was fine at home. I was starting to heal. Now I've ruined it, I've ruined everything. Oh, Jac, sweetheart, I'm so sorry.

Minutes drag as I sink into deeper mud and involuntarily sprawl across two chairs, tingling all over, my eyes glue on the spot where I last saw William. Please Will, you have to get here soon, so I know our baby will be safe. I close my eyes for an instant, trying again to calm myself, and when I reopen them Will, Mom, Meagan, and Brenna, and a wagon loaded with suitcases, carry-ons and laptops appear around the corner.

He takes a look at me and leaves the cart instantly.

"I'm having a problem," I say stupidly as he bends over me.

He reaches for my arm. I shake my head. "I can't walk."

Mom hovers close, her face strained with concern. I smile weakly.

"I'll get a wheelchair," Will says quickly and disappeared. Mom starts quizzing me, but I don't want to talk. I just want to be quiet, really quiet, but she wants me to reassure her. I'm not able to.

"I guess you shouldn't have come," she says wearily. "I tried to tell you it was too early. But you wouldn't listen."

Oh, well, that's helpful. Thanks Mom. And please, God, please if you let me live past tonight, just help me remember never, ever to say something like that to anyone who's lying in front of me completely incapacitated.

I clamp my jaw and try to slow my racing, erratic heart. William returns quickly and easily transfers me into the chair. He opens a quart bottle of water and hands it to me.

"You're dehydrated. Drink it."

"I've been drinking the whole trip," I argue.

"Drink it."

"I can't. I'll throw up."

"Then sip it!"

"Will." My voice falters. "My arm's numb. My heart's funny."

"Just try to sip it," he repeats patiently, then he picks up Jacqueline and balances her limp, inert body expertly over his shoulder. He begins pushing my wheelchair and somehow pulling the huge cart of luggage. The twins are milling close, weaving and exhausted. It is one-thirty a.m. our time, and the girls are always sound asleep by seven-thirty. Mom is worn out and clearly worried. And the little clique of young men roams near.

William is in charge of five vulnerable females, and he has this look on his face that if anyone messes with him or any of his family, they are going to be sorry. Some guy would have a death wish to tangle with him now, but then some guys do, and William knows that even better than I.

Oh, what have I gotten us into? All because I had to attend a seminar? I was the tough guy who could travel just fine all on my own. And now we're all in trouble.

I reach my right hand back to William's hand on the chair.

"I'm sorry." I say softly, but he doesn't answer. He doesn't even hear me; a man hears little in "commando mode". Will watches the halls and the gates as if he is walking through a war zone. He spots a security guard and walks away for a few seconds, but his eyes remain glued on me as he talks. And the guard stands right beside us while William leaves to find transportation.

William pushes me out to the van that is supposed to take us to the hotel forty minutes south. He bends down to me, again.

"Just sip it."

I sigh. "I have to go to the hospital, if they even have one. I'm not doing okay. Really."

His face and voice are strained. "You did too much getting ready for the trip and the seminar, and the trip was way too long. I'm wasted too. You just need water, and you need sleep. Relax."

"And if you're wrong, I'm dead. Are you listening to me? My arm's completely gone." And my voice suddenly rises. "Do you think I want to go there?"

His face looks hard. "Okay. I'll get you to the hospital."

He loads us all in, talks to the driver, and I sink into a heap on the seat. Mom sits close beside me; she leans down. Just leave me alone. Please Mom, please, just don't talk or anything right now. I'm struggling here.

"Are you all right?" she asks.

And I feel myself snap. "No, Mom, I am not all right. I can't walk. I can't even sit up, and my arm's numb. But beside that," I add sarcastically, "I'm doing fine."

Mom starts crying quietly beside me. Oh Melissa…That's perfect. Real good call. Dad would be angry with you for upsetting your mother like that.

"Watch after your mother," he told me. "If something happens to me, watch after your Mother."

And I told him I would.

"I will, Dad, you know I will." He nodded silently.

And now the woman he so dearly loved, the woman he took great care of for over fifty years is elderly and exhausted, with a broken arm that is probably throbbing though she would never complain about it. She weeps softly beside me. Because of me.

Oh Mom, I didn't mean to hurt you. Just give me a little space for a while. Please, I've just insisted William take me to a place that makes an icy ball of fear curl inside my stomach. I act like it's no big deal. But Mom, I just can't tell anyone how I feel. Please Mom, please don't cry.

I know right then that somehow my dad would have been able to calmly reassure her that everything was fine, no matter how he felt. But I can't. I don't have your strength, Dad. I don't even have a measure of my own right now. I'm too imploded.

The hospital towers before us. The driver stops at the emergency room entrance to let us out. He's proved helpful in every way possible. He and William have been talking the whole trip. William asks him to take the rest of his family to the hotel and to see that the luggage is delivered. He asks him to make sure everyone gets safely inside. I notice the men looking steadily at each other in the dim light. And I see the message communicated in that simple nod.

Then I watch my mom and three sleeping little girls drive off into darkness with a stranger. Please take care of them, I think as he leaves.

God, please watch over them. And please let the driver be as nice as he seems.

Different hospital, same routine, same IV, blood tests, and EKG. Same fear overpowering me. Don't be afraid, I keep urging myself. Just nod and smile a little and answer questions. Breathe. A cardiologist is called in immediately. He arrives, looked at my chart, asks questions about my surgery, and tells me he wants me on nitro immediately and a blood thinner.

I balk. The nitro will put me out instantly. It did twice before, I guess because my blood pressure runs low. And I don't want my blood thinned because I'd had severe bleeding problems before. The doctor must be thinking I have a blockage in a bypass graph. But that doesn't feel right.

"I don't want nitro," I say politely, "It'll knock me out. And I don't think it's the best thing to take if an artery's dissecting, which was my problem before."

"I won't give you a large dose," he says pleasantly, trying to reassure me.

He's been called in late for an unknown patient who is now not going along with his recommendations. But I'm still balking. I don't have even a crumb of his medical knowledge or experience, and I don't like making decisions short of facts and vital information, but I do have a sense of what works for me. That sense is shouting, *NO!*

The doctor's jaw works tensely. I try not to watch the metamorphosis in his face, but I look away just a shade too slowly. I figure then that he is from the old school and is clearly not accustomed to waiting for patients while they are thinking. Thinking is not something we really are supposed to do. And from the look on his face he figures we're obviously less intellectually qualified to attempt it than the men with a stethoscope draped around their neck. *They* think. *We* follow. Preferably with a sense of awe and unwavering appreciation. But scared or not, I've never been a good sheep.

"I really don't want to take anything right now," I say again gently. "And I'm feeling a little better," I add helpfully. "Maybe my fluids were just low." I glance at William. "I know that can happen flying."

I look back at the doctor as he goes completely rigid. His eyes fix on me with profound irritation. I glance back at him as demurely as possible. I can't blame him, and I'm not trying to insult him, but I am not changing my mind.

In the same situation, I wouldn't keep arguing with Dr. Jamisen. He was beside me in the cath lab and during the heart surgery when I was bleeding, and they were trying so hard to stop it. He and Dr. Davis pulled me through. I don't want to take anything to decrease my blood viscosity, and I just don't believe Dr. Jamisen would immediately throw me on nitro and blood thinners. Maybe it is standard protocol, maybe he would. I wish Dr. Jamisen were here to tell me what would be best to do.

The cardiologist glares at me. "You could be making a very, very big mistake here," he says slowly, just barely keeping a handle on himself.

I see the battle lines again. It would be clear to an idiot that this doctor doesn't tolerate patient participation. But it's my body, and I pay the ultimate price for stupidity.

Why do you do this when I'm frozen with fear? Maybe I'm not strong enough now to keep my ego out of this, but you should be able to, because it's your job. If it were mine, I'd have the presence of mind to be professional enough not to treat a sick, scared patient like this. I wouldn't need to scare them more.

A very big mistake, you say. Taunting me with the horror of making a mistake is supposed to pin me into meek submission. Well, I can live or die with my own errors. I can't live with doing anything that goes against what my gut is screaming, not ever again. That cost me. Big time. Talk about mistakes. We all make them. You don't look like you've ascended yet either.

So, I'm not going along. If that means you don't like me, tough. You could be making a mistake too, because you don't know me or my case enough to be sure what you should do. I can do the straight, hard, unsmiling stare just as well as you can, even as scared as I am.

"If I make a mistake," I say levelly, "it won't be the first."

"If you start having chest pains," he counters rapidly, "you won't have any choice."

"Well, if I start having chest pains, I'll probably take the blood thinner, but then I still have a choice. Unless I'm unconscious."

"Who's your doctor in Boulder?" he asks brusquely. "I don't like the look of this EKG, and I need to talk to him to find out if it looked like this after surgery."

I gave him the information, and he leaves asking William to come with him while he puts in the call. What? Does he think he can convince William to force me to take nitro?

The cardiologist returns after a long delay. He tells me that Dr. Jamisen isn't on duty. The doctor on duty says that he's not familiar with my case, and that I'm not his patient. He has refused to get my chart or any information until morning.

Oh, that's great. This cardiologist is working late, putting up with my obstinacy, and he's probably wondering why this other physician won't even help by getting my records. He seems genuinely puzzled by his lack of assistance, but I could probably enlighten him.

This has to be the same doctor who wouldn't even drive five minutes to see me in the ER. And the same one I saw in between having four heart attacks who told me I was fine and suggested I just put it all behind me. What in the world did I do to him? If anybody should be holding a grudge, it sure seems like it should be me, not him. "It's not your heart, just go home and forget it." Well, I do try, trust me, but it's gotten a little hard at times. But forgetting sure comes mighty easy for you.

Okay, Dr. Hawaii Cardiologist. As I look at him, I know what he's thinking. That maybe I'm not too popular with the doctors at home either. Maybe I don't have any interested players on my team.

So what? It doesn't change how I feel about the blood thinners and the nitro. The doctor tells me he'll try to get a security guard at Boulder Hospital to locate my records and fax the information he needs.

"Maybe your EKG looked like this before tonight, but I need to know, because if it didn't, you could be having a very, very big problem."

Oh good. I nod. Good rapport again, Melissa. Strike out one more time. Sorry I can't die a little more complacently.

Maybe I'm just off track again, I tell myself. Overreacting because I'm so scared. I look at William, knowing I'll get instant feedback with or without words.

He looks ticked, fuming, and not at me. Well at least somebody is finally on my team.

"This guy's a total flake," William says, "And if you want to stay here with him that's your business, but I'm going to check on the kids and your mom. And then I'm going to get some sleep. Are you coming with me or not?"

I hesitate before I shake my head. "I don't think I should, I'm still too weak, and I'd be forty-five minutes away if something serious happens."

"Then, I'll be back in the morning. I'll leave the name of the hotel in case they need to reach me."

We nod at each other before he disappears. I wouldn't have thought the fear inside me could double until I watch him fade from the room. Oh, William, please don't leave me! I know you need sleep, but I'd never leave you all alone in some place that terrifies you.

But I nod instead. William seems distant again, his tenderness cast aside. Nodding feels easier than trying to talk. Telling him how I feel and watching him leave me anyway would hurt far, far worse.

The cardiologist returns after reaching the security guard and getting the information he needed. He is attempting to be amiable again. Attempting to make another effort. I do too. He looks around before asking about my husband.

"He was tired," I say quickly. "We've been traveling all day, and we have three little girls at the hotel." I wish I didn't have to explain why William left so abruptly, and I wish too that I had a doctor on duty at home who'd pretended he cared, even a little. But I guess he needs his sleep too.

I get transferred to the intensive care floor, yet I tell myself it isn't that bad. Just because I'm in intensive care again, it's not bad. But I also know they put you in here when you're dying, or they think you might be dying real soon. I can't lie to myself about that.

The blood tests come back, indicating my potassium is extremely low. I get three large pills, and within thirty minutes of taking them, I feel good again, just like before I stepped off the plane. So, this drama was all due to a lack of potassium. Why would my potassium be that low? I have no idea, but the problem is resolved. I want to go rejoin my family. But I'm stuck in ICU for the rest of the night. And it proves to be a very, very long one.

I'm awake every moment as the patients on either side of me are suffering through various stages of heart attacks. An older woman I can't see through the curtains of my glass room gasps and moans piteously. I hear when the doctor is called in. I hear him suctioning her, and I know these sounds don't bother the doctor or nurses, because this is their work and they detach emotionally to tune it all out as the crisis demands, but every sound digs into me like a meat hook.

As they attach a respirator into this poor woman, I'm right beside her. I'm with her in a way medical staff would never want to be; I hear the machine rising to life, that awful, rhythmical, rasping sound, and my skin crawled. I keep swallowing; I keep trying to clear my swelling throat. I close my eyes listening to the doctor's voice as he speaks to the woman, as he talked in vacant tones that told me he was unsure if she could hear or even understand. But he isn't present anyway. Every sound in his well-rehearsed voice communicates that he doesn't want to be there. He has all the words down right. But every word lacked feeling. Is there a test medical worker must pass for basic human compassion?

Honest feelings of compassion can seldom be trained into an adult, yet perhaps they can be thoroughly trained out. I open my eyes to the curtains that separate me from this lady who is dying all alone. And I weep for her. No family member or dear friend stands near. No Dr. Davis forms an umbrella as he had for me. Please God; please don't let her hear that her doctor plainly doesn't care. Please let her be too far gone to hear. People shouldn't leave this world without someone leaning down to whisper loving words.

A hideous machine speaks instead. "Uh-Whooosh.... Uh-whooosh... Uh-whooosh..." And some switch flips inside me.

I suddenly feel like throwing up. I tear off my sheet and bolt from the bed, heading for the window. It is black outside, but I peer down at least five stories to the lighted cement walk below. I look for a ledge. I've got to get out of here. Let me out of here! I spin, scanning the room and the nurses' station and the hall. Everyone is working on the dying patients, perhaps they wouldn't even notice if I just eased out the front.

My heart rate is climbing. Calm down. Calm down or someone will notice and come in. How do I get out? I'll never make it out the front. And if I do, what then? I'm not in Boulder. If I were, I'd find some way out right now, and I'd be heading toward the mountains. Going home. Melissa, just try to calm down. Try...

I return to bed, looking at the walls, the hospital equipment surrounding me, and I start trembling. I cover my ears with both hands…pressing hard…holding my breath while I wait. No, the sound is still here. I try humming softly. It's still here. Please, don't ever put me on a respirator again. Please, William, come back now and get me. I made another horrible mistake. Just take me with you.

In desperation, I pick up the phone to call William. But it rings and rings and rings. No one answers. I call back and ask the hotel clerk to check that I have the right room. I do. They put the call through again. I hold my breath again, listening.

The phone rings forever, and then they tell me it must be off the hook. As I hang up, I wipe away a tear. How would they have reached him if I were dying? Was sleeping so much more important than me? I'm alone. Utterly alone. No one cares. Not even my own husband.

A nurse comes in unexpectedly to check on me. No one has been in for most of the night, and she sounds highly apologetic for ignoring me. I think of Terry, and I know that's not normal fare for ICU.

"Believe it or not, you're the healthiest one in here," she tells me. "It's been a really bad night."

"It's okay. I'm really okay," I say quickly. "I want to go now. Can I just call a taxi and go?"

She pauses completely startled. "Well, you can't go anywhere until the doctor says you can, and he won't be here for hours yet. And then he may want to do other tests or put you on medication."

I nod before she leaves. She leaves me a few seconds before the uncontrollable shaking starts again. It's the hospital thing, the trapped, helpless thing, crescendoing again. I hear the respirator again and again. I glance at the clock. Six o'clock here. That means nine o'clock in Boulder. I sit up.

I need to talk to Dr. Jamisen. And I feel right then if I can't talk to Dr. Jamisen, I'll go crazy listening to that machine and what it reminds me of. I reach for my purse to look up his number… If I can just talk to him for a couple minutes, I believe I can pull myself together. I imagine his voice while I dial the number. I try to calm myself imagining his calm voice.

But the answering service tells me he isn't on duty. The same doctor who wouldn't help last night is still on duty. The same one who never seems to want to help me. Oh God.

"Would you please ask Dr. Jamisen if I can talk to him just for a minute? Please, I don't mean to bother him," my voice falters, and I look up at the ceiling, blinking hard, hating myself that my voice is dissolving and there is no hope of controlling it. "Please tell him I'm in intensive care in Hawaii, and it would really help if I could talk to him."

"Okay," the woman says, apparently hearing my plaintive desperation. "We're not supposed to ever call when they aren't on duty, but I'll ask him."

I hang up and try to breathe. I try not to listen to that tortuous respirator breathing inside my neighbor. But it is all I can listen to. Please talk to me, Dr. Jamisen. Please, I believe I am losing my mind.

A call comes through quickly. It isn't Dr. Jamisen. It is the doctor on duty who doesn't care to review my file last night. My heart sinks.

He obviously hasn't bothered to get it this morning either. He asks who I am. He asks me to tell him a little about my situation. I explain a little about myself. Nothing appears to be ringing any bells. I know there can't be too many forty-three-year-old women in their practice with a spontaneous dissected left main artery and a triple bypass within the last two months. Boulder isn't that big. You'd think my cardiac event was unusual enough that it might create some vague sense of recognition, yet I might as well have been a complete stranger. I stop talking.

He tells me I should listen to the doctors and do whatever they were suggesting. He is sure they are very well qualified to treat my case.

"Thanks for calling," I say almost inaudibly. He hangs up.

As I put the phone down, I try to keep swallowing, so my throat won't close completely. I'm alone. Alone. Dr. Jamisen doesn't want to talk to me, I think over and over and over. I thought he cared a little about me, but he doesn't want to talk to me for even one minute.

Melissa, Melissa, they do that when they aren't on duty, so they can maintain a personal life, and a little balance so there's something left of them when they are on duty. You'd do it too, if you were a doctor. They have to do it. It's nothing personal. What did you expect? He's a very busy doctor with a thousand patients and you're just one of them. It's how he plays his game. And he's not on duty. Why would he want to talk to you when he's not working? I moan and sink deeply into the bed.

Because I think of him as a friend. I need to think of him as some kind of friend, because I can't deal with him as a doctor. Because I would have done just about anything to help him if he ever needed me to. Just like Dr. Davis. Well, Dr. Davis wouldn't have talked to you either.

I keep blinking; I keep hoping no one walks into the room right now. No one does. I feel more alone than I have ever been in my very long life. No one seems to care. And it gouges me deeply.

They transfer me out of intensive care later that morning, and I don't want to see the cardiologist who put me there. I just want him to sign the discharge papers. Physically I feel fine. I have ever since taking the potassium pills, but the night has trimmed me considerably, but then, I guess he wanted me trimmed. I am quiet when William comes to pick me up.

The doctor wants me to do a treadmill echocardiogram test before I leave. I finish jogging and lay down on the table for the echocardiogram, but the way he lifts my arm so high and the way he pushes on my chest hurts my sternum. It hurts in a way Dr. Jamisen and Dr. Davis have never once hurt me, even when I was far more tender. The doctor continues hurting me, until I even admit it quietly, hoping he will let up the pressure, but he dismisses my comment and tells me just to bear with him.

After he is satisfied with the test results, he says he'll release me.

"Why wasn't this test done in Boulder?" He questions me.

"I did a stress test after surgery but not an echo stress."

He indicates his disapproval. He isn't being entirely professional with his disapproval. I didn't ask for his critique of my medical care. Maybe he thinks I'll be more comfortable with him and his supposedly superior expertise. But I am not.

After being too busy to discharge me for the entire morning and part of the afternoon, he spends nearly twenty minutes writing suggestions for nice places to eat, places to snorkel, and fun places to take the kids. I know he's trying to be helpful. He has a break in his scheduled day, and now he is helping two tourists enjoy the island. I know he doesn't need to spend his time doing any of this, yet he is. I wish I hadn't made him so mad at me last night. He seems congenial now, but I just want out. I know I'm not thinking rationally, and I'm not capable of making good decisions any more. Asking Dr. Jamisen if he'd talk to me off-duty demonstrated that. Remembering my call to his office makes me wince. I turn away from the long list of restaurants the cardiologist has just handed William.

"Are you hungry?" William asks, as we drive away from the hospital.

"No . . . not really."

"Did you eat?"

"I . . . I couldn't eat those artificial eggs."

"You need some food. You need some clean carbs and protein."

I nod, and then I turn toward him slightly. "Maybe I was just low on fluids like you thought and low on potassium," I say, trying to find my way back to the way I was yesterday morning.

It seems impossible that so much has changed inside me in just one day. My voice sounds different now. Lacking life and luster now. And I listen listlessly as William tells me about how great hotel is, how it is right on the ocean, and how the kids went swimming with him this morning in the pools and went down the water slides. They're having a good time. You'll love it.

Yes, I used to love islands, beaches, and pools.

I nod as I glanced out the window. William and I vacationed here every year before the kids. We'd scuba and snorkel and parasail hundreds of feet in the air behind a ski boat, we'd horse around doing fun stuff all day and into the night. But all those years we arrived mid-winter. Now it is late, hot, humid summer. Heat drains me dry. I'm empty and far past drained dry.

Melissa, you've got to try. Will is here because he wants to help you. Just look around, it's so pretty. You love flowers. Remember? Oh, Melissa where have you gone again?

I reach over and turn on the radio, hoping it will muffle that pumping noise that lives again inside my head. I remember to answer William, knowing if I do, he won't realize I'm not here anymore.

⊰❖⊱

The seminar begins later in the day. I look around. No one knows me here, so they don't realize I'm running on one cylinder. Then during the second morning, right after William walks me to the meeting room, the weakness starts unexpectedly. I reach for water and notice my hand shaking. It is happening again. Not the numb arm, just weakness. I tear off small pieces of the Power Bar Will bought me. They energize me at home whenever my blood sugar feels off.

I start writing a note, listing my husband's name, his room number, and the name of the cardiologist I saw. The woman next to me notices my note. She leans over, and I quietly tell her I recently had surgery for a heart problem, and I tell her I think some Gatorade might help, or any sports drink with electrolytes and potassium. I can't stand up.

She leaves and returns with the seminar director who brings Gatorade and tells me to let her know if they can help in any way. I try to pay attention to the speaker standing right in front of me. I try to learn what I came here to learn, but most of all I keep hoping the weakness won't get worse. I keep hoping I won't have to go back into that hospital.

I keep drinking and nibbling. The weakness slowly passes. Will is kneeling unexpectedly beside me. Someone has called him.

"It's better," I whisper.

"Okay. If you need me, I'll be in one of the pools with the kids. They have beepers at the front desk. I'll get one and bring you the number so you can reach me right away."

Anxiously I watch him leave. I watch him go. I'm sitting a wide ocean away from the woman who was telling her husband about the wolf whistle and insisting he didn't need to come. I could take care of myself.

Yes. I used to be able to take care of myself. I felt strong once. Strong and independent and exceptionally capable. The door starts closing as William in his swimming trunks fades away into the heat, blinking bright sunlight and blue water that must lie somewhere close by. The door is almost closed in this carefully lighted, carefully cooled room. I turn away from the light and the heat. I can't tolerate life's heat anymore.

William is waiting for me with a wheelchair that afternoon. I get into it without comment. I am exhausted as he pushes me the long way back to our air-conditioned room. All week long, he pushes me to every seminar, he pushes me to breakfast, he brings healthy snacks, so I don't get hungry or weak, and he arrives at the seminar door right on time for every break. He pushes me to lunch, he takes me back to the seminars, and he brings me to the hotel bedroom and gets my dinner. And he is taking care of the kids whenever he isn't trying to take care of me.

"Just rest," he tells me encouragingly. "You're doing fine."

Oh, Will, am I really? I am never in a wheelchair at home.

Yet I am getting accustomed to the feel of a chair and the feel of dependence on it. And watching people as they watch you in it. And I learn there are only two types of people watching an approaching wheelchair. There are those who absolutely will not look at you. They look everywhere except down into your eyes, as if perhaps you have something contagious and they know only that they do not want to catch it. They know only that they do not want to catch your eye or any of the pain you might be feeling.

And then, there are those people who smile and, in some way, acknowledge that you're sitting or rolling right in front of them. You always feel more human with the type of people who feel comfortable enough with the weak side of themselves to face you.

If I ever get out of this chair, please never let me forget the days that I spent in it and all the people in this world who never get out of it. Let me take a second to talk to them if they seem to want to talk. Let me smile if they don't want words. Let me at least send silent prayers and good wishes.

Will isn't exaggerating; the kids and Mom are having fun. We celebrate Jacqueline's birthday together in the hotel room, with a store-bought chocolate birthday cake with green palm trees and a train trailing across it. The family gathers around me on the bed as I help Jac cut it. And I am glad I've lived long enough to see three candles on her cake.

For the first time, Will had to arrange a birthday party by himself. He did an outstanding job, never complaining and never once questioning why we were here.

The next day I sit beside Mom at lunch as William helps all three girls through the buffet line. Mom studies him, and then she turns to me. She's spent the week with him and the girls, at the pool, the beach, and all in very close quarters with a door connecting our rooms. I saw something was on her mind. I know I won't have to wonder long.

"William's a marvelous father," she tells me emphatically. "He played all morning with them, and then the girls were getting a little sassy and very whiney, but he was extremely patient." She pauses. "Your Dad never would have put up with any of this."

"I know he wouldn't." I sigh and watch them working their way through the line and working their dad. Jacqueline has decided that she has to have strawberry crepes daily for breakfast, and she's suddenly just as insistent about something else she's spotted on the line. People are always learning and either we're teaching our kids or they're training us. William attempts to keep things pleasant, yet I am thinking whenever we shirk lessons to maintain the peace and extend the quiet, life surely will not. Life doubles as a mighty hard teacher.

I've always been the day-to-day disciplinarian because I've been there day-to-day. But I'm not there much anymore. I'm guessing it's also because William's afraid of his strength and the strength of his focus, so he backs off a little from correcting his little girls, so he won't overdo it.

"Please, Mom," I say suddenly on some urgent need, "when you're around, don't let them act sassy. Say something. Let them know that's not right. I hate that spoiled kid stuff."

After lunch during a break in the seminar, William offers to push me down to the pool, so I can be near the water for the first time. I get my suit, feeling a little less tired than I have all week.

William and the girls start playing on the water slides. Cascading down in a series of little eddies and big laughter. Slides Jacqueline can do in her father's arms, but I cannot. For a few minutes I watch, and then I move toward the pool. Slowly I wade in up to my belly.

"You're not going in all the way, are you?" Mom asks nervously. "You won't go completely under?"

I tell her no. And I turn back to look at her after I am partway in. I do not know what torturous impulse makes me look back at my mom. I know what I'll find looking at her. I know Mom's eyes will be riveted to me. I turn away again quickly because of the look in her eyes and the memories it brings instantly to me.

"Watch your mother," Dad said, and I stopped what I was doing, stopped packing up for another day at the pool to listen to him. I was in high school and had been swimming since Mom and Dad taught me when I was just one year old. They would laugh recalling how I didn't know enough to come up to breathe. They'd have to pick me up for air, but I swam like a little tadpole, they said, like a little dolphin way down deep.

By high school, I was a competitive swimmer, used to endless laps and water that suddenly drains from an ear in a flush, waking me at night.

"Watch your mother, watching you," Dad said then. "And just glance around the pool. You'll see other mothers talking with each other, eating and playing cards. But your mom's eyes will be on you whenever you're in that water."

So, I watched that day, just like he told me to, and I noticed that day for the very first time. She never let me out of her sight. If she was talking to a friend, she still had her eyes on me. If she was eating, she still had her eyes on me. Watching her watching me so closely throughout that day, felt like seeing love.

Years later, when I was in my thirties, Mom and I took a trip to Taiwan, and I asked at a local shop where the best bodysurfing beach was. Some guy named a remote, out-of-the-way spot no tourist would know about. We parked and climbed down a tricky ravine with big bushes. I went back to help Mom because it was so steep and awkward. She made it down without complaint. Mom sat on that beach as I swam out and surfed hard waves in deep blue water.

Between the swelling, breaking waves, whenever I looked to shore, Mom was there. She was sitting up, her face focused on me. And I knew her eyes would be too, only I couldn't see that far. I came in breathing hard after about an hour. I felt good that day. Radiant and strong. Mom had a wide grin as she watched me jog in from the shoreline with my wet suit plastered down on a body trimmed with taunt, tested muscles. I was back to shore. I was safe. Only then did she lie down and rest in the sun for a few minutes before we started back to our hotel.

I neglected to think about the lack of time she had until later. I don't like just sitting on beaches. I don't think there is anything my mom loves more in this world than lying down on a beach and sunning herself. Except I guess there is something she loved more.

And now, Mom's eyes still train on me, only my back is wasted and bony. I wear fresh, vivid scars, and I don't even feel strong enough to go out to dinner with the family. Oh Mom, I know it must break your heart, yet you smile at me. Before I turn away from your anxious eyes, you manage another smile for me.

And it is like hearing you say when you taught me to swim, "You can do it, Lissy, just come up for another breath." But sometimes I just don't know how to come up anymore.

Yet I smile back, thinking again you deserve that. You deserve far more than that. I'm a mom now too, so I realize what you did, you never did for recognition or even for remembrance. But I won't ever forget, Mom. Long after I'm gone from this body, the memory of your loyal love will live on somewhere in some deep part of me. It's the gold I want most to pass along to my kids.

I'm afraid now I won't have the chance. Yet I am thinking that I will try to be a good role model for them. The way you were for me. But they won't ever know me as I once was. They won't know a mother who once won at the game of life. They'll only see a scarred, scared woman who watches from the sidelines. And maybe they won't see me long enough to even remember me at all.

Come on. Don't start thinking like that again. You know it tears you up; it's not the thing to think about with the family all around. I dab water quickly on my face. Then I turn to wave at the woman sitting on the far side of the pool. The woman who gave me hazel brown eyes, long black lashes, and the dark hair that shines auburn in bright sunlight. I'll try, Mom. I'll keep trying not to slip and go completely under. For I know you'll always be watching.

Chapter Twelve

That night I am again too weak again to go out to dinner.

"No, don't bring me anything," I answer William. "I'm just not hungry." They gather up mounds of dirty clothes, planning to stop at a laundromat after dinner. After a long time, when they return, I finally tell William what I've been trying not to tell myself.

My chest hurts. For the first time since surgery, I have chest pain. Not a sharp pain, but a bad, dull ache, that has been going on for almost three hours. It isn't going away. My anxiety will not go away. I can't look at Mom. I can't look at anybody.

William pushes me downstairs in the wheelchair. I almost pass out in the heat of the open-air lobby waiting for him to bring the rental van around. Waiting and thinking about the growing pain and where I am going again. Why? Why can't I get better?

William helps me into the van. I lay down with the pain on the bench seat behind him. I cry silently in fear and thundering frustration. I don't want to go back there, but I feel I need help again. I don't know who can help me. It is dark. We have close to an hour's drive on roads we aren't comfortable with, and William doesn't see well at night. I used to be the navigator. I used to be the eyes of the team, and now I can't even sit up. There will be no way he'll ever find the hospital.

"You're upset," he says with a shade of irritation in his voice.

"Well, you'd be upset too!" I snap back. "Wanna switch places and try it? Cause I'd sure like to be driving." My voice sounds unusually high pitched.

"Maybe it really is a panic attack this time," Will says. He seems to be talking to himself more than to me.

I put my hands over my face, not that he can see me in this darkness. Well maybe it is. I'm a real natural for panic attacks now. It's the same hated agony again. This hating being so weak and not being able to find any strength. This hating myself and knowing I don't fit into my life or any real life anymore. We ride the rest of the way in bumpy silence.

William gets me checked in at the hospital, and he leaves to get back to the kids. There is a different cardiologist on duty.

"He's very good," the nurse tells me as I am settled into my room. "And he doesn't get as easily excited." There is no need to elaborate; I understand what she means.

Nothing new shows up on the EKG, so I am released the next day, without pain but still weak. William brings me back to the cool room where I collapse. He spends two hours sitting beside me on the bed, rescheduling airline flights home. We cancel the rest of the trip and the vacation plans. Getting home as soon as possible becomes the only priority. I doze on and off beside him. Mom entertains the girls again. William gets us scheduled on a flight in three days. Please God, let me last three days. I just want to make it home, so I can see the mountains once more.

William keeps feeding me, making sure I have enough water. The weakness continues. I skip the remaining seminars. But then the day before we are supposed to fly home, chest pains start again. After several hours, I pull out the card the cardiologist gave me the first night we arrived in Hawaii. He calls me back quickly, obviously concerned.

"Do you realize weakness and fatigue are the number one complaints I hear before a heart attack?" He asks me.

The doctor asks me to call him every three hours that entire day. And I do. He asked me how I feel each time I call. He asks me if the pain goes away when I move or change positions. It isn't bad, just there, and no, it doesn't go away in different positions.

"I was afraid of that," he tells me. "I want you to come into the hospital right now."

"I want to go home. We fly home tomorrow."

He sighs. "You're a nice lady, and it's my job to get you home safely. But you belong in the hospital! Do you know what it would be like to have another heart attack on that plane? There's little or no medical help they can give you. And after they get far enough out, they won't turn around. You'd be stuck there in pain. Do you want to die like that on the airplane in front of your children?" Silence is on the end of the line.

"Please just come in. I can move my scheduled patients, and we'll have you in the cath lab first thing in the morning, so I can see what's going on."

"I'd want Dr. Jamisen to do that if it really has to be done again," my voice falls quieter. "And you don't have surgery backup if I needed it, do you?"

"No, but that's not a problem, we can have you on a plane to Oahu. Your lungs may be filling with fluid."

"I have a little cold..."

"That has nothing to do with it!" he interrupts, impatiently. "Your bypass graphs may be crimping. Or your aorta may be dissecting."

"Well if my aorta's dissecting," I say wearily, "I should be dead pretty quickly."

I can't get used to his shotgun style, his pelleting me with every possible worse-case scenario. I want to say, please listen, I understand that you know what can happen to me. I understand blood may not be flowing well through the bypass veins and they be narrowing, but can you keep it to yourself until you're reasonably convinced it's actually happening?

I liked it better when Dr. Davis and Dr. Jamisen kept me thinking I was doing okay. Because thinking I am doing okay, up the odds of me doing okay. Surely, I am in greater danger right after surgery, but they never felt the need to describe in detail all the possible ways I might die.

Listening to him, my nervousness grows. I suddenly doubt my ability to even make it home alive on that plane. My chest aches, and Will won't look at me.

"Please, just come in!" the doctor says. "You have three young children, I have a bad feeling about this. I have over thirty years' experience, and I've learned not to ignore it when something's telling me things are not right."

He has a bad feeling. Oh Lord. This I understand; I can't ignore feelings either. Why would he keep pushing this if he weren't seriously concerned?

Will and Mom look at each other; I see them shake their heads before they leave the room. They don't want me to go in again. They want me to fly home tomorrow. But I'm not sure I can make it now. And I don't want to die in front of everyone with that kind of pain. I don't want to die like that in front of my daughters.

"Just come in for some tests," the doctor pleads. "Let me do it right this time, so we can see what's wrong. Then if nothing's wrong, you can fly home safely the next day. And I'll know I've done my job. You're a nice lady," he repeats. "I don't want anything to happen to you."

"Okay," I agree finally. "I'll come in."

⊰❊⊱

Will drives me in again in silence. Finally, I turn to him, with a lump in my throat, a lump so large I can barely speak. He doesn't look at me while I talk. But he doesn't make fun of me either. When we were first together, he made fun of me if I ever cried, or even if my voice trembled even slightly. It is trembling now, yet he just listens while he drives to the hospital for the third time in ten days.

"I wish, just once, I could tell you how scared I am and it would be okay with you. I wish I could share it with you and think you'd love me just the same. I wish I could think you still loved me even though I'm not great at anything anymore." Tears well up so thickly I can't see, but I just keep talking, because I need to say this.

"William, I know a better person could will this all away. That they wouldn't keep doing this sick person stuff, and I know they wouldn't have created all this in the first place. But I'm not a better person, and I'm doing the very best I can. It's just that the …the very best I can do has never been so pathetic." A full minute of complete stillness follows.

"I know you're doing the best you can," he says at last. He keeps driving. "I'll get the flights rearranged so we can leave as soon as you're done at the hospital. We'll spend the night in San Francisco to break up the trip."

"Please just get me home."

"I'll get you home."

"Promise?"

"I'll get you home."

We didn't talk again, but I am thinking, I don't want to have more surgery. I don't want to fly to Oahu tomorrow and be carved up by strangers. I can't go through it. I cannot do this again. Please, please do not ask it of me.

William keeps the motor running in front of the emergency entrance. It takes a moment for me to realize that he isn't even walking in with me this time.

"Maybe we could get this down to a rolling stop," I tell him as I open the car door.

The dullness in my dropping voice is a heavy weight to hear. His seeming lack of emotion feels like a heavier weight.

"I'll talk to you tomorrow," he says, "after you get the test results."

I close the door and walk into the hospital. We don't wave or even say good-bye to each other.

And I remember right before I left the hotel room just a short time back, Mom bent over me in the wheelchair. "Do you want me to come in with you tonight?" she asked with tears in her eyes. "I can sit up with you, so you aren't alone in that place this time."

Mom hates "that place" too, but she was offering to come into it with me. She couldn't imagine what her offering meant to me.

I reached out and patted her shoulder. "No, Mom, it's okay. I can do it. Get your rest and just take care of the kids for me."

As I walk through the hospital doors, my stomach flips one more time and sweat runs trickling down my sides before I even make it to the elevator. I wish William had wanted to stay with me, so I had to work hard to convince him it wasn't necessary, and I could tell him I'd rather he stayed with the kids too. Convincing him didn't take much skill tonight. Well, I don't have much anymore.

The tests begin within the hour. The cardiologist stops by, peers at me oddly and turns to the person beside him. "Did you see that? Did you see the way her color shifted? I don't like her color." Then he asks me for Dr. Jamisen's office number again.

"I want to talk to him first thing in the morning," he says. "I'm extremely worried about you."

Thanks, that's comforting. Yet somehow thinking he might be able to get in contact with Dr. Jamisen helps. Somehow thinking Dr. Jamisen is involved even long-distance makes me feel in safer hands than being in this doctor's hands alone.

I've never met such a nervous man. He must be able get the job done in a crisis, but he does not inspire my confidence. The last time I saw him, right before I left the hospital, he was listening to my heart, when he gasped, "What's that?" and leaped back a full foot from me.

I turn to look at him thinking, well in layman's terms, I'd tell you my heart just skipped a beat, a very big beat, but I don't think that's what you medical guys call it when you're trying to sound technical. Come on. Steady yourself! Then I glanced at William and saw him staring at the doctor with disgust and disbelief.

The first test came back indicating my blood sugars were way off again. They switched the IV drip for one that has a 5% glucose solution, and almost miraculously, after twenty minutes, the weakness I'd been struggling with for nearly five days vanished. I tell everyone who comes in that I suddenly feel better. But no one acts the least bit interested. I now realize how important this IV drip is for my trip home...

After the MRI is completed, I get wheeled back to my room. A nurse appears to tell me the doctor has ordered a sleeping pill and a tranquilizer. I pass on both.

"Really?" she says in a surprised tone. "The doctor wants you to take them." "Really," I answer.

Perhaps the doctor should take a tranquilizer or two himself. I'll struggle with my emotions until I figure out how to get them right. I don't want drugs making me think I've got it right before I do. My body feels stronger, and I'm not making a scene here or doing anything negative you people need to concern yourselves with. I know I won't be sleeping tonight but leave me alone.

The next day is filled with tests and waiting for results. My lungs aren't flooding with fluid, so my heart must be pumping sufficiently. They're clear, the doctor tells me. I only wish I didn't hear regret in his voice as he bring me this information. But I hear it.

I am just about to start the treadmill test again. A young female intern, who is visiting, is making the rounds with the doctor. She seems quite impressed with all he is handling this busy day and appropriately voices her esteem.

"You just learn to do it," he tells her calmly. I nearly gag. They start discussing my case as if I'm not there. As if I am a specimen already bottled.

I catch the cardiologist's attention. "I'm not sure if I told you, but I've always had an usually strong aversion to heat and humidity. Maybe that partially caused the weakness, and then my potassium levels and my blood sugars were way off and...."

"This is not about the humidity," he snaps disdainfully. "You should be feeling better at sea level. This is your heart!"

He appears to have a great deal invested in all this being my heart. I am trying hard hanging on to thinking that it isn't.

The doctors wander away to more pertinent discussions. Hours pass laboriously, and I have to convince myself to take the thallium test. The doctor insists it must be done. I know it probably never bothered anyone else, but when they bring something radioactive, the technician wears a lead coat, the needle sits tucked away in a protective case, and they inject what they don't want any contact with right into your veins, I am left wondering how beneficial it is for you. The technician empties the syringe. I keep myself calm. I keep trying not to think about the years I just wasted carefully eating only organic food.

I'm wheeled back again to wait for the results. I wait for hours, knowing the thallium test is the most important because it will show if my bypass graphs are compressing or if blood isn't flowing through them properly to supply enough blood for my heart. When my own arteries dissected and failed, these three bypass vessels taken from my legs became my heart's lifeline.

I've never been more jittery in my life, but I'm holding a false face of calm, trying not to think about the only thing I can think about. If they were crimping, the cardiologist told me a little while ago, you'll need surgery. You won't be flying home. I feel desperate to get home. And I'm scared having so much riding on the outcome of this test. I feel far safer waiting when I can handle outcomes either way they come out.

An unexpected call from Dr. Jamisen comes through to my room. We talk a couple minutes. His voice sounds calm and steady and friendly the way it always is. He tells me he has talked to the cardiologist and after talking to him, he has confidence in him and I should do what he recommends.

I sit very quietly a moment thinking that these two doctors have absolutely nothing in common except a medical degree. And just because he conned Dr. Jamisen with all the appropriate terminology on the phone, I really don't think Dr. Jamisen would have so much confidence in him if he heard what he has been telling me. Dr. Jamisen would never have tried so desperately hard, in so many ways to shake me up.

Trust is not an easy thing for me to give, and now he is handing it over to a perfect stranger without a second thought. But I guess I'm the stranger here. I'm the patient, the odd man out.

"I don't think it's the graphs," Dr. Jamisen continues.

His comment stands as the first positive thing I've heard in ten days, and I weld to it instantly. If Dr. Jamisen doesn't think it is the graphs, then I can start to believe it might not be. Thank you. Thank you for being my doctor instead of him. Because I'd be dead now if he was, for I'd have given up trying long ago.

"But if the test results come back bad," I say, "if he thinks I need surgery, can I call you and talk about it?" I'm thinking only that I should know the results almost any time now.

There is a sudden pause on the phone. Dr. Jamisen is articulate, and there are usually no uncomfortable breaks in his communication. He's normally smooth on the phone, like William can be smooth. But seconds keep ticking, and I feel him thinking. It grabs me, and it is like I am in his head suddenly. Just as suddenly I realize I've done it again, made the exact same faux paux that slaughtered me the first time. I've forgotten the time change, and he must be getting ready to go home. And now, right now he's thinking I'm asking permission to call him at home when he's off duty.

No! I want to shout. I would never do that again. I thought you'd be in your office for hours still, because it's still early here. I want to drop the phone before I have to hear what is coming out of his mouth. I can feel it before he says the words. It is charring me already.

"I'm on duty Thursday, Friday, and Saturday," he says very politely. "And you can call me, anytime, day or night then. Just call the office and they'll get in touch with me."

I thank him softly for calling before we hang up. It is Tuesday, September 2nd. And it's okay with Dr. Jamisen if I call him at the office on Thursday, Friday, or Saturday. Day or even night. That will help a lot making the decision I might soon have to be making, but I guess it doesn't really matter to him if it helps or not. Dr. Jamisen is just covering himself as tactfully as he can with me stepping so far out of bounds again. I'm naked once again.

I would have helped you anytime, I think again, starting to crumble. If you ever needed my help, I wouldn't have told you the days I was available. But I've made that same mistake before, thinking people are my friends when they are not.

I push the phone and the table far away from me, as some hard shell tightens over me and over my heart. I won't call you. I will never ever call you again. Because I don't trust you either, not anymore.

I cringe and sink into the bed. What is wrong with me? Why do I set myself up to be crushed like this? Why do men work so hard to get you to trust them and when you do, it means nothing to them? *You* mean nothing to them. And I moan involuntarily from a deep wound.

"William, can you help me?" I call without thinking.

"It depends what it is."

Dr. Jamisen, can you help me?

It depends what day it is. It depends what time it is. No, I will not help you. Not if I am not on duty. Not if I'm not being paid to help you.

I hurt so much I want to run screaming from the room, but I sit very quietly wishing the way I care about people would be more lightweight. Like their caring is toward me. Because then I'd have fit better into this life. I wish I hadn't hung up the phone so soon. If I were still talking to Dr. Jamisen, I would tell him if I were dying of a heart attack on the same street he was walking on, I wouldn't call out his name, or make the mistake of thinking he cared. I'd bite my tongue off before I ever asked him to help me again.

I sit up stiff like solid ice, feeling frozen deep inside me. The test results hardly matter anymore. I've made my decision. I'll have William take me home either way. I'm not having any more surgery. I am done.

Very late that afternoon the cardiologist pulls up a chair close to my bedside. I can hardly breathe as he begins talking.

The graphs are fine. The aorta is fine. My lungs are clear.

"You can go home tomorrow," he tells me.

So, all this has been a waste. A very costly waste. And I am completely wasted.

"Did Dr. Jamisen ever call you?" he asks.

"Yes."

"What did he tell you?"

I look at him carefully. Do you think I feel like giving you that satisfaction? Well, I don't and so I'm not telling you that you spoon-fed him well, and that he swallowed it, because swallowing it was the easiest thing for him to do long distance. I am not going to tell you that I'm supposed to be good and listen to whatever you suggest. What did he tell me?

"Not too much," I answer.

"Has anyone told you about your heart damage?"

"No," I hesitate a moment before continuing. "My mom told me they said my heart looked stunned during surgery. But she said they thought it would be fine."

"Well, it's far more than stunned," he says quickly. "Fifty to sixty percent of your heart muscle is damaged, in the most critical area. It's very unlikely to regenerate at this point, and if you ever have another heart attack, you'll either be dead or a cardiac cripple." He pauses. "You have to realize your life can never be the same."

I have heard this one before, from a nurse. Yes, I have heard it. And in that instant, I keep thinking of Dr. Jamisen, I am only thinking of him not wanting to talk to me for a second time.

I keep thinking about this man sitting in front of me, and of all that he's eagerly told me the past ten days, and his pleasure in telling me. I have slept precious little the past week and a half, and I've waited on pins all day for this test result, exhausting myself further by trying to pretend I'm not nervous at all. Praying I'll be flying home tomorrow. And now you are telling me that my heart is never going to be okay, not ever again, because fifty to sixty percent of it is completely gone.

Everything falls in on me in a way it never has before. I drop my face into my hands, and I cover it tightly, sobbing in utter desperation. I have never cried like this in front of anyone. Not in front of Jan or Sara or any member of my family.

Only once, like this in front of William for about ten seconds, the ten seconds, just after I got the call that my daddy died a few minutes after I left the hospital.

I wailed then, an inhumane keening wail I hadn't thought myself capable of, but it sprang from me and William moved to my side as I collapsed over the kitchen countertop and sobbed hysterically.

"I wasn't there," I cried over and over. "He never let me down once, and I wasn't even there when he needed me."

I pounded my opened palm over and over into the hard counter.

"I just wanted to be there with him. I wanted to be there."

And after that first huge wave passed, I sobbed in its eddy just like I'm doing now, and then a couple seconds later, there was a voice telling me that I needed to pull it together, that my Mom needed me, that I'd promised Dad to take good care of her, and I pulled it together instantly. I raised myself up from the white counter and I drove dry eyed to the hospital to my mom, and I made phone calls all the way there, notifying family and close friends who needed to know. And I was there and strong for Mom, arranging the funeral and all that needed to be done.

But I am broken now. Broken in front of a stranger who tried hard to break me whether he knows it or not. Like a missionary, trying to break my heathen spirit, and thinking all the while of his good intentions. I am broken, I tell myself as if from a distance, I am finally irretrievably broken, and I will not ever be coming back.

From a long way off, the doctor begins talking to me. And I can hear only from a very long way off. He is suddenly a man with a weak woman in front of him. A weak woman in tears and he is back peddling rapidly, the way men do when a woman cries unexpectedly in front of them.

"You haven't faced it until now, have you?" He says. "Well, it's good to face it," he adds softly. He starts telling me things I can only partially absorb. He talks about support groups to help me emotionally. He talks about the possibility that if I work hard during the next year, I have a chance to live a near normal life.

I never wanted to be normal, let alone near normal. Normal is four hours a day in front of the television. No, I just want to be me. I am no longer crying because there is nothing, absolutely nothing in the hole left inside me anymore. I take my hands away and look up into his face.

I can see on some level he feels badly now. He didn't mean to lose such a large dam. It splashed on him a little more than he anticipated.

"But I gave you hope, didn't I?" he asks.

I sit dumbstruck. And then I nod because I can see he thinks it is somehow important that I have hope. I can see too that it is even more important that he thought he gives it to me.

But hope is what I've had with me all my life. Hope is what I came to this island with, and it does not feel like hope is what I'll be taking home with me in my suitcase. It does not feel like hope will ever travel with me again.

But I nod. I don't care anymore. Let him think he gave me hope if it makes him happy. Someone should be happy. I don't care about trying to communicate honestly with anyone ever again. I don't care.

"I want you to do something for me," he says quietly. "You're a very nice lady. I want you to drop me a card when you get home, so I know that you're okay. Then I want another one in two weeks, and another one in two months. Would you promise to do that for me? Three cards."

He actually wants me to respond, so I nod again. But I know that I won't be able to write him one note. I know that I will break a promise for the first time in my life. Even that which I hold most dear feels worthless now.

Get me home, Will. Just get me home, so I can die at home because I will never, ever heal with over half of my heart destroyed. I will never heal. Any chance for a real life is over. They should have let me die, I thought again. It is no kindness leaving me a cardiac cripple. I need to be outside. I need to ski and swim and take long walks in the foothills I love. I would rather die than become who I've become, but then, no one asked me.

I guess it made them all feel a little better that I didn't die right on the table that day. But they are on to other cases now. I am stuck with mine. And I can never forgive myself for breaking down in front of this man who tried so hard to break me. That I did tells me how very far from home I'm floating now. The tether snapped clean through, and so have I.

2 Maccabees 8-18

They trust in weapons and acts of daring
    but we must trust in almighty God,
    who can by a mere nod destroy
    not only those who attack us but the whole world.

2 Maccabees 8:23

After reading to them from the holy book
    and giving them the watchword, "The Help of God,"
    he himself took charge of the first division
    and joined in battle with Nicanor.

Chapter Thirteen

The day arrives hot and exceptionally bright. We walk toward the airplane at noon. I step inside knowing the doors will close in a few minutes. We'll be over the Pacific soon, and there will be little anyone can do to help me if I have another problem. The picture the cardiologist sketched so clearly for me plays out in my mind. I keep walking back, going down the aisle with William and the girls, going all the way back to where we'll be seated together in the tail section. Mom isn't with us on this full flight. She flew home the day before.

They pack us in tightly and pack in carry-ons even tighter. The big, metal doors swing shut. They lock. And then we sit. For twenty minutes or more we sit with the sun baking the plane and cooking us inside it. The ventilation is not on, and the flight attendant talks over the intercom apologizing profusely for the long, overlong, delay and the terrible temperature.

We sit. Sweat rolls past a man's temple. I scan flushed faces all around growing redder from the heat and growing impatience. William leans forward from behind me, peering around the side of my seat cushion.

"Are you okay?" he asks.

I smile as I nod quickly because I hear his concern, and I've already given him enough to worry about; there is no need to add to it.

Will stands and starts fanning me with a magazine. And when he stops fanning, he reaches down to rub my neck and my shoulders. Five minutes later, when he finishes the massage, he hands me a quart of water he's brought for me. He keeps fanning while I drink it.

I notice a woman a few seats over, intently watching my husband as he does all these things for me. Her eyes develop a wistful look that soon shifts to exasperation, yet she keeps staring until finally she turns away with a frown. But I can't stop studying her and the hard, deep lines on her face that appear to deepen as she flips pages, snapping them fast and erratically in the magazine she is not reading.

I am sorry for the sadness you must have known. But each of us know sadness and disappointment, so please don't begrudge my husband's kindness. I still cling to believing there's more than enough love in this world to go around, and surely, me receiving some does not mean less lies available for you.

I look away as we broil inside the airplane. I reach back to hold Will's damp hand that still rests upon my shoulder, knowing that I could easily begin dwelling again on the things the doctor planted in my mind. I could panic enough to have another heart attack in this stifling heat, right here, right now. I squeeze Will's hand as another choice shows itself to me, brightened by his love and concern. I begin focusing my remaining memory of will on it for him and for my little girls.

Will leans around the side again, to look into my eyes. I hold them smooth and steady. "I'm okay," I whisper. "It's okay." I won't let you down, here. I know it's entirely possible for me to create another heart attack. I feel that potential with unwavering certainty. Suddenly I wonder if such a thing is possible, and I know it is, then why can't I harness the same force to create perfect health? Surely that must be equally possible too.

William caresses my shoulder as the flight attendant informs us we've been given the go-ahead. And I soon lose the insight about health with the sound of cheers and sighs of relief from the sweltering passengers. All thoughts about creating health float away as I think they'll have to get the air on quickly before someone collapses inside this tin can. But it is not going to be me. God willing. Not this time. Not in front of my kids or my husband.

You can do this, I urge myself. Just concentrate on staying alive for the next six hours and don't think about any of the rest that might follow. Do it. Stay firmly planted in the present.

I let go of fear. I trust in God.

And then I realize with a sense of disappointment that I did not remember this mantra once when it could have served me. All that time I'd spent in the hospital, it was lost to me when I was completely lost. And I had told myself over a month earlier, if I got tired of working on it before the work was done, then fear wins and I lose. And I have never once been keen on losing. So, I will just need to keep working.

"Keep listening for the pipes," I whisper, while cooling air rushes over me from overhead vents. Don't quit when it's black outside and just as bleak in. Let go of fear. Over and over again.

Sometime during that flight, I notice the plane has passed the point of no return. I can't reach out for help behind me. I remind myself to release the anxiety that thought stimulates, and I lean deeper into the seat cushion supporting me. Go ahead. Surrender. Breathe. There will be no turning back on this journey. The tether snaps, indeed it does, yet you fly home.

We arrive in San Francisco, to milder, dryer air, and some oppressive weight shifts from my body. I feel better instantly just breathing in this air, breathing deep air that hints of the Rockies lying not far away.

Smiling I tell William that I don't need the wheelchair that he's arranged for me. He stares at me. "You'll sit in it," he informs me as we de board. "And you won't argue with me."

Fine, I think. I'll sit. If it's that important to you, I can sit. An attendant pushes my wheelchair out to the shuttle that takes us to the hotel nearby. Will rolls me upstairs into the room.

"May I get out now, if it pleases Your Majesty?"

He laughs and orders dinner from room service while I crawl into bed and ease off my shoes. Their imprints show deep groves in my swollen feet. I cover them quickly, so William doesn't notice the swelling. I don't want worry to fade his smile tonight.

The kids crowd in all around us. After dinner is delivered, we eat snuggling together on the bed and we even turn on the TV, a rare treat for them.

The next day, I don't need the wheelchair when we arrive in Boulder. William doesn't argue with me this time. As the Flatirons come into view, I know my family has been spared watching me die on this trip.

Thank you, Lord, for granting that. I don't need to be putting in any more requests. I'll never leave Boulder again. Me, the world traveler who flew to Europe for the fifth time on my twenty-first birthday with tickets paid for by cleaning houses and waiting tables. Traveling was once worth working hard, long hours. But I guess I've traveled far enough because traveling farther feels impossible. Our home behind the Flatirons pulls like a massive magnet.

Inside our house, my wiggling Rottweiler, Tess, nuzzles me. Salutations arrive from my aloof, non-wiggling cats. I take a quick head count of all the pets. Sara has obviously taken good care of everyone. I have to grin. "I made it home," I whisper. One of my tortoiseshell females, Gwen, jumps up on my chair and rubs her side against me.

"Yes, I can see that you did. I've been expecting you," she whispers back.

"Upstairs," William says pointing, "just go up and rest. I'll take care of the kids and all the unpacking." Dutifully I walk to my bedroom. But I can't rest. I have made it back to this land I love. My kids begin laughing downstairs as they chase each other through the house. Hearing them I tell myself that they can still be just children for another day. I spared them tears and loss on the trip home. I accomplished what I had focused on so hard, yet my body feels too frail to accomplish anything more. My mind wanders too splintered to imagine more. Now what? I flounder adrift.

Unexpectedly I start thinking of Dr. Jamisen and how I must have annoyed him thoroughly with my neediness. I didn't use to be a worm people needed to step over to avoid getting goop on the soles of their shoes. Yet I couldn't blame him for stepping over me. I'm sure his life overflows with sick and needy people. Even though I can't ever go in for another appointment at his office, I might at least apologize for intruding on his free time, and I could certainly assure him that it wouldn't ever happen again.

So, I reach for a piece of plain paper as I sit on the bed; I begin writing out how sorry I am that I have disturbed him and that I hadn't ever meant to disrupt his sleep or his private time...I know I'll never send this note. I know I'm writing to try to reach some understanding that I do not have. So, I keep writing, and the tears start coming. Understanding does not. I tell him the other doctor says fifty to sixty percent of my heart is gone. I do not write that I've lost my motivation for living. I put the pen and paper by the side of my bed, and I watch the pen slowly roll off the table and fall to the floor. And I lie down.

But I can't rest. There is a voice inside my head saying, Send it. Send the note.

No, I'm not sending it. He'll know I'm nuts, and he must be leaning far in that direction anyway. I'm not sending it. It's fine to write it, to get it out of my system, but I'm still lucid enough not to send this type of thing. You wait at least a couple days, and then if you're still possessed, you read it again and see, that, yes indeed, you were a little maudlin and a lot melodramatic and naturally you don't send it. Which was the right thing to do all along. Because you wrote it knowing full well that you'd never have such a sorry lack of brains to send it.

Send it now. Before you even read it again.

I am not sending it! Don't ask me to do that. I've been stripped bare lying under bright lights on an operating table in front of him and Dr. Davis. I don't need to fillet myself too.

You promised you'd never vaporize your voice again. You promised you wouldn't hide what you're feeling just because it's easier to hide, safer to hide and not risk people's disappointment. You claim that you are honest.

I cannot rest. Begrudgingly I go downstairs. I put the letter into an envelope, and I look up the address, write it down and stamp the letter. And then William says he needs to go back into town and stop by the office.

"Mail this for me, would you? Mail it right away."

"Sure."

❧❦

Knowing I actually mailed the letter eats at me. Just like not mailing it would have. I grow consistently quieter as the afternoon and evening wears on. Knowing something has happened to my mind, and I can't even begin to feel what is right to do anymore.

I thought I'd found bottom in the cataclysm of Hawaii. Yet I keep plummeting lower, knowing now I merely paused a moment in my dramatic, endless descent. I was lingering at the way station of self-loathing. Waiting for the final impact of the disintegrating crash I had already felt. And I can't conceive trying to rebuild. You need strength and you need vision for rebuilding. But what does any of it matter? Rebuilding isn't possible without a heart.

Hours later, after the kids are securely tucked into bed and William is catching up on work in his office, I go back into my bedroom and walk over to the windows on the north side. I open them both wide, and I open the roll screen clear to the top and then I sink down onto the carpet that used to be so creamy white. Pulling my legs in close, a moment later, because I don't want them close to touching that invisible spot on this floor where I collapsed in such god-awful pain. That spot and everything connected to it still feels clearly visible to me.

I take a breath of cool mountain air. I made it home, I kept telling myself. I didn't want to die so far from home. Tears keep coming as I stare at the Big Dipper and Cassiopeia. I have always loved the stars so much, yet I know I won't be watching them much longer. But watch them now, I tell myself gently, and appreciate the simple, magnificent sight of them. Be thankful that you made it home. Your kids smile in sleep... I am thankful. I truly am. That is all I wanted.

William steps softly into the darkened room. He sits quietly behind me. I know he must be way past ready to have me in a body bag, a bag all zipped up so he doesn't have to see my eyes go wide again, or suffer any more late night frantic trips to emergency rooms. He could start over with someone new and healthy. I want that for him. All of their lives would soon be better off without me. And when he started over, he'd always be a great dad. Mom was right on that.

I'm ready to let go. They don't need me. And what they do need their daddy can give them far better than I can. I don't have anything left inside to give.

Will stretches out, and I realize he's watching me, just like he was watching me that day I told him I wanted to start dating. And I feel suddenly like I could talk to him like an old friend, just like I did on that other day that seemed so very long ago.

"Thanks for helping me," I begin slowly without once looking at him. "Thanks for helping and never once needing to tell me how stupid I was to think I could make that trip. I don't know what would have happened to me without you."

"I wanted to do it," he says quietly. "I wanted to be there in case you needed me."

We sit silently for several minutes until I swallow again. I look at Draco in the sky, following the dragon's winding tail with my eyes. "William, I have to tell you something."

He waits, letting me compose myself somewhat in the darkness.

"In the hospital in Hawaii that last night, right before the doctor let me out ... when he came to talk with me, to tell me about the heart damage ... I ... I cried in front of him." I instantly wipe away tears again at the thought of it.

"You were tired," Will says quickly.

"No, I mean I really cried. I cried like some baby."

"Anyone would have been tired. And he was horrible. I told you that from the beginning."

"And I never told you that I tried to call Dr. Jamisen that first night in the hospital. After the other doctor wouldn't help get my records. You know Dr. Jamisen was always so nice to me, I thought he'd want to know I was having a problem, and then I asked his answering service to ask him if he'd talk to me just for a minute ... but he ... he didn't want to talk to me." I don't bother to wipe my face.

"Anyone would want to talk to their doctor."

"Do you think they would, really? I mean do you really think so?"

"Yes," he says emphatically.

I slowly turn from the window, and I see him now in the darkness. "Will... I know you'll be good to the kids and that you'll be fine too. I don't want a slim chance to be near normal, I want to be me, and I'd rather just go if I can't be me. I'm not afraid to die, and I know you'll be good to the kids and that you'll be fine too."

There is a long pause. I hear him exhale in the silence.

"Let me call Jamisen."

"No. I can't see him again. He just wanted me to do what the other doctor told me to do. He doesn't understand. And he doesn't really care anything about me."

"Then let me call Davis. You always liked Davis."

"No, please don't call. He's a surgeon. I don't need surgery and even if I do, I'm not having it. I'll handle it on my own."

Abruptly I get up and walk to the bed. Will follows.

"Thanks for listening," I say softly as I slip beneath the covers. William gets in on his side.

There is another pause. And then there is something I have to ask. And I have no idea why I even think of it.

"Why did you take the phone off the hook, that first night in the hotel when I was in intensive care?

"What are you talking about?"

"I tried to call because I was losing it, and when I called, they said it was off the hook."

"I didn't take it off the hook. It got bumped by a bag I put down, and I was so tired I never even noticed till I woke up the next morning. Then I called you right away to make sure you were okay."

"But it was almost eleven by then. I wasn't okay."

"You didn't tell me that. But I called as soon as I woke up," he repeats. "I'd never intentionally take it off the hook with you in the hospital. Why would you think I would?"

I have no answers. And I try to sleep, but I can't breathe well. I feel like I'm not getting any air, that I am slowly suffocating. Then I sit up and find I am a little more comfortable sitting, propped up on a bank of pillows. I doze on and off that way until morning. Thinking on and off that I was starting to heal the last time I slept in this bed. I was trying to heal the last time I slept in this bed. And now I'm not.

⚜

In the early morning, I open my eyes and see William sitting close to me, staring anxiously at me.

"Let me call Jamisen," he says again as if there haven't been hours between our conversations. "You always felt better when you talked with him."

I shake my head and move away a little.

"There might be something he could give you," William says, "something that would help. There might be some window where you could take something to help your heart muscle rejuvenate."

"There isn't any magic pill, or he'd have given it to me. I think he knew all along. He isn't dumb. He saw my heart, and there must be signs they notice when they're in there that indicate it's pretty well damaged."

"Maybe they thought it might come back."

"Maybe. And maybe they knew they couldn't tell me yet because I couldn't handle it. And they were right. I wouldn't have tried so hard if I thought I couldn't come back all the way. And they sure made a point of trying to convince me I could."

"But there could be something that would help. At least find out. I want to call his office and set up an appointment. I want to find out. Please see him for me. Will you do this for me?"

The seconds tick. William has never been so near begging. I am not looking at him. I do not want to look; yet I feel him pulling me toward him with that indomitable determination. William reaches out his hand and waits for me to take it. He waits for me to shake to seal the deal.

"Ok," I agree as strong fingers close around mine. "I'll do it for you."

I take a walk in the meadow that day. Twenty minutes and I feel a little stronger. The wheelchair is feeling farther away. And the following day, I take another, longer walk.

But that night, after I'm in bed I feel a sudden sharp pain in my heart. The same type of pain I had before surgery. As it twists me into the sheets, I remember once during a post-op visit when Dr. Davis asked me about the chest discomfort I felt, asking if the character of the pain was similar to what brought me in originally to see him. It wasn't then, but it sure is now. And I know immediately if this pain continues, it will kill me or have me in surgery again. And I cannot do surgery again.

But my mantra comes to me, and somehow, magically, I relax to it, I completely surrender to trust. I open to the pain, too, and just as miraculously, it vanishes within six or seven seconds. I feel the power of opening my heart, the way it instantly disperses pain, yet before I can fully gather the gift of this treasure, another sensation of suffocation rolls over me, and I am depleted again. Falling far back on defense again. But for the first time in my life I feel the power of surrender in my heart, opening to its presence and purpose. I have felt a high level of pain fully blurring in natural childbirth and learned to encompass it. You need to open to the pain before it can pass.

I lie awake for another hour, trying to relax, trying to breathe and practice willing away fear. I know a carb drink will help my energy level, but I can't manage walking downstairs to get it.

"William," I say softly, touching his arm.

He wakes with a start. "Is something wrong?"

"I need a drink. I'm weak and I can't breathe."

He turns on the light.

"I'm sorry," I apologize immediately. "I hate to wake you."

"It's okay," he assures me. "I'll be right back. Do you need anything to eat too?" A little brown rice, maybe? Oatmeal?"

"No, I don't think I could get it down. Just the drink."

William returns from the kitchen about five minutes later, and he sits up with me while I sip the liquid. Thirty minutes later, the weakness abates, and I know I can sleep.

"Will you hold me?" I ask. "Just for a couple minutes?" I add quickly as I slip down a little farther on the pillows. "I was a little scared."

"Sure, I'll hold you." His arm moves around me gingerly. He is always careful now not to hurt me. Yet even the slightest weight of his arm across the incision site or the numb area where they took the mammary artery would be too uncomfortable. He positions his arm with precision as if he knows I might break too easily now. William seems to understand clearly that I might shatter if I'm not handled delicately.

⁓⧽⧼⁓

Waking the next morning, my first half-conscious thought is remembering the searing pain of the night before. I have forgotten how trust could eliminate pain: I've forgotten the brief glimpse of that treasure, because I was orienting myself with the outlines of my new reality. I remember the heart attacks and the surgery... I am a sick person now. I take a breath and my chest aches, like a bad bruise touched too hard and too often.

Slowly I open my eyes. I open my eyes on the life that is now mine and on another day. In weak light, I admit to myself again that since over half of my heart is gone and since I am having horrific pains again, there is probably a very good chance I'm not going to make it much longer.

Beth Kelly had told me before I left Boulder Hospital after the surgery I wouldn't have any pain as soon as the sternum healed. But I am having them. So, I make a decision right then. Without even talking to William, yet I am completely confident he'll see the wisdom of it, just as soon as he wakes up. Then I'll have to tell my twins, and Meagan will cry for sure.

Seeing her tears and knowing I've let her down again will hurt me too. It will hurt, but I love them all so dearly that I have to start making other arrangements for them. Other arrangements in place which might help to mean losing me will be a bad earthquake instead of a nuclear blast. It's sure hard recovering from a nuclear blast. And I want my girls to be survivors, even if I'm not.

❧

As Meagan crawls up onto my king-sized bed, I silently say a prayer that I'll somehow find a way to tell her without traumatizing her.

"Meagie, there's something we need to talk about."

"Yes, Mom."

"Your dad and I have decided it would be best for you to go to school this year instead of doing school at home."

Her eyes pools instantly and color to a bright, unusually bright, husky blue. Huge tears cascade down her cheeks. "Oh no, Mom."

I open up my arms, and she climbs into them sobbing as if I have broken her heart. And I have, for I had promised her after a disastrous year in preschool, when one boy exposed himself repeatedly and other boys kept tackling her on the playground, and my happy, healthy daughter developed hives and stomach aches every morning, I promised her that we could learn well at home at least through elementary school, and we'd have fun learning without all that kind of nonsense.

We had a wonderful time last year. Both girls had progressed far ahead of their grade level even though I hadn't done anything with them since I got sick over two months ago. Meagan's hives and stomach aches long ago left; her smile long ago returned.

I love teaching. I'd gotten a teaching degree when I first graduated from college and had planned to make it a career before I got so involved in business. And now I am violating a promise to one of my daughters and telling her she has to go to school.

I ache deeply listening to her sobs. Soon I am crying right along with her. She pulls back in surprise and looked at me.

"I'm so sorry, honey," I say, alternately wiping my face and hers. "You know how much I wanted to teach you, but I can't sweetheart. I just can't with my heart problem."

"Oh, Mom, why not? I'll try really hard, I'll listen." She sniffles.

"It's not you, honey. You always listen. It's me. I can't be sure I can do three hours a day consistently. And then there's time needed for planning and buying books and supplies. And I just can't do it anymore. I'll make you get behind, and I'd never want that. Education is too important."

"Oh, Mom, please, I don't want to go."

"I know you don't. And I wish you didn't have to, but you do. There's no other way. Everyone has challenges to deal with, and this is one for you, but I know you can do it. Dad called this morning and they have two openings in the first grade at Divine Mercy in Boulder which is very unusual because it's such a good school and there is normally a long waiting list. We told them you'd start right away."

She leans into me sobbing again, inconsolable for another minute, and then she says in a desolate voice, "Can Brenna and I be together?"

"Of course you can. And we'll pick you up each afternoon about 2:30, and then we'll have the rest of the day together."

She stops crying. "But can you teach me again when you feel fine?' I pat her back a couple times.

"Let's see. But for this year for sure, you'll go to school. You're a very smart girl. You're strong and you're great at sports already. This is a good school and the people teaching there believe in the importance of learning and in good behavior. It's not poorly supervised like the last time. No one will be sitting around undressing or asking you to take off your clothes, trust me. And if they did, they'd be in big trouble."

"Are you sure."

"I'm sure. And you'll do great there."

"But the other people aren't always nice the way you are." Her eyes are still full of tears.

"I know you can do it. On the first day, just remember that everyone gets a little nervous meeting new people, and they are scared too, just like you are. All you have to do is pay attention to the teacher, do your schoolwork, and be friendly with the kids. In a couple days you'll see its okay."

She stops crying.

"You can do this Meagie, I know you better than anyone knows you, and I have total confidence in you."

Right after she leaves, Brenna comes into my room, wide-eyed with curiosity. But I know this will be easier, because Brenna has always been more outgoing and negotiates new situations with more ease than her twin does.

"Mom, why's Meagan so upset?" She asks a bit nervously.

"Because I explained to her that I can't teach you at home because of the heart problem, and you both need to start school in town."

Her apprehensive eyes mix with excitement, brightening despite the tugging of loyalty to her sister. "It's a good school," I continue enthusiastically. "And they'll have sports like basketball and soccer. You'll both do well there."

"How far away is it?"

"Just at the bottom of the hill."

"Will they have a playground?"

"A nice one."

"What did Meagan say?"

"She was upset at first, but now she's okay."

"And I'll have my own desk?"

"I think so."

She grins. "Okay, Mom, can I go now?"

I nod. "And you'll watch out for Meagie for a little while until she gets going? Sit next to her at lunch and don't let any boys be mean to her on the playground."

"How can I do that, Mom?"

"Well, just stick together. And if any boys get rough, if they push her down, you help Meagan and you do whatever you have to do to get them off her and you let them know they don't mess with either of you because you're a team. Besides boys won't keep doing that rough stuff much longer. Pretty soon, they'll get a whole lot nicer. I promise."

My firstborn nods. "Okay, Mom, got it."

Proverbs 3:5-6

Trust in the Lord with all your heart,
    On your own intelligence rely not;
In all your ways be mindful of him,
    And he will make straight your paths.

Chapter Fourteen

(M)y physical fatigue lingers. Late afternoon Sara and her husband Tim drop by to visit, so I force myself out of bed. Tim brings me one of his college textbooks, because Sara mentioned to him that I want to understand more about the body and how the heart works. He hands me a huge, meaty volume, three inches thick with small print. This would certainly satisfy even my curiosity.

Everyone meanders out onto the porch to talk and watch the kids play, yet I stay in the kitchen a few minutes with the book, because I've just opened it, rather it opened itself to a section on the circulatory system and the heart.

My eyes scan the first paragraph they happen to land on, and that paragraph explains heart failure and the symptoms of it. Most of the symptoms described sound exactly like what I've been struggling with. My heart pumps faster as I read that the long-term prognosis is extremely poor. Heart failure predisposes the patient to a dramatically shortened life span...A shortened life span and a prolonged, lingering death... Progressive debilitation, repeated hospitalizations, constant drugs, oxygen tubes, and ultimately, the respirator...

William comes in for more water.

"Would you feel my left arm," I ask as casually as I can when he walks by. He reaches out to touch it. I know what he'll discover. I discovered it hours ago.

"Now feel my right one."

He does, and then Will looks at me steadily.

"The left is substantially colder isn't it?" I ask.

"Yes, it is." Then he fills up his water and walks out to rejoin our friends.

I make the mistake of reading more, yet I have to sit down as I keep reading, because I remember again the rasping, rhythmical sound the respirator makes. I choke, feeling restraints pinning down my arms and my legs. I lie with tubes and needles, helpless again. Trapped again. Then I close the pages slowly and carry the heavy medical book to the farthest corner of the room, yet the words hover with me. The tug of the whirlpool suddenly feels far stronger. Fear ties fast and hard into my area of dread where it could most find a vulnerable area. It has mysteriously doubled its power as if in response to my fledgling efforts to fly free of it. Tying onto my areas of dread where it can easily connect. It feels inescapable. My hand shakes with the fear that is promising to draw me under, but I reach for the phone.

Jan answers on the third ring.

"Jan, it's me. I know this is a major imposition, I know it's five-thirty and you're making dinner, but could you possibly come up and work with me. My arm feels like ice, and I need you."

"Of course," she says quickly. "Of course, I'll do that for you. I'll be right there." And I know "right there" will still take her thirty-five minutes to come across town and up the mountain.

I walk out to the patio to sit for a few minutes. I am able to join in the conversation often enough that I decide no one is noticing how scared and miserable I feel.

Jan rings the doorbell, and only then do I tell everyone that we will be working together.

William stares at me perplexed. "What about dinner?"

"I can't make it. I'm not doing very well."

Without hesitating a moment longer, Jan and I go upstairs to the massage table. I lie down on it, watching while Jan looks over my body.

"Do you want a pillow?" she asks unsmiling.

I nod. Jan gets one and props it behind me so I can sit up slightly and can breathe better.

"You're not in your body," she tells me.

"I guess being there hasn't felt great lately."

"Well, we need to get you back in. And we need to release some of this fear, right now. I can see it lodged here, here, and here," she says as she touched me. "It's completely blocking your energy, and it doesn't need to live here anymore."

Jan says a prayer for guidance and one in gratitude for the help that always surrounds us. For the light that always shines available to us.

She pulls up a chair and moves once more to my feet. Her face sets up hard like a serious mask. Her eyes tell me she is battling for me. Good. I need her fighting for me while I'm too weak to wage war by myself.

I need her now because I'm too close to crying. I close my eyes, trying to relax. I tell myself I am strong enough to make a call for help. Before the heart attack, despite physical appearances, I would not have been that strong.

Jan does not leave my feet until almost an hour has past, and when she does, they feel warm. My feet tingle with life again.

She sighs heavily. "There," she says satisfied at last. "We got you back in your feet." She begins working on the rest of my body while I consciously attempt to release negativity from every thought. Yet hordes of negative thoughts and a definitive negative prognosis assault me. Believing my wavering pep talk over that authoritative scientific book proves daunting. An echo forms within my mind, calling out incessantly. You must have heart failure...You must have heart failure...

"Jan" I say quietly, as she continues working. "I don't think I'm going to be able to do this." And I know she understands me completely.

"I'm right here with you, baby girl, you know that. You're doing fine. And I don't see you going anywhere."

I smile at her. "That's because you don't want me going anywhere," I tell her.

She laughs. "That's true, but you know I support you completely. And you do look pretty good to me right now. A little off in a few areas, but we're working on it."

I don't want to risk asking if she'd ever admit to me if she thought I still looked bad, so I relax again, surrendering at last. And I feel a lift from the cold, darkened heaviness fear has draped across my thoughts. Two and a half hours pass as I pray my mantra.

"That's enough this time," she tells me after saying a final prayer of blessing and protection. "Most people can't take that much, and we don't need an overload," she smiles. "I'm glad you called. If you need me, I'll be right over. I told Paul tonight, "Melissa needs me," And he said, 'then you go,' and I said, 'I'm already going.' I don't care if it's two in the morning."

We hug each other, and then I walk her downstairs where she gives hugs to the girls and calls out a good-bye to William.

I linger a little longer than necessary by the window watching her car driving away. I linger knowing William's not supportive about this type of thing. He likes Jan, but her work is just not the kind of thing anyone can lay out easily on a spreadsheet.

I stretch out my arms in front of him.

"Feel them," I say trying to respond to his unspoken disapproval.

He takes both arms in his hands.

"They're warm, aren't they? And they're the same temperature."

"Yes."

"I feel better."

"I'm glad you feel better."

"I want to keep working with Jan every week."

He frowns.

"Will, the body is energy. And Jan is able to see that energy. She can see where it isn't moving well anymore. What, you think she's lying?"

"No, I know Jan's not lying."

"You could try to keep an open mind. Just because you can't see the energy doesn't mean it isn't there or that Jan doesn't see it. Just think, if you tried to explain to a blind person who's been blind since birth all the beautiful colors you see when you look outside, he might think you had an overactive imagination too. But the colors would still be there."

"I don't like things sprung on me at the last minute," he says dryly. "Things like no dinner and I'm suddenly expected to make it. And I'm supposed to put the kids to bed. I have work to do, and it's piling up."

"Look, I needed to do something. And it really helped. I believe moving the energy better can facilitate healing, and I want to keep doing it. My health seems more important than dinner. And I didn't exactly know in advance that my left arm was going stone cold."

"We still need to eat."

I watch him turn from me, knowing we still have love between us but it is camouflaged in fear. And after the first flood of fear, an enemy is best dealt with in the light of day. I shine another light on a dark side of myself. Then I release one more layer of the fear still rooted deep within me.

I know I was being inconsiderate about dinner and the kids. I knew Will would be upset with me, yet I value myself enough to make that call for help. Dinner or not, I'd do it again.

William and the girls go out to do errands for a few hours and he promises them a stop by the playground before they come home. I wave to them cheerfully out of habit, yet as I move away from the window, a voice hints that I'm alone in the house. Totally alone for the first time since we returned from our trip. Hawaii.

I feel my vulnerability suddenly escalating again. Knowing I'm no more capable of fending for myself than I did the day my cat Tom pinned me to my chair right after I got home after surgery. I feel myself mentally slipping backward again. I pace, trying to stabilize by not thinking about all the things that could happen to me and succeeding only in imagining more of them. Discouraged with my roller coaster resolve, I walk to my desk to sit down weakly. I sit there head in my hands and then I close my eyes, to work once again with my mantra. I work to unharness the intricate, knotted lacings of the yoke of fear I know so effortlessly now.

Ten minutes later I can stand, so I load dishes into the dishwasher and clean up the kitchen, but I carry the phone with me everywhere I go, every step I take, knowing fifteen feet would be impossible to walk if something goes wrong with my heart. I hate this compulsive need to cling to the phone, yet I allow myself to hold it. I tell myself as long as I keep trying to move, clutching the phone to my breast may move along too. Some other day.

My arm doesn't turn to ice. I check it several times as I work. Minuet knots relax each time I do. I remind myself that Jan will be up again in a few days. That thought relaxes me further. I put music on, knowing singing even methodically may lift me enough that I can compete a few tasks. I want to contribute when I can. I feel the desire to contribute to feel less like an anchor hindering my family's forward progress in life.

When everyone returns, I hang up the phone. We sit down to the dinner I made, and for just a moment, in light of this ritual so steeped in my past and the countless nights I have sat here healthy and strong, I feel myself as I was such a short time ago. The strength of the past vibrates so strong and so real, I imagine I feel better. I can believe that I'm healthy, but when I breathe, tightness and aching pain fills my chest.

Words of the doctor in Hawaii fill my mind, telling me again that

I will never be the same. My mirage of health dissipates. I unfold my napkin neatly onto my lap, and I glace up to meet William's concerned eyes focusing on me. I smile briefly in response before turning toward Jacqueline. He wants me back the way I was too. He remembers the woman who once sat across this table from him. But I can't bring her back. She is gone from us both. I understand the sadness that fleets across his eyes. No one chooses the consolation prizes. I rarely provide much consolation.

I lead the family in the blessing, longing to linger within the brief gaps between breaths, between pain; any gap in my pain stimulates flickers of euphoria, yet they flicker out far too soon. Reality returns with every intake of air. I do understand.

This lesson within this pain lingers for my learning. It lies folded within an inlayed mahogany box, hidden from my view and my full comprehension. If someone offered me the key to unlock this mystery to healing, I would jump to grab it and claim it for mine. Yet you can claim only what you rightfully possess. I have not earned this key yet. Someday it will appear before me.

Book Two Preview
A Silent Voice Sings

Chapter One

Will and I climb the steps of Divine Mercy School to register Brenna and Meagan. To our surprise, we discover that one of the mothers who learned about my heart problem has purchased backpacks and stuffed them full of all the school supplies both girls need for first grade.

"She made me promise I wouldn't tell you who she is," the principal, Mrs. Hamilton, explains. "She said she just wanted to do something to help you."

That unknown angel couldn't know how much her thoughtfulness touches me, because the idea of going into a store and sorting through racks of lined paper and folders overwhelms me. Everything still overwhelms me because I travel with hidden companions at all times: Pain and incapacitating weakness reveal themselves at unexpected moments, and I can't take a step or even stand. These travelers rob me of confidence, yet I am able to rest this afternoon instead of shop. I can rest within the wings of unknown angels instead of worrying about being stranded between isles.

We wait in the principal's office while the staff eagerly gathers together enough uniforms so the girls can make it through their first week without us having to buy anything or do anything more. I sigh with relief.

As we drive away from the girls' new school, I look at William. "It'll be okay for them won't it?" I ask him. "With people that nice it will be okay."

He nods and smiles reassuringly. "They'll do fine. And the basketball program is great."

I laugh. "Well, let's hone right in on all the really important things. You want the girls to start playing this year? It seems a little early."

"The earlier the better or they'll never handle the ball the way kids do who grow up with it."

"They're very coordinated."

"I know they are. But if they want to be good, they need to start now."

"Maybe they won't want to be good at basketball."

"Maybe not," he says.

"And what's so important about basketball?"

"They need to start now because it will help them in any other sport they ever play."

"Well, they probably won't be pro ball players. And I did fine without it."

"Do you mind if I enjoy this?"

"No, of course I don't mind."

"What did I buy the day you told me you were pregnant?"

I laugh. "A basketball backboard. But I can't believe you'd even admit to that one, let alone mention it. Then you put it up six years too early, and even after you found out we were having girls."

He is looking at me.

"Okay, alright. I got it, but you'll have to help take them to practices and games I can't do all that extra driving yet.

"I already figured that out."

"But wasn't that nice of the lady to buy all those school supplies. I'm sure she's busy with things of her own. I don't know who she is, but I'll never forget it. It kinda brings back your faith in humanity doesn't it?'

"I go all tingly inside just thinking about it." He pretends to sniff. "I'm...I'm not even sure I can see well enough to drive."

"Well, you can't ever see to drive and that doesn't stop you, so just shut up and keep focused on the really critical, manly stuff, like basketball."

⁓∰⁓

I sit down that evening to skim a *Reader's Digest,* and my cat Gwen drapes herself across the back of my chair. She is always there whenever I sit down. I make myself sit there sometimes, just to take a moment to visit with her, but that evening I am reading quickly and not paying attention to her.

I find the main story, about a Frenchman in his early forties, who's been a successful publisher before suffering a massive stroke. He's written this book with the help of a friend who runs through the alphabet and notices when he lifts his eyebrow, because the man can't move any other part of his body. The words I read has been spelled out laboriously and mutely, letter by agonizing letter.

He lived "locked in" as it's called medically: a man left hopelessly trapped inside the tomb of a numb and useless body, yet he still thought clearly, too clearly; he felt all the amplified emotions deeply, far too deeply. Poignantly expressing his pain until I sensed every lonely minute stretching eternally while he waited for visitors or waited for someone to think to move his chair from the over bright sunlight. All the long while, the respirator gasped and breathed inside him.

I draw into his suffering and my own when two days on a respirator lasted two lifetimes. And the fear of being kept alive like the remains of this man wrenches my stomach. I could only have lifted my eyebrow to write, Tube out. Tube out ... please, please let me go!

He endured over a year in that condition, and I endure nearly an hour of reading before I walk into the bathroom to throw up into the toilet.

I catch sight of my chalky pale face in the mirror. This is stupid, I tell myself as I walk back to my chair and sit in it unsteadily. Gwen moves into my lap, and I pet her with a hand that still trembles slightly.

"Oh Gwen," I whisper.

"It's alright," she whispers. "You're doing fine."

But I know I should have put that magazine down as soon as I realized what was going on. I need to be careful about what I read and who I see and talk to. To make sure every moment feels as positive and uplifting as possible. Don't read this stuff again. Don't read the newspaper and learn about rapes, murder or child molestation either. Keep everything coming in as clean as possible because you've got way too much of your own garbage to sort through, you don't need to process fresh contributions from anyone else.

Will and I carry the video of the echocardiogram to the appointment with Dr. Jamisen. I hold the paperwork from the hospital in Hawaii for him to review as I am thinking, if I can survive the embarrassment of this meeting with him, it will be miraculous. I am thinking it is a good thing for William that he made me shake on this deal.

Dr. Jamisen comes into the room pleasantly; he reaches out his hand to me, and I shake it. He sits so we can talk a few minutes while he looks through the copies of my Hawaii chart.

"I tried to call you eight times," he says nonchalantly while turning pages, and I am hoping he doesn't say anything more in reference to my moronic letter, because then I'll have to explain it fully to Will, and I'd rather just try to forget it. Yet something inside me warms a few degrees because I know he wouldn't have bothered saying that he tried to call unless he cared a little about my situation and he wanted me to understand that he did.

Thanks, I think. Thanks for telling me. I don't believe I will ever be able to ask for your help again, but I greatly appreciate you telling me that you tried calling. It will help me move along more easily.

Dr. Jamisen takes the echocardiogram video and returns a few minutes later.

"How much heart damage did you say he told you?" he asks me.

"Sixty percent," I answer.

"Fifty to sixty percent," Will corrects.

Dr. Jamisen sits down again. "Well, I disagree. It looks more like twenty to twenty-five percent."

I am stunned. He actually voiced disagreement with another doctor. I glance at William: doesn't twenty-five percent damage sounds a world better than sixty? Twenty-five percent sounds like there might be some hope of recovery. In that moment I remember how I'd felt one afternoon when a blizzard lifted.

I'd pulled off a road I could no longer see while traveling in a sudden, spreading storm. Huddling there for hours, I mentally thanked Dad for teaching me to keep a blanket and boots in my car during winter. I stayed low until the howl of the winds and the horizontal sheets of snow slowed. I started up the car again, the road still treacherous, but I could see a little way ahead, so I breathed easier the next few miles. Dr. Jamisen has just offered me a little breathing room. I clamp down on an expanding Cheshire cat smile, but I feel the delirious energy of liberation gathering momentum inside me.

Then Dr. Jamisen says, "There are things we don't understand - why some people do better than others." He continues talking about patients who do well and live active lives with substantial valve damage and other serious problems that contradict standard medical prognosis.

I am bubbling inside like a geyser. I want to say, I understand why some people do better, and I think you do too. It's called a will to live. Some call it a positive attitude. And you've casually just kick-started mine one more time. But I don't tell him this. I stay quiet.

William asks if there is something he can give me that will help the muscle regenerate.

"There's no magic pill," Dr. Jamisen says. I have to smile at that because his words mirror mine to William the other morning.

Dr. Jamisen checks if my ankles are swollen and he asks a few more questions. I explain that I am having to sleep sitting part way up to be able to breathe, yet after he listens to my heart, he tells me he thinks I am doing well. He says he wants me to start taking Advil for the chest pain three times a day for a week, and he also wants me to try a medicine that will help my heart beat stronger.

He gets a sample and asked me to call his nurse Patty to let them know how I'm doing with it.

"I'm very sensitive to medication," I explain cautiously.

"Just break a pill into eighths," he says. "Start with that. It'll be a little more than a grain."

I hold the package in my hand as Will and I say good-bye to him. I walk faster and easier than when I'd entered into his office a half hour earlier, just like I used to whenever I talked with Dr. Jamisen. Looking at William I notice he seems to be feeling better too, and I wonder if Dr. Jamisen's contagious optimism affects everyone that way. I wasn't certain whether he felt it fully himself or if he carried it only for the benefit of others. Yet, he routinely passes it along to his patients. No greater gift can be given.

I secure my seatbelt, thinking I should thank William for making me shake on this deal. A mature person would make a point of thanking him for forcing her past the embarrassment of this first meeting, but I haven't even waded into admitting to him how I am feeling. I'm wanting to duck from ever seeing Dr. Jamisen again after my desperate phone calls and my near as desperate note. I squeeze Will's arm instead.

I sit up straighter, even though I risk increasing the tightness in my chest with that simple motion, yet I feel a faint humming inside, despite the tightness. The humming feels like my engine firing again. It feels like I believe in the possibility of healing again.

Good. I need this fire and this hum. Without an engine, without any rudder, I wallowed, and I drifted too long after Hawaii. Yet I know I need to find a way to consistently nurture and fuel myself or I'll be wallowing again. I lower the window, savoring the fresh, invigorating air, telling myself that the person I was is gone, and new strengths wait to be discovered and built upon. Closing the doorway of the past opens new views to the future. I am finding the courage to hold a vision of a new me.

"Twenty percent sounds so much better," I say cheerfully as we start home. "Unless it's return on investment and then I'd prefer the sixty."

William chuckles. "Most people would be happy with twenty. Want to get some lunch before we go home?"

"Sure."

Smiling I turn toward William. "You know, if I can just keep my attitude intact then I'll have salvaged the best part of me anyway. And if I do, my potential for healing is stronger. And if I can't, perfect health would be wasted on me anyway."

William grins as he reaches out to pat my leg.

⚜

Will continues working daily with a counselor, spending long hours in discussions and reflection. He reads and seems to both digest and internalize the mounds of books she gives him. The books deal with varied issues of self-improvement, ethics, managing anger, and family commitments.

Will studies them every chance he gets. He even reads at night while he brushes his teeth. From the shower, I see him through the steamy glass, leaning over a book and leaning over the sink at the same time. He takes notes on a nearly full piece of paper. He is, without doubt, the most tenacious creature I have ever known. A badger would give him wide berth.

※

A few weeks later Jan arrives at our house to work with me again. After we are alone, she asked, "What's going on with William? His colors are better. There's not as much gray as he used to have."

"Don't tell him that," I say laughing. "Please. And I'm not entirely sure what's going on, but whatever it is," I continued, "it's not a band-aid fix. He's fundamentally changed. He hasn't lost his temper with me once."

Jan smiles. "Well I'm very happy for you both. I see you're still not wearing your ring."

I remain silent for a moment. "It's in the jewelry box. I just can't put it on yet... I'm not even sure why. I thought about it the other day, I even slipped it on, and I was telling myself, go ahead and wear it, but then I took it right off again." I pause, confused.

"It's just not time yet," she said. "You'll know when it's time."

※

I miss the kids while they are at school. Their absence leaves me feeling detached from motherhood and the focus, which has both motivated and dominated my daily life since they were born. But from every appearance I can monitor or measure, they are thriving.

With excitement they bring home books to read and spelling lists to practice. They bring home smiles and tales of new friends. One night at dinnertime, Brenna announces there's a group of about four boys that have just started running into some girls as hard as they can during recess, and they all pile on top and won't let the girl up.

"Aren't there any teachers supervising?"

"They don't ever do it when the teacher's out there."

"Naturally."

"What should I do, Mom?

"Well, it seems to me you have three options. You can go find a teacher and tell the teacher what's happening. And that will help, as long as you can keep running to get a teacher. Or you can learn to take it, but I don't think you'll like being a victim much. Or, when the boys pile on, then you can figure out how to make them think twice about it next time. Just like I told you before."

"You have to be willing to hit them back harder than they hit you," William interjects enthusiastically. "And if you are, then they'll leave you alone."

"I really don't want to hit anyone," Brenna says, and Meagan quickly echoes her sentiment.

"I understand." I tell them.

"So, do I," Kike says. "That's why they're jumping on girls and not boys. Well, when you get tired of it, tell your Mom and she'll teach you how to punch." William smiles.

They turn to me admiringly. "Really Mom?"

"Your Mom has a great punch," William says interrupting my answer. "Hasn't she told you that she took second place in an open Karate tournament when she was only a white belt?"

"Really, Mom?" They say simultaneously.

"And it was embarrassing," he continues grinning at me, "because I was sitting there talking to this guy and his wife comes up and her face is all swollen, and then Mom walks up to me and the woman gets a funny look." William starts laughing. "And it turns out your Mom had just fought her."

"Oh, please Will," I say cringing. "It was all in the heat of battle and I got a little carried away."

"Mom got called for unnecessary roughness."

"Will! Anyway, it was a point deduction if I remember right. But let's not talk about it.

"Were you a black belt, Mom? Meagan asks.

"Oh, far from it. I quit."

"Why?" Brenna asks.

"The instructor told Mom he'd taught for twenty years and never seen a woman with her ability," William said. "I think he liked you," he continues, with a smirk.

"So, his comment wasn't valid because he liked me?"

"No, I'm sure it was. I never saw anyone else out there like you."

"To answer your question Brenna, if your Dad would quit interrupting me, I quit because I really didn't want to hurt anyone. I didn't want to spend hours practicing kicking and hitting people.

But let's get back to the playground problem. And do you all notice how Jacqueline isn't eating with her elbows on the table? That's quite impressive for such a little girl." Meagan and Brenna immediately get their elbows off the table.

"So, what about the playground?" Brenna asks. And I'm suddenly stuck, feeling there must be better ways to handle things. Only every time I've tried to teach them the other way, it doesn't seem to handle it for long.

"You hit them back harder," William says again. "Don't ever start something, but don't take a bunch of nonsense either."

"William!"

"Cause if you take it," he adds, ignoring me, "you'll just keep getting it."

"Show me how to punch, Mom. Would you?" Meagan says as she's standing up from the table.

"Me too," Brenna says. Jacqueline is now climbing down from her high chair.

I glance at William. "Oh, this is real Christian."

"Just a couple minutes, Mom, please!" Meagan insists and I'm still hesitating.

William raises his eyebrows. "Do you want wimp daughters who can't defend themselves if some guy's trying to hurt them?"

"Of course not."

"Then show them, or I will. I'm not going through another year hearing you tell them not to let someone's bad behavior effect theirs." He sticks his finger down his throat, and pretends he's gagging. I frown.

"That's fine when you're talking to most adults," he tells me, "But it doesn't work with little boys pushing you around the playground. And then all you'll end up with is little tattle tale girls who think they can't care of themselves."

William is really on a roll. "I'm telling you," he says, staring hard at me. "Most seven-year-old boys have absolutely nothing between here and here," he says pointing to his temples.

"And they won't either for about another thirty years," I interject. Will laughs.

"The point is," he says, "you don't try to reason with boys the same way you do girls. At least you don't expect them to hear you."

He looks at his daughters carefully, looking into one captivated face after the other, "what you do when they're crashing into you, is you elbow them real fast," Will's elbow flies out, "and they won't know where it came from but something inside them will make them veer and crash in some other direction next time on the playground."

I'm still sitting down. The only one sitting down now. "Are you going to show me how to punch, Mom?" Brenna asks impatiently.

"Okay." I stand and motion for Will to come closer. He raises his hands and holds them up for a target. I move in front of him as my daughter's crowd around.

"Notice how Mom's left hand's up by her chin," William says, "that's to block a punch coming in."

"They hit you back?" Meagan asks in shocked tones.

"If you don't discourage it really quick," William answers. "But you have to be willing to take a punch."

"Did you ever get hit, Mom?" Brenna asks excited.

"We'd spar in Karate."

"With men?" Meagan asks, as her eyes go wide.

"Sure," I tell her nonchalantly. "What good would it do to just spar with women? No woman's ever going to hit you. We're too smart."

"But a guy hit you?" Brenna says really interested now.

I laugh. "Yes, but never very hard because whenever we'd line up to spar, your Dad always made a point of going up to the man who was supposed to spar with me and he'd tell them, "That's my wife." I smile at Will.

"Why'd you do that, Dad?" Meagan asks.

"Because I saw a woman get her nose broken once when we were practicing, and I wanted the guy to know if he ever hit Mom like that, then he'd have to answer to me."

"No, they never hit me hard," I say laughing again.

And then I jab a couple times with my left checking my distance before moving in quick and hard with my right.

William grins. "Wow. That's a great right. Your mom really has a great right."

"That was way cool, Mom," Brenna says. "Show me."

Will and I bend down simultaneously to all of them, checking their fists and making adjustments and they all practice.

"Stand sideways just a little. Use your whole body, like Mom does," William tells them, and we keep practicing. Then I notice I'm breathing a little heavily, and I slow it down.

"We've got a full body punching bag. Dad can put it up downstairs and some gloves if you want to do more later." I say sitting back down. The family rejoins me. As we finish dinner, they all agree they want to practice more, and Dad agrees to put up the bag.

The next week, they start practicing while Will works out. And I go down to watch them one afternoon. Brenna finishes her turn, shakes her gloved fist painfully and comes to sit wearily beside me on a weight bench.

"Feel my forehead," she says, laboring for breath.

"Pretty damp."

"You know Mom," she says. "I think I'd rather just get a teacher."

"Great, then get one," I tell her, but William catches my eye and I nearly crack up. The girls wander upstairs and the two of us are alone.

"Maybe we over did it?" I say with a smile.

"We usually do." He answers and then he gets really quiet because he's doing squats, and we both know anyone who can carry on a conversation doing squats, is not doing deep squats.

⚜

There are no more complaints about boys piling on at the playground, only talk of new friends and how nice everyone is. In the afternoon, Meagan appears at my bedroom door.

"Hi, sweetheart," I say, sitting up a little in bed. "Everything okay?"

She nods, yet I know instantly she wants to tell me something. But it will take a little warm-up before she gets to it. I'm familiar with the technique.

"Do you want to read one of your books out loud to me?"

"Maybe later."

"Something's going on at school?"

"No, it's okay. It's not as fun as you though."

"Well, I am fairly amusing."

"Oh, Mom." She gives me an impatient look. "I just wanted to tell you," she starts, and her words arrive slower then, suddenly much more deliberate and harder to get out. "I thought about it, and I think your heart attack happened so I could realize I could go to school and not be afraid." Meagan smiles very brightly at me.

"I think you're right," I tell her. She leans into me for a quick hug.

"I knew you could do it," I say. Meagan nods before moving off the bed. "They're practicing basketball," she explains as she leaves me. I listen to her run down the stairs to join William, Brenna, and little Jacqueline at the hoop Will bought the day I told him I was pregnant.

I sit back in awe a moment, wondering about Meagan's comment. And it floors me because just last night William told me he thought my heart attack happened to help him know he needed to change. And I am thinking in that moment, if it really helped either of them, I'd willingly do it all again. But before this magical moment, I'd been imagining it all happened, so I'd know that *I* needed to change...So I could learn not to be afraid. So, I could learn how to trust in God.

We hurt so we can learn and grow together. Good comes from all things. Just trust. Just keep leaning on trust.